George McCall Theal

South Africa

The Cape Colony, Natal, Orange Free State, South African Republic, and all other territories south of the Zambesi

George McCall Theal

South Africa
The Cape Colony, Natal, Orange Free State, South African Republic, and all other territories south of the Zambesi

ISBN/EAN: 9783744752251

Printed in Europe, USA, Canada, Australia, Japan

Cover: Foto ©Andreas Hilbeck / pixelio.de

More available books at **www.hansebooks.com**

The Story of the Nations.

SOUTH AFRICA.

THE STORY OF THE NATIONS.

Large Crown 8vo, Cloth, Illustrated, **5s.**
The Volumes are also kept in the following Special Bindings:
Half Persian, cloth sides, gilt top; Full calf, half extra,
marbled edges; Tree calf, gilt edges, gold roll
inside, full gilt back.

1. **ROME.** By ARTHUR GILMAN, M.A.
2. **THE JEWS.** By Prof. J. K. HOSMER.
3. **GERMANY.** By Rev. S. BARING-GOULD, M.A.
4. **CARTHAGE.** By Prof. ALFRED J. CHURCH.
5. **ALEXANDER'S EMPIRE.** By Prof. J. P. MAHAFFY.
6. **THE MOORS IN SPAIN.** By STANLEY LANE-POOLE.
7. **ANCIENT EGYPT.** By Prof. GEORGE RAWLINSON.
8. **HUNGARY.** By Prof. ARMINIUS VAMBÉRY.
9. **THE SARACENS.** By ARTHUR GILMAN, M.A.
10. **IRELAND.** By the Hon. EMILY LAWLESS.
11. **CHALDEA.** By ZÉNAÏDE A. RAGOZIN.
12. **THE GOTHS.** By HENRY BRADLEY.
13. **ASSYRIA.** By ZÉNAÏDE A. RAGOZIN.
14. **TURKEY.** By STANLEY LANE-POOLE.
15. **HOLLAND.** By Prof. J. E. THOROLD ROGERS.
16. **MEDIÆVAL FRANCE.** By GUSTAVE MASSON.
17. **PERSIA.** By S. G. W. BENJAMIN.
18. **PHŒNICIA.** By Prof. GEO. RAWLINSON.
19. **MEDIA.** By ZÉNAÏDE A. RAGOZIN.
20. **THE HANSA TOWNS.** By HELEN ZIMMERN.
21. **EARLY BRITAIN.** By Prof. ALFRED J. CHURCH.
22. **THE BARBARY CORSAIRS.** By STANLEY LANE-POOLE.
23. **RUSSIA.** By W. R. MORFILL, M.A.
24. **THE JEWS UNDER THE ROMANS.** By W. DOUGLAS MORRISON.
25. **SCOTLAND.** By JOHN MACKINTOSH, LL.D.
26. **SWITZERLAND.** By Mrs. LINA LUG and R. STEAD.
27. **MEXICO.** By SUSAN HALE.
28. **PORTUGAL.** By H. MORSE STEPHENS.
29. **THE NORMANS.** By SARAH ORNE JEWETT.
30. **THE BYZANTINE EMPIRE.** By C. W. C. OMAN.
31. **SICILY:** Phœnician, Greek and Roman. By the late Prof. E. A. FREEMAN.
32. **THE TUSCAN REPUBLICS.** By BELLA DUFFY.
33. **POLAND.** By W. R MORFILL, M.A.
34. **PARTHIA.** By Prof. GEORGE RAWLINSON.
35. **AUSTRALIAN COMMONWEALTH.** By GREVILLE TREGARTHEN.
36. **SPAIN.** By H. E. WATTS.
37. **JAPAN.** By DAVID MURRAY, Ph.D.

LONDON: T. FISHER UNWIN, PATERNOSTER SQUARE, E.C.

GATEWAY OF THE CASTLE OF GOOD HOPE.

SOUTH AFRICA

(THE CAPE COLONY, NATAL, ORANGE FREE STATE, SOUTH AFRICAN REPUBLIC, AND ALL OTHER TERRITORIES SOUTH OF THE ZAMBESI)

BY

GEORGE M. THEAL

OF THE CAPE COLONIAL CIVIL SERVICE

London

T. FISHER UNWIN

PATERNOSTER SQUARE

MDCCCXCIV

COPYRIGHT BY T. FISHER UNWIN, 1894
(For Great Britain).

COPYRIGHT BY G. P. PUTNAM'S SONS, 1894
(For the United States of America).

PREFACE.

THE chapters in this volume upon the Cape Colony before 1848, Natal before 1845, and the Orange Free State, South African Republic, Zululand, and Basutoland before 1872, contain an outline of my *History of South Africa*, which has been published in England in five octavo volumes. In that work my authorities are given, so they need not be repeated here. The remaining chapters have been written merely from general acquaintance with South African affairs acquired during many years' residence in the country, and have not the same claim to be regarded as absolutely correct, though I have endeavoured to make them reliable. In preparing the book I was guided by the principle that truth should be told, regardless of nationalities or parties, and I strove to the utmost to avoid anything like favour or prejudice.

GEO. M. THEAL.

CAPETOWN,
    September, 1893.

CONTENTS.

I.

ANCIENT INHABITANTS OF SOUTH AFRICA — PAGE 1–7

Hottentots—Bantu—Constant warfare.

II.

DISCOVERY OF THE SOUTH AFRICAN COAST BY THE PORTUGUESE . . . 8–16

Discoveries of the Portuguese—First ships in Table Bay—Portuguese maps.

III.

EVENTS THAT LED TO THE OCCUPATION OF TABLE VALLEY BY THE DUTCH EAST INDIA COMPANY 17–24

Rise of the Dutch Republic—The Dutch East India Company—The Eastern trade route—Wreck of the *Haarlem*—Advantages of Table Valley—Loss of life by scurvy—Mr. Van Riebeek.

IV.

FORMATION OF A REFRESHMENT STATION IN TABLE VALLEY BY THE DUTCH EAST INDIA COMPANY 25–31

Trade with Hottentots—The first cattle raid—Extension to Rondebosch.

V.

FOUNDATION OF THE CAPE COLONY   32–44

Introduction of slaves—Introduction of Asiatics—The first Hottentot war—The first Church—Purchase of territory.

VI.

THE SECOND HOTTENTOT WAR AND ITS CONSEQUENCES   45–59

Origin of the cattle farmers—Extension of the settlement—Arrival of Huguenots—Form of government—System of taxation—Exploration.

VII.

PROGRESS OF THE CAPE COLONY FROM 1700 TO 1750   60–79

Life of the early settlers—Wilhem Adrian van der Stel—First outbreak of small-pox—System of Administration—Effort to improve Table Bay—Growth of the settlement.

VIII.

COURSE OF EVENTS IN THE CAPE COLONY FROM 1750 TO 1785   80–95

Second outbreak of small-pox—Exploration of Namaqualand—Villages in the colony—Tour of Governor Van Plettenberg—First Kaffir war—Arrival of French troops—Complaints of the colonists—Agitation in the colony.

IX.

THE END OF THE EAST INDIA COMPANY'S RULE IN SOUTH AFRICA   96–112

Reckless expenditure—Second Kaffir war—Churches in the

colony—Affairs in Europe—Arrival of a British force—
Fruitless negotiations—Feeble defence of the colony—Review of the Company's rule.

X.

THE FIRST BRITISH OCCUPATION . . 112–128

Character of the colonists—First days of British rule—Surrender of a Dutch fleet—Insurrection of Graaff-Reinet—The third Kaffir war.

XI.

THE COLONY UNDER THE BATAVIAN REPUBLIC 129–137

Dealings with Kosa chiefs—Attack by the English—Capitulation of Capetown—Departure of General Janssens.

XII.

EARLY YEARS OF ENGLISH RULE IN SOUTH AFRICA . 138–147

Powers of the governor—Condition of the Hottentots—Fourth Kaffir war—Establishment of a circuit court—Cession of the colony.

XIII.

THE ADMINISTRATION OF LORD CHARLES SOMERSET 148–161

Slachter's Nek rebellion—Fifth Kaffir war—Arrival of British settlers—Success of the British settlers—Signs of progress—Resignation of the governor.

XIV.

THE WARS AND DEVASTATIONS OF TSHAKA . 162-174

Genius of Tshaka—The Mantati horde—Murder of Tshaka—Rise of the Matabele power—Genius of Moshesh—Condition of the tribes in 1836.

XV.

EVENTS IN THE CAPE COLONY FROM 1826 TO 1835 . 175-194

Injudicious measures—The Kat river settlement—Condition of the slaves—Emancipation of the slaves—Effects of the emancipation—Treaty with Waterboer—Sixth Kaffir war—The province of Queen Adelaide—Action of earl Glenelg.

XVI.

GREAT EMIGRATION FROM THE CAPE COLONY. EXPULSION OF MOSELEKATSE FROM THE TERRITORY SOUTH OF THE LIMPOPO . 195-203

Fate of the first party—Attack by the Matabele—The first constitution—Defeat of the Matabele.

XVII.

DESTRUCTION OF THE ZULU POWER AND FOUNDATION OF THE REPUBLIC OF NATAL . 204-218

Natal and Zululand in 1837—Arrangement with Dingan—Massacre of emigrants—Desperate fighting Invasion of Zululand—Death of Pieter Uys—Destruction of the Natal Army Arrival of Andries Pretorius—Defeat of a Zulu army—Revolt of Panda—Destruction of the Zulu power—Final defeat of Dingan.

XVIII.

SEIZURE OF NATAL BY BRITISH FORCES. CREATION OF TREATY STATES ALONG THE FRONTIER OF THE CAPE COLONY . 219–231

Conduct of the Natal government—Siege of the British Camp—Relief of the British Camp—Project of treaty states—The Griquas—Effects of the treaties.

XIX.

EVENTS TO THE CLOSE OF THE SEVENTH KAFFIR WAR 232–243

Expedition to aid Adam Kok—Arrangement with Adam Kok—Marks of progress—Seventh Kaffir war—Course of the war—Results of the war.

XX.

EVENTS DURING THE ADMINISTRATION OF SIR HARRY SMITH . . 244–257

End of the treaty states—Battle of Boomplaats—Anti-convict agitation—Eighth Kaffir war—Settlement of British Kaffraria.

XXI.

ACKNOWLEDGMENT BY GREAT BRITAIN OF THE INDEPENDENCE OF THE SOUTH AFRICAN REPUBLIC, AND ABANDONMENT OF THE ORANGE RIVER SOVEREIGNTY 258–270

First Basuto war—The Sand River convention—Condition of the Basuto tribe—Battle of Berea—Wise action of Moshesh—Arrival of Sir George Clerk—Abandonment of the Sovereignty—South Africa after 1854.

XXII.

The Constitution of Cape Colony . . 271–276

The Cape parliament—The Dutch language.

XXIII.

The Province of British Kaffraria . 277–289

Policy of Sir George Grey—Self-destruction of the Kosas—Annexation to the Cape Colony.

XXIV.

The Colony of Natal and the Dependency of Zululand 290–312

Influx of Bantu—The Hlubi tribe—Rebellion of Langalibalele—Importation of Indians—Mode of life of Europeans—Constitution of Natal—Cetewayo—Isandlwana—Invasion of Zululand—Battle of Ulundi.

XXV.

The Orange Free State and Basutoland . 313–331

Presidents Hoffman and Boshof—Second Basuto war—Conduct of Moshesh—President Brand and Moshesh—Discovery of Diamonds—Orange Free State and Basutoland—President Brand's visit to England—Basutoland.

XXVI.

The South African Republic . 332–352

Lawlessness—Dr. Livingstone—War with the Baramapulana—President Burgers—Rebellion of the Bapedi—British rule—Struggle for independence—British disasters—Rich goldfields—Railways.

XXVII.

DEPENDENCIES OF THE CAPE COLONY . . 353-364

Transkeian territory—Ninth Kaffir war—Port St. John's.

XXVIII.

VARIOUS TERRITORIES NOT ALREADY DESCRIBED 365-376

British Bechuanaland—Chartered Company's territory—German sphere of influence—Portuguese possessions.

XXIX.

THE PRESENT CONDITION OF THE CAPE COLONY 377-387

Exports of South Africa—Missionary labour—Courts of justice—Modern improvements—Need of European immigrants.

CHRONOLOGICAL TABLE OF EVENTS . . 388

INDEX 391

LIST OF ILLUSTRATIONS.

	PAGE
MAP OF SOUTH AFRICA, 1893	*Facing* 1
GATEWAY OF THE CASTLE OF GOOD HOPE	*Frontispiece*
SOUTH AFRICA AS OCCUPIED BY BUSHMEN, HOTTENTOTS, AND BANTU IN 1650	7
CROSS ERECTED BY DIAS ON PEDESTAL POINT	9
THE CAPE OF GOOD HOPE	11
PORTRAIT OF A BUSHMAN	16
TABLE MOUNTAIN AS SEEN FROM ROBBEN ISLAND	24
PLAN OF THE CASTLE OF GOOD HOPE	41
EXTENT OF THE SETTLEMENT IN 1700	58
SOUTH AFRICAN TENT WAGGON	62
HOUSE ON W. A. VAN DER STEL'S ESTATE	66
EXTENT OF THE CAPE COLONY IN 1750	78
THE OLD BURGHER WATCH-HOUSE, CAPETOWN	84
CHURCH OF LAST CENTURY IN CAPETOWN	102
SIMONSTOWN IN 1795	106
SOUTH AFRICAN FARMHOUSE OF THE BETTER CLASS IN 1795	114
EXTENT OF TERRITORY UNDER EUROPEAN RULE IN 1800	127
VIEW IN THE KOWIE VALLEY, BELOW GRAHAMSTOWN	144
FORT WILLSHIRE. BUILT, 1820; ABANDONED, 1837	154
A ZULU WARRIOR IN UNIFORM	163
PORTRAIT OF DINGAN	168

LIST OF ILLUSTRATIONS.

	PAGE
THABA BOSIGO	172
PORTRAIT OF HINTSA	190
UMKUNGUNHLOVU	206
SCENE IN PONDOLAND	226
GRIQUA MAN AND WOMEN	229
SCENE IN MONTAGU PASS	238
PORTRAIT OF SIR HARRY SMITH	245
EXTENT OF TERRITORY UNDER EUROPEAN RULE IN 1850	256
THE GIANT'S CUP, AS SEEN FROM THE SEAWARD SIDE OF THE DRAKENSBERG	264
PARLIAMENT HOUSE, CAPETOWN	273
THE GREY HOSPITAL, KING-WILLIAMSTOWN	278
PORT NATAL AND DURBAN IN 1860	298
SCENE IN ZULULAND	311
PORTRAIT OF PRESIDENT BRAND	319
COMMON STYLE OF SOUTH AFRICAN FARMHOUSE	329
COMMON SOUTH AFRICAN BOULDER	354
THE BOYS' SCHOOL, LOVEDALE MISSIONARY INSTITUTION	381
INNER DOCK, CAPETOWN	384

EXPLANATION OF TERMS.

EXPLANATION of words in common use in South Africa, but that may not be understood elsewhere, at least in the same sense :—

Assagai, a javelin or dart used by the Hottentots and Bantu in war and the chase. The word is a corruption of the Portuguese "azagaya," which was derived from the Latin "hasta."

Boer, Dutch for a tiller of the ground. The word is applied in this country to cattle-breeders as well as to agriculturists, and is frequently used in the plural form to signify the whole rural population of European blood speaking the Dutch language.

Burgher, a European male, no matter where resident, who is in possession of the franchise and liable to all public duties. It corresponds to the civis Romanus of old.

Calabash, the hard rind of a gourd, used by the Bantu for various purposes, such as water-pots, jars, dishes, basins, snuff-boxes, &c.

Commando, a body of burghers called out for military purposes.

Heemraden, burghers appointed by the government to act as assessors in the district courts of justice. A Dutch word.

Induna, an officer of high rank under a Bantu chief. The word is Zulu.

Kraal, a cattle-fold. The word is a corruption of the Portuguese "curral." It is also used to signify a collection of either Hottentot or Bantu huts, as these are usually built in a circle, within which the cattle are kept at night.

Lager, a Dutch word meaning an enclosure for protective purposes, such as a circular wall of stone, or a number of waggons lashed together.

Landdrost, a stipendiary magistrate, who administers justice and receives the revenue of a district. The word is Dutch.

Tsetse, a fly whose sting destroys domestic cattle, but has no effect upon wild animals. The word comes from one of the Bantu dialects. The *tsetse* disappears from a district when the game is exterminated or driven away.

Volksraad, a Dutch word meaning the people's council, an elected legislative body.

THE STORY OF SOUTH AFRICA.

I.

ANCIENT INHABITANTS OF SOUTH AFRICA.

The aborigines of South Africa were savages of a very low type. They were pigmies in size, yellowish-brown in colour, hollow-backed, and with skins so loose that in times of famine their bodies were covered with wrinkles and flaps. On their heads were rows of little tufts of wiry hair hardly larger than peppercorns, and leaving the greater portion of the surface bald. Their faces were broad in a line with the eyes, their cheeks were hollow, and they had flat noses, thick lips, and receding chins. They anointed their bodies with grease when any was obtainable, and then painted themselves with soot or coloured clay. The clothing of the males was the skin of an animal hung loosely over the shoulders, and often cast aside; that of the females was little more than a small leathern apron. To the eye of a European no people in any part of the world were more unattractive.

These savages were thinly scattered over every part of the country from a very remote period, for implements—such as arrow-heads and perforated stones similar to those which they had in use when white men first met them—have been found in positions where the overlying materials must have been undisturbed for an incalculable time. The Bushmen —as the pigmies are termed by Europeans—had no domestic animal but the dog, and they made no effort to cultivate the soil. They lived by the chase and upon wild plants, honey, locusts, and carrion.

They were without other government than parental, and even that was not respected after they were able to provide for themselves. So weak in frame as to be incapable of toil, they possessed great keenness of vision for detecting objects at a distance, and marvellous fleetness of foot and power of endurance in the chase. Their weapon of offence was a feeble bow, but the arrow-head was coated with poison so deadly that the slightest wound was mortal.

In addition to the Bushmen there lived on South African soil, from a period long anterior to the arrival of Europeans, a body of people much more advanced towards civilisation, the people now known as Hottentots. Where they came from, and how they got here, are questions that no one has yet been able to answer. Some have supposed that they sprang originally from a Bushman stock, others that the Bushmen were simply Hottentots who became degraded by the loss of their domestic cattle, but neither of these theories is now tenable. It has been ascertained that their languages are differently constructed, though both abound with clicks. The Bushman was a strict monogamist, the Hottentot customs admitted of polygamy. Then their skull measurements do not correspond. The head of the Hottentot is longer and narrower than that of the Bushman, and his face is more prognathous. The lower jaw of the Bushman is only surpassed in feebleness by that of the Australian black, while that of the Hottentot, though far from massive, is much better developed. The Bushman ear is without a lobe, which the Hottentot ear possesses, and the cranial capacity of the Hottentot is higher.

On the other hand, against these differences several points of resemblance can be placed. The colour of the skin is the same, and the little balls of wiry hair with open spaces between them are in general common to both, though sometimes the head of a Hottentot is more thickly covered. The one has small hands and feet, and so has the other. Their power of imagination is similar, and differs greatly from that of other Africans.

All this seems to point to the supposition that at a time now far in the past an intruding body of males of some unknown race took to themselves consorts of Bushman blood, and from the union sprang the Hottentot tribes of Southern Africa. There are other reasons for this conjecture, but they need not be given here.

The Hottentots were never very numerous, and they occupied only the strip of land along the coast and the banks of the Orange river and some of its tributaries. There was a constant and deadly feud between them and the Bushmen. Only in one locality—along the banks of the lower Vaal—are they known to have mixed in blood with those people in modern times, and in that case the amalgamation arose from wars in which the vanquished males were exterminated and the females were seized as spoil.

They lived in communities under the government of chiefs, who, however, possessed very limited authority, for public opinion was freely expressed, and was the supreme law. They depended mainly upon the milk of cows and ewes for their subsistence, and did not practice agriculture in any form. Their horned cattle were gaunt and bony, and their sheep were covered with hair—not wool—and had fatty tails of great weight. Their only other domestic animal was the dog. The men lived in almost perfect indolence, moving with their herds and flocks from one place to another as pasture failed; and when the supply of milk was insufficient it fell to the lot of the women to gather bulbs and roots with which to eke out an existence. The huts in which they slept were slender frames of wood covered with mats, and could be taken down and set up again almost as quickly as tents.

These nearly naked people, living in idleness and filthiness indescribable, were yet capable of improvement. During the last century a vast amount of missionary labour has been concentrated upon the natives of South Africa, and though to the present day there is not a single instance of a Bushman of pure blood having permanently adopted European habits, the Hottentots have done so to a considerable extent. They have not indeed shown a capacity to rise to the highest level of civilised life, but they have reached a stage much above that of barbarism.

Before the arrival of Europeans yet another branch of the human family was beginning to press into South Africa. Tribes of stalwart people practising agriculture and metallurgy, under strict government and with an elaborate system of law, were moving down from the north, and by the middle of the seventeenth century had reached the upper tributaries of the Orange river and the mouth of the Kei.

These people formed part of the great Bantu family, which occupies the whole of Central Africa from the Atlantic to the Indian ocean. They were certainly of mixed blood, and one branch of their ancestors must have been of a very much higher type than the other. This is shown in various ways. Among them at the present day are individuals with perfect Asiatic features, born of parents with the negro cast of countenance. In almost any little community may be found men only moderately brown in colour, while their nearest relatives are deep black. Here and there one may be seen with a thick full beard, though the great majority have almost hairless cheeks and chins. And a still stronger proof of a mixed ancestry of very unequal capability is afforded by the fact that most of these people seem unable to rise to the European level of civilisation, though not a few individuals have shown themselves possessed of mental power equal to that of white men.

These Bantu were of a healthy and vigorous stock, and were probably the most prolific people on the face of the earth. The tribes were seldom at peace with each other, and great numbers of individuals perished yearly through charges of dealing in sorcery, but the losses thus sustained were made good by a custom which provided that every adult female should be married. There was no limit to the number of wives a man could have, and thus in a state of society where the females outnumbered the males, all were provided for.

The three classes of people referred to in this chapter enjoyed the lives they were leading quite as much as Europeans do, though their pleasures were of a lower kind. Given freedom from disease and a slain antelope, and there could be no merrier creature than a Bushman. He was absolutely devoid of harassing cares. A Hottentot kraal in the clear moonlight of Africa, with men, women, and children dancing to the music of reeds, was a scene of the highest hilarity. The Bantu woman, tending her garden by day, and preparing food in the evening which she may not partake of herself until her husband and his friends have eaten, is regarded as an unhappy drudge by her European sister. In her own opinion her lot is far more enviable than that of the white woman, whom she regards as being always in a state of anxiety.

The chief element of disturbance in their lives was war. The hand of the Bushman was always against every man, and every man's hand was against him. The Hottentot tribes were continually robbing each other of cattle and women, and on their eastern border were struggling in vain against the advancing Bantu. Every Bantu clan was usually at feud with its nearest neighbours, whoever these might be. But life without excitement is insipid to the savage

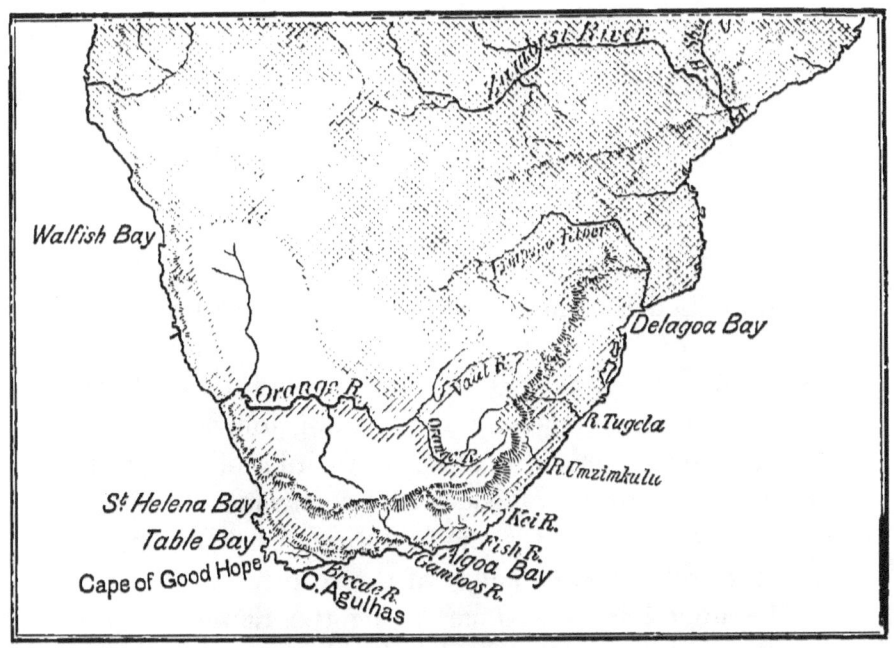

SOUTH AFRICA AS OCCUPIED BY BUSHMEN, HOTTENTOTS, AND BANTU IN 1650.

Bushmen were the only inhabitants of the parts unmarked, and they lived also in all the rugged and mountainous sections of the parts occupied by Hottentots and Bantu. The territory in which the Hottentots roamed with their cattle is marked , and the territory occupied by the Bantu .]

as well as to the civilised man, and these wars and animosities, though sometimes causing great suffering and loss of life, in general provided just that excitement which was needed to prevent the minds of the people from sinking into complete stagnation.

II.

DISCOVERY OF THE SOUTH AFRICAN COAST BY THE PORTUGUESE.

IN 1486 two little vessels, under command of an officer named Bartholomew Dias, sailed from Portugal in search of an ocean road to India. Pushing his way down the western coast, Dias passed the farthest point previously known, and sailing onward with the land always in sight came to an inlet of no great depth with a group of islets at its entrance. There he cast anchor, and for the first time Christian men trod the soil of Africa south of the tropic.

The inlet has ever since borne the name Angra Pequena, or Little Bay, which its discoverer gave to it. The surrounding country was a desolate waste of sand, and no signs of human life were seen, nor was other refreshment than seabirds' eggs obtainable. Having set up a cross as a mark of possession for his king, the Portuguese commander proceeded on his voyage. He tried to keep the land in sight, but when he was somewhere near the mouth of the Orange river a gale from the north sprang up, and for thirteen days he was driven helplessly before it.

As soon as it abated the prows of the vessels were turned to the east, with a view of getting near the shore again, but after sailing a long time without reaching land Dias began to think that he must either have passed the end of the continent or have entered a great gulf like that of Guinea.

He therefore changed the course to north, and after a while came in sight of the coast, which he found trending away to the east. The exact spot where he made the land cannot be stated, but it was

CROSS ERECTED BY DIAS ON PEDESTAL POINT.
(*From a Sketch by H. M. Piers.*)

one of the curves in the seaboard between Cape Agulhas and the Knysna. Large herds of cattle were seen, which the natives drove inland with haste, as they seemed in terror of the ships. It was not found possible to open intercourse with the wild people.

Sailing again eastward Dias reached an islet where he found fresh water and where he set up another cross. It was the islet in Algoa Bay which is still called on that account Santa Cruz, or, as it is usually written in the French form, St. Croix. Here the sailors objected to proceed farther, and it was with difficulty that they were induced to press on a couple of days longer. At the mouth of a river—either the Kowie or the Fish—the expedition turned homeward, and on its way back discovered a bold headland which Dias named the Cape of Storms, but which was renamed by King John the Second the Cape of Good Hope. As seen from the sea this cape is much more conspicuous than Agulhas, the true southern extremity of the continent.

Ten years passed away after the return of Dias to Portugal before an expedition was fitted out to follow up the discovery he had made. Four small vessels were then made ready, and were placed under command of Vasco da Gama, a man of proved ability.

It was not quite five years after Columbus sailed from Palos to discover a new continent in the west, when Da Gama's little fleet put to sea from the Tagus. Five months and a half later he reached a curve in the African coast about one hundred and twenty miles north of the Cape of Good Hope, to which he gave the name St. Helena Bay. Here he landed and by a little strategy managed to obtain an interview with a party of natives, whose friendship he tried to secure by making them presents of trinkets. All went well for a time, but at length a misunderstanding arose, which resulted in the Portuguese attacking the natives, and in a skirmish Da Gama himself and three others were wounded with

THE CAPE OF GOOD HOPE.

assagais. Such was the first intercourse between white men and Hottentots.

On the 17th of November 1497 Da Gama set sail from St. Helena Bay, and three days later doubled the Cape of Good Hope in fine weather. Turning eastward, he anchored next at a cape which he named St. Bras, and which is probably the same as the present St. Blaize. There he found a number of natives similar in appearance to those he had first seen, but who showed so little symptom of alarm that they crowded on the beach and scrambled for anything that was thrown to them. From these people some sheep were obtained in barter, but they would not sell any horned cattle.

Keeping within sight of the shore, on the 25th of December Da Gama passed by a beautiful land, to which he gave the name Natal, in memory of the day when Christian men first saw it.

On the 6th of January 1498 the fleet reached the mouth of a river which enters the sea on the northern side of Delagoa Bay. Here the Portuguese landed, and found a friendly people, black in colour, who brought copper, ivory, and provisions for sale. During the five days that the fleet remained at this place nothing occurred to disturb the friendly intercourse between the Portuguese and the Bantu residents.

Sailing again, Da Gama next touched at Sofala, where he found people who had dealings with Arabs, and thence he continued his voyage until he reached India.

The highway to the East being now open, every year fleets sailed to and from Portugal. In a short time the Indian seas fell entirely under Portuguese dominion, and an immense trade was opened up.

In 1503 a small fleet, under command of an officer named Antonio de Saldanha, put into a bay on the African coast that had never been entered before. On one side rose a great mass of rock, over three thousand feet in height, with its top making a level line more than a mile in length on the sky. This grand mountain was flanked at either end with peaks less lofty, supported by buttresses projecting towards the shore. The recess was a capacious valley, down the centre of which flowed a stream of clear sweet water. The valley seemed to be without people, but after a while some Hottentots made their appearance, from whom a cow and two sheep were purchased.

Saldanha himself climbed to the top of the great flat rock, to which he gave the name Table Mountain. The bay in which he anchored was thereafter called after him the watering place of Saldanha, until nearly a century later it received from the Dutch sea-captain Joris van Spilbergen its present name of Table Bay.

No effort was made to explore the interior of the country, and, indeed, setting aside danger from the natives, it would have been beyond the power of any man to have gone far from the coast at this period. The land rises in a series of steps from the seashore to a great interior plain, and until that plain was reached the traveller would have had everywhere a rugged and seemingly impassable range of mountains before him. If by great exertion he had made his way to the summit of one, he would have found himself on the edge of a broken plateau, with another range—the front of another terrace—shutting in his view. It follows from this conformation of the country that there are no navigable rivers. The streams—even the very largest—are all of the nature of mountain torrents, obstructed with rapids and falls, and varying in volume with rain and drought. There is an utter absence of secure natural harbours on the coast, except in positions where they could be of little service in the early days of exploration. And, in addition to all this, a very large portion of the land along the western seaboard, as well as of the interior plains, is so arid that it could only be traversed by degrees, as its slender resources became known.

In returning with the fleet which left India at the close of 1509, Francisco d'Almeida, first Portuguese viceroy of the eastern seas, put into Table Bay for the purpose of obtaining water and refreshing his people. Some natives appeared on the beach, and a party of ships' people went ashore to barter some cattle from them. Traffic was carried on for a time in a friendly manner, but at length a quarrel arose, and two white men were badly beaten. This caused an outcry for vengeance, to which D'Almeida unfortunately lent a willing ear.

Next morning, 1st of March 1510, the viceroy landed with one hundred and fifty men armed with swords and lances. They marched to a kraal and seized some cattle, which they were driving away when the Hottentots, supposed to be about one hundred and seventy in number, attacked them. The weapons of the Portuguese were useless against the fleet-footed natives, who poured upon the invaders a shower of missiles. A panic followed. Most fled towards the boats as the only means of safety; a few, who were too proud to retreat before savages, attempted in vain to defend themselves. The viceroy was struck down with knobbed sticks and stabbed in the throat with an assagai. Sixty-five of the best men in the fleet perished on that disastrous day, and hardly any of those who reached the boats escaped without wounds.

After this event the Portuguese avoided South Africa as much as possible. With them the country had the reputation of being inhabited by the most ferocious of savages, and of furnishing nothing valuable for trade. Their fleets doubled the continent year after year, but seldom touched at any port south of Sofala. They made a practice of calling for refreshment at the island of St. Helena, which had been discovered in 1502, and then pressing on to Mozambique without a break, whenever it was possible to do so. They never attempted to form a station below Delagoa Bay.

Now and again, however, their ships were driven by stress of weather to seek a port, and occasionally a wreck took place. Curiosity also prompted some of them, and orders from the king required others, to inspect the coast and make tracings of it. The principal bights and headlands thus acquired names. Nearly all of these have been replaced by others, Dutch or English, but a few remain to our day.

With the regions north of the fifteenth parallel of latitude the Portuguese were well acquainted. Their traders crossed the continent from Angola to Mozambique, and the quantity of gold which they exported from their factories on the eastern coast shows that they must have had an intimate knowledge of the territory along the Zambesi. But of the interior of the country south of the tropic they knew absolutely nothing, and what they imagined and laid down on their maps was so very incorrect that after the territory was explored the whole of their delineations of Africa were regarded as valueless.

PORTRAIT OF A BUSHMAN.

III.

EVENTS THAT LED TO THE OCCUPATION OF TABLE VALLEY BY THE DUTCH EAST INDIA COMPANY.

AFTER a long interval English, Dutch, and French ships followed the Portuguese to India. Drake and Candish passed in sight of the Cape of Good Hope when homeward bound on their celebrated voyages round the world, but did not land on the African coast. In July 1591 the English flag was seen there for the first time. Three ships—the pioneers of the vast fleets that have since followed the same course—then put into Table Bay on their way to India. Their crews, who were suffering from scurvy, obtained good refreshment, as in addition to wild fowl, shellfish, and plants of various kinds, they bartered some oxen and sheep from Hottentots. One of the ships, commanded by Captain James Lancaster, reached India in safety, another returned to England shorthanded from Table Bay, and the third went down in a gale at sea somewhere off the southern coast.

In 1601 the first fleet fitted out by the English East India Company, under command of the same Captain James Lancaster mentioned above, put into

Table Bay on its outward passage. Thereafter for several years the fleets of this Company made Table Bay a port of call and refreshment, and their crews usually procured in barter from the natives as many cattle as they needed.

During the closing years of the sixteenth century the people who were destined to form the first European settlement in South Africa were engaged in a gallant struggle for freedom against the powerful Spanish monarchy. The northern Netherland provinces had entered the sisterhood of nations as a free republic which was rapidly becoming the foremost commercial power of the age. While the struggle was being carried on, Portugal came under the dominion of the king of Spain, and the Dutch were then excluded from Lisbon, where they had previously obtained such eastern products as they needed. Some of their adventurous merchants then thought of direct trade with India, but it was not until 1595 that a fleet under the republican flag passed the Cape of Good Hope. It consisted of four vessels, and was under an officer named Cornelis Houtman. This fleet touched at Mossel Bay, where refreshment was procured, the intercourse between the strangers and the natives being friendly.

After Houtman's return to Europe, several companies were formed in different towns of the Netherlands, for the purpose of trading with the Indies. No fresh discoveries on the African coast were made by any of the fleets which they sent out, but to some of the bays new names were given. Thus Paul van Caerden, an officer in the service of the New Brabant

Company, when returning to Europe in 1601, gave their present names to Mossel, Flesh, and Fish bays, all of which he entered.

The fleets sent out by the different small companies gained surprising successes over the Portuguese in India, but as they did not act in concert no permanent conquests could be made. For this reason, as well as to prevent rivalry and to conduct the trade in a manner the most advantageous to the people of the whole republic, the states-general resolved to unite all the weak associations in one great company with many privileges and large powers. The charter was issued at the Hague on the 20th of March 1602, and gave the Company power to make treaties with Indian governments, to build fortresses, appoint civil and military officers, and enlist troops. The Company was subject to have its transactions reviewed by the states-general, otherwise it had almost sovereign power. The subscribed capital was rather over half a million pounds sterling. Offices for the transaction of business, or chambers as they were termed, were established at Amsterdam, Middelburg, Delft, Rotterdam, Hoorn, and Enkhuizen.

The general control was confided to an assembly of seventeen directors, whose sessions were held at Amsterdam for six successive years, then at Middelburg for two years, then at Amsterdam again for six years, and so on.

The profits made by the Company during the early years of its existence were enormous. The Portuguese ships, factories, and possessions of all kinds in India were fair prize of war, and the most valuable were shortly in the hands of the Dutch. Every year fleets of richly laden ships under the flag of the Netherlands passed the Cape of Good Hope outward and homeward bound.

In 1619 the directors of the English East India Company proposed to the assembly of seventeen that they should jointly build a fort and establish a place of refreshment somewhere on the South African coast. This proposal did not find favour in Holland, and each company then resolved to form a station of its own. Instructions were issued to the commanders of the next outward-bound fleets of both nations to examine the seaboard and report upon the most suitable places for the purpose. Thus it happened that in 1620 two English captains, by name Fitzherbert and Shillinge, inspected Table Bay, and believing that no better place could be found, they proclaimed the adjoining country under the sovereignty of King James. They did not leave any force to keep possession, however, and the directors in London having changed their views with regard to a station in South Africa, the proclamation of Fitzherbert and Shillinge was never ratified. English ships still continued occasionally to call for the purpose of taking in fresh water, but from this time onward the island of St. Helena became their usual place of refreshment.

The assembly of seventeen also allowed its resolution concerning the establishment of a station in South Africa to fall through at this time. Some of the advantages of such a station were already in its possession, and the expense of building a fort and maintaining a garrison might be too high a price to pay for anything additional that could be had. Its fleets usually put into Table Bay for the purpose of taking in fresh water, giving the crews a run on land, catching fish, and getting the latest intelligence from the places they were bound to. Letters were buried on shore, and notices of the places where they were deposited were marked on conspicuous stones.

Table Valley was also sometimes occupied for months together by parties of Dutch seal hunters and whale fishers. Among others, in 1611 Isaac le Maire, after whom the straits of Le Maire are named, left his son with some seamen here for this purpose.

Early in 1648 the *Haarlem*, a ship belonging to the East India Company, put into Table Bay for refreshment, and in a gale was driven on the Blueberg beach. The crew got safely to land, and succeeded in saving their own effects and the cargo. When everything was secured against stormy weather they removed to Table Valley as a better place for an encampment, leaving only a guard with the stores. Beside a stream of fresh water, somewhere near the centre of the present city of Capetown, they made themselves huts, and threw up an earthen bank for shelter around them. The rainy season was setting in, and as they happened to have various seeds with them they made a garden and soon had abundance of vegetables. They were fortunate also in being able to procure in barter from the natives more meat than they needed, so that their experience of South Africa led them to believe that it was a fruitful and pleasant land. After they had been here nearly six months a fleet returning home put in, and took then on to Europe.

Upon their arrival in the Netherlands, Leendert Janssen and Nicholas Proot, two of the *Haarlem's* officers, drew up and presented to the chamber of Amsterdam a document in which they set forth the advantages that they believed the Company might derive from a station in Table Valley. This document was referred by the chamber of Amsterdam to the directors, who, after calling for the opinions of the other chambers and finding them favourable, in August 1650 resolved to form such a station as was proposed. A committee was instructed to draw up a plan, and when this was discussed and approved of, three vessels were made ready to bring the men and the materials to South Africa.

The post of commander of the station about to be formed was offered to Nicholas Proot, and upon his declining it, a ship's surgeon named Jan van Riebeek, who had been for some time in the Company's service and had visited many countries, was selected for the office. A better selection could hardly have been made. Mr. Van Riebeek was not a man of high education or of refined manners, but he was industrious and possessed of good natural ability. He had been in Table Bay with the fleet in which the *Haarlem's* crew returned home, and upon the document drawn up by Janssen and Proot being submitted to him for an opinion, he endorsed all that was in it concerning the capabilities of the country.

Things were not done in such haste in those days as they are now, and the year 1651 had nearly come to an end before the three vessels set sail from Texel. It must not be supposed that they were bringing people to South Africa with the intention of founding a colony, for nothing was then further from the thoughts of the directors of the East India Company. Their object was merely to form a refreshment station for the fleets passing to and from the eastern seas.

Six months was considered a quick passage between the ports of the Netherlands and the roads of Batavia, where their ultimate destination was made known to the skippers by the governor-general and council of India; and it was no uncommon circumstance for one-third of the crews to have perished and another third to be helpless with scurvy when the ships arrived there. The loss of life was appalling, as the Indiamen were fighting as well as trading vessels, and usually left Europe with two or three hundred men. The crews were very largely composed of recruits from Germany and the maritime states of Europe, or the population of the Netherlands could not have borne such a tremendous drain of men for any length of time.

Table Bay was regarded as two-thirds of the distance from Amsterdam to Batavia, and the directors thought that by establishing a refreshment station on its shores many lives could be saved and much suffering be avoided. The design was first to make a large garden and raise in it vegetables for the supply of the fleets, secondly to barter oxen and sheep from the Hottentots for the same purpose, and thirdly to build a great hospital in which sick men could be left to recover their health.

Every man at the station was to be a servant of the East India Company. Mr. Van Riebeek, who had the title of commander, was to hold a position similar to that of a sergeant in charge of a small military outpost at some distance from the head-quarters of a regiment. Every admiral of a fleet that called was to supersede him for the time being, and he had hardly any discretionary power even when no superior officer was present.

TABLE MOUNTAIN AS SEEN FROM ROBBEN ISLAND.

IV.

FORMATION OF A REFRESHMENT STATION IN TABLE VALLEY BY THE DUTCH EAST INDIA COMPANY.

In April 1652 Mr. Van Riebeck and his people arrived, and at once set about the construction of a fort by raising banks of earth round a hollow square, within which they erected some wooden sheds brought from Holland. The rainy season at and near the Cape of Good Hope usually commences in the month of April, but this year the summer drought lasted until towards the close of May, and consequently there was a good deal of suffering among the people. Scurvy was showing itself and no sorrel or wild plants of any kind could be found, nor could a garden be made.

The only permanent inhabitants of the Cape peninsula when the Dutch landed were some sixty Hottentots, who were without cattle, and who lived chiefly upon shell-fish. Where as many thousands now exist in comfort, these wretched beachrangers— as Mr. Van Riebeck styled them—were barely able to exist at all. The chief man among them was named Harry by the white people. He had once been taken to Bantam in an English ship, and he spoke a little broken English, so Mr. Van Riebeek employed him as an interpreter. The others made themselves useful by carrying water and gathering firewood, in return for which they were provided with ships' provisions.

Two large clans of Hottentots, consisting together of about five thousand souls, roamed over the country within a radius of fifty miles from Table Bay, but they were then far from the peninsula, and very little could be ascertained concerning them.

When the winter rains at last set in, much discomfort was the immediate result. The tents and wooden buildings were all found to be leaky. With the change of weather came dysentery, which the people were too weak to resist, and now almost every day there was a death from that disease or from scurvy. By the beginning of June the party was reduced to one hundred and sixteen men and five women, of whom only sixty men were able to perform any labour. Fresh meat and vegetables and proper shelter would have saved them, but these things were not to be had. They were almost as solitary as if they had been frozen up in the Arctic sea. The two largest of the vessels had gone on to Batavia, leaving the other—a mere decked boat—at Mr. Van Riebeek's disposal, and for many weeks no natives were seen except Harry's miserable followers, from whom no assistance of any kind was to be obtained.

But the rain, which had brought on the dysentery,

in a very short time brought also relief. Grass sprang into existence, and with it appeared various edible plants. They were all correctives of scurvy, and that was mainly what was needed. The strong and the feeble went about gathering wild herbs and roots and declaring there was nothing in the world half so palatable. As soon as the first showers fell, a plot of ground was dug over, in which seeds were planted; and soon the sick were enjoying such delicacies as radishes, lettuce, and cress. Then they found good reeds for thatch, and when the buildings were covered with these instead of boards and torn sails, they could almost bid defiance to the rains.

The pleasant weather which in South Africa is termed the winter passed away, and in October a large Hottentot clan—called by the Dutch the Kaapmans—made its appearance in the Cape peninsula with great herds of horned cattle and flocks of sheep, which were brought there for change of pasture. These people and the Europeans met openly on the most friendly terms, though each party was so suspicious of the other that a constant watch was kept. A supply of copper bars, brass wire, and tobacco had been brought from the Netherlands, and a trade in cattle was now opened. On the European side the commander conducted it in person, assisted only by a clerk and the interpreter Harry. All intercourse between other white men and these Hottentots was forbidden under very severe penalties, with the twofold object of preventing any interference with the trade and any act that might lightly provoke a quarrel.

Parties of the Kaapmans remained in the Cape peninsula nearly three months, during which time Mr. Van Riebeek procured in barter over two hundred head of horned cattle and nearly six hundred sheep. Before they left, they proposed that the commander should help them against a tribe with whom they were at war, and offered him the whole of the spoil whatever it might be. Mr. Van Riebeek replied that he had come to trade in friendship with all, and he declined to take any part in their quarrels.

By the end of the first year's residence of the Europeans in Table Valley the station had made very satisfactory progress. A large garden had been planted, and the stream that ran down from the mountain had been dammed up in several places, so that the whole of the cultivated ground—several acres in extent—could be irrigated. A plain hospital had been built of earthen walls and thatch roof, large enough to accommodate two or three hundred men. And another clan had visited the peninsula, with whom a cattle trade had been opened, so that there was plenty of fresh meat for the crews of all the ships that put into the bay.

The second winter was uneventful. Some building was carried on, oxen were trained to draw timber from the forests behind the Devil's peak, and much new ground was broken up. Wild animals gave more trouble than anything else. The lions were so bold that they invaded the cattle pens by night, though armed men were always watching them, and leopards came down from the mountain in broad daylight and carried away sheep under the very eyes of the herdsmen. One morning before daybreak there was a great noise in the poultry pens, and when the guards went to see what was the matter, they found that all the ducks and geese had been killed by wild cats. The country appeared to be swarming with ravenous beasts of different kinds.

A good look-out was kept over the sea, for the Netherlands and the Commonwealth of England were at war, and it was necessary to guard against being surprised by an English ship.

The Europeans had been living in Table Valley about eighteen months when the first difficulty with the natives occurred. One Sunday while they were listening to a sermon Harry and his people murdered a white boy who was tending the cattle, and ran away with nearly the whole herd. As soon as the event became known pursuing parties were sent out, but though the robbers were followed to the head of False Bay, only one cow that lagged behind was recovered. This occurrence naturally produced an ill-feeling towards the Hottentots on the part of the European soldiers and workmen. One of their companions had been murdered, and his blood was unavenged. The loss of their working oxen imposed heavy toil upon them. The fort was being strengthened with palisades cut in the forests behind the Devil's peak, and these had now to be carried on the shoulders of men. Then for some time after the robbery the pastoral clans kept at a distance, so that no cattle were to be had in barter; and the want of fresh meat caused much grumbling.

The directors had given the most emphatic orders

that the natives were to be treated with all possible kindness, and so, after a few months, when the runaways began to return to Table Valley, each one protesting his own innocence, no punishment was inflicted upon them for their bad conduct, but they were allowed to resume their former manner of living by collecting firewood and doing any little service of that nature.

As everything was now in good working order at the station, Mr. Van Riebeek began to send out small exploring parties, not so much to learn the physical condition of the country, however, as to make the acquaintance of Hottentot clans who could be induced to bring cattle to the fort for barter. This object was attained without crossing the nearest range of mountains, and therefore no one tried to go beyond that formidable barrier. During the next few years names were given to the various hills scattered over the western coast belt as far north as the mouth of the Elephant river, the Berg river was inspected from its source to its mouth, and acquaintance was made with several Hottentot tribes; but there was little or no advance in the knowledge of South African geography.

By this time nearly every garden plant of Europe and India was cultivated at the Cape, though potatoes and maize were not yet introduced. Oaks and firs, fruit trees of many kinds, several varieties of vines from Southern Germany and from France, and strawberries and blackberries were thriving. The foreign animals that had been introduced were horses from Java, and pigs, sheep, dogs, rabbits, and poultry from Europe.

Every season wheat and barley had been sown, but the crop had always failed. Just as it was getting ripe the south-east wind came sweeping through Table Valley, and destroyed it. But it was noticed that even when it was blowing a perfect gale at the fort, nothing more than a pleasant breeze was felt back of the Devil's peak. The commander therefore tried if grain could not be raised in that locality. At a place where a round grove of thorn trees was standing, from which it received the name Rondebosch, a plot of ground was laid under the plough, and some wheat, oats, and barley were sown. The experiment was successful, for the grain throve wonderfully well, and yielded a large return.

The Cape establishment was thus answering its purpose admirably, but the expense attending it was found to be greater than the directors of the East India Company had anticipated, so they cast about for some means of reducing its cost. After much discussion they resolved to locate a few burgher families on plots of ground in the neighbourhood of the fort, and instructed Mr. Van Riebeek to carry this design into execution. They were of opinion that the men, though not in their service, would assist in the defence of the station, so that the garrison could be reduced, and that from such persons vegetables, grain, fruit, pigs, poultry, &c., could be purchased as cheaply as the Company could produce them with hired servants. The plan was to select a few respectable married men from the workpeople, to send their wives and children out to them, and to give them a start as market gardeners or small farmers.

V.

FOUNDATION OF THE CAPE COLONY.

IN February 1657 nine of the Company's servants took their discharge, and had small plots of ground allotted to them along the Liesbeek river at Rondebosch. They were the first South African colonists in the true sense of the word. They were provided on credit with everything that was necessary to give them a fair start as agriculturists, and in return they bound themselves to deliver the produce of their ground at the fort at reasonable prices until the debt was cleared off.

Within a few months thirty-eight others took their discharge on the same conditions. But it soon appeared that many of these men were not adapted for the life of independent gardeners, and it became necessary to take them back into the Company's service, when the ground that they had occupied was given to others on trial. In this manner a selection was constantly being made, in which only the steady and industrious remained as permanent colonists. There was a rule that only married men of Dutch or German birth should have land assigned to them, but it was not strictly observed, and single men who were mechanics or who would take service with gardeners were frequently discharged by the Company. As soon as a man proved himself able to make a competent living, he had only to apply for his wife and children to be sent out from Europe, and with the next fleet they were forwarded to him. The descendants of many of those who at this time became colonists are now scattered over South Africa from the Cape of Good Hope to the Zambesi and Benguela.

In this manner the colonisation of South Africa was commenced, but as yet there was no intention of forming a European settlement of any great extent. A few gardeners, fruit growers, and poultry breeders within four or five miles of the fort comprised the whole scheme which the East India Company had in view. These people were to pay tithes of any grain they might produce after twelve years' occupation, but were otherwise to be left untaxed. It was still supposed that as many cattle as were needed could be obtained from the Hottentots.

In 1658 the great mistake of introducing negro slaves was made, a mistake from which the country has suffered much in the past and must suffer for all time to come. There was no necessity for the introduction of these people. The climate for nine months in the year is to Europeans the pleasantest in the world, and even during the other three—excepting from twenty to thirty excessively hot days—white men can labour in the open air without discomfort. The settlement could have been purely European.

But in the seventeenth century it was the custom of all colonising nations to make of the negro a hewer of wood and drawer of water, and the Dutch merely acted in the spirit of the age.

From a Portuguese slave ship captured at sea the first negroes brought to the Cape settlement were taken, and shortly afterwards a number arrived from the coast of Guinea in one of the Company's vessels. Some of them were sold on credit to the burghers, but the greater number were kept by the government to do whatever rough labour was needed. This fixed the character of the colony, for the system once entered upon could only with great difficulty be altered. The white man and the black cannot work side by side on equal terms, hence manual labour came to be regarded by the Europeans as degrading, a sentiment that has not died out at the present day.

The Dutch laws at that time made manumission extremely easy, and freed negroes had all the rights of colonists, though they were without the hereditary training necessary to enable them to make proper use of their privileges. As soon, however, as it was ascertained by experience that they were too indolent and thriftless to put by anything for sickness or old age, when they became a burden upon the community, a law was made that any one emancipating a slave under ordinary circumstances must not only give security that he or she would not become a dependent upon the poor funds within a certain number of years, but also pay a sum of money into the poor funds as a premium on the risk of his or her requiring aid after that period. This checked manumission considerably, still as many slaves were emancipated by the testaments of their owners, and others obtained their liberty under special circumstances, the free negroes would have become a large body in course of time if they had not been swept away by imported diseases, to which their habits of living made them an easy prey.

Besides negroes, the East India Company at this time began to introduce Asiatics—chiefly natives of Malacca, Java, and the Spice islands—into the settlement. These persons were criminals sentenced by the high court of justice at Batavia to slavery either for life or for a term of years, and were then sent to South Africa to undergo their punishment. In intelligence they were far above the natives of Guinea or Mozambique, many of them being able to work as masons, harness makers, coopers, and tailors. They all professed the Moslem religion. Being without women of their own nationality, they formed connections with African slave girls, and thus arose one of the many classes of mixed breeds in the country.

At a little later date the Company made of South Africa a place of banishment for Indian political prisoners of high rank, who were often accompanied by their families and numerous attendants, male and female. These people had fixed allowances from the government for their support. Sometimes families of their dependents became attached to the country, and preferred to remain here when the time came for their return to Java if they had chosen to go back. A race of pure Asiatics thus arose, never very numerous, though for more than a century political offenders continued to be sent from Batavia to Capetown. The last were some natives of high rank in the islands of Tidor and Ternate, who made their escape from this country in 1781.

One of these exiles was the Sheikh Joseph, who took a leading part in the Bantamese civil war of 1682, and who was a determined opponent of the Dutch. He was a man of great repute for sanctity, and was believed by his Moslem followers to have performed some extraordinary miracles. He died near the head of False Bay, and his tomb there is still a place of pilgrimage for Mohamedans in South Africa.

Thus early in the history of the Cape Colony three varieties of human beings were introduced: Europeans, negroes, and Javanese. The aboriginal Hottentots formed a fourth variety. As years passed away mixed breeds of every colour between these four extremes were to be seen, side by side with the pure races, so that nowhere else could such a diversity of hue and of features be found as in the Cape peninsula. The crosses between Europeans and the lower races did not increase in number as rapidly as pure breeds, however, owing to a lack of high fertility among themselves, and unless connected again with one of their ancestral stocks, they often died out altogether in the third generation. The same may be said of the half-breed Asiatics and negroes, but the cross between the others was more fertile.

The pastoral Hottentot clans looked upon the

European settlement along the Liesbeek with a good deal of jealousy. It was not alone the ground under cultivation that was lost to them, for the government had given the burghers a free right of pasture, and thus the ancient owners were excluded from the best patches of grass along the base of the mountain. Early in 1659 the two clans that had always been accustomed to visit the Cape peninsula in the summer season with their flocks and herds appeared there as usual, and were informed that they must keep away from the grass that the Company and the burghers needed. This announcement was not at all to their liking. They had ample pasture left in the peninsula for ten times the number of cattle in their possession, and all the country stretching away beyond the isthmus as far as could be seen was theirs to roam over; but they were like other people, they did not relish being deprived by force of anything that they regarded as their own.

So they commenced to drive off the burghers' cows, and murdered a white herdsman. The beachrangers in Table Valley, though they were certainly gainers by the presence of the Europeans, and though they had a long-standing feud with the pastoral clans, now joined their countrymen. In this manner what the colonists termed the first Hottentot war began.

In fact, however, it could hardly be termed a war, for the natives were careful to avoid a pitched battle, and the Europeans were unable to surprise any large body of them. On two occasions only were small parties met, when six or seven were killed and a few more were wounded. The pastoral clans then abandoned the peninsula, and the beachrangers, upon begging for peace, were allowed to return to Table Valley.

A strong fence, through which cattle could not be driven, was now made along the outer boundary of the settlement, three watchhouses were built to defend it, and in these were stationed companies of horsemen, whose duty it was to patrol the border. Some powerful dogs were imported from Java, and the Europeans then considered themselves secure.

The Hottentots were the first to make overtures for a restoration of friendship. About a twelvemonth after the first breach of the peace they sent messengers to the fort to propose a reconciliation, and as these were well received the chiefs followed, when terms were agreed to. These were that neither party was thereafter to molest the other, that the lately hostile clans were to endeavour to induce those living farther inland to bring cattle to the fort for sale, that the Europeans were to retain possession of the land occupied by them, that roads were to be pointed out along which the Hottentots could come to the fort, and that any European who molested a Hottentot should be severely punished.

After the conclusion of peace the cattle trade went on briskly. Bartering parties were sometimes sent out, but Hottentots often came from a distance of eighty or a hundred miles with troops of oxen and flocks of sheep for sale. They were very eager to obtain bright coloured beads and other trifles. The quantity of beads given for an ox cost only from eight to ten pence, but there were other and larger expenses connected with the trade. Presents, consisting of flat pieces of copper, wire, iron rods, axes, tobacco, pipes, and other articles, were frequently made to the chiefs to secure their friendship, and all who came to the fort were liberally entertained. The burghers were strictly prohibited from holding intercourse of any kind with other Hottentots than the beachrangers, but in defiance of the law some of them found means to carry on a petty cattle trade.

After ten years' service in South Africa Mr. Van Riebeek was sent on to India, where he received promotion, and Mr. Zacharias Wagenaar took his place at the Cape. During this commander's term of office—which extended over four years—a few events occurred that are worthy of notice.

In earlier years a catechist, who was also a schoolmaster, held services on Sundays, and the chaplains of ships that called administered the sacraments. But now the settlement was provided with a resident clergyman. From this time onward there was a fully organised church, subject to the spiritual control of the classis or presbytery of Amsterdam.

In 1664 the island of Mauritius was taken into possession by the Dutch East India Company to keep it from falling into other hands, and it was made a dependency of the Cape station. A few men were sent there to cut ebony logs, and once a year a packet took supplies to them from Table Bay and brought back a cargo of timber.

Owing to the threatening attitude of England, the directors resolved to build a strong fortress in Table Valley, as the walls of earth, which were considered ample protection against Hottentots, would be a poor defence if a British force should land. The castle of Good Hope, which is still standing, was commenced in 1666, and was completed in 1674. It is now useless for military purposes, but for some time after its construction it was considered almost impregnable. The directors, who were beginning to realise that the French and the English might prove formidable rivals in the eastern seas, had come to regard their station in the Cape peninsula as a strategic point of great importance. "The castle of Good Hope," they wrote, "is the frontier fortress of India," and as such they provided it with a strong garrison.

Commander Wagenaar's successors for some time were men of very little note, and nothing of much consequence occurred to disturb the quiet course of life in the settlement. All was bustle and activity when the outward or homeward bound Indian fleets were in the bay, but after their anchors were raised there was nothing to create excitement. The workmen engaged in building the castle and the garrison when it was completed increased the demand for food, so that more servants of the Company took their discharge and set up for themselves as market gardeners. Soon the best plots of land within the boundary fence were all taken up, and then the fence was disregarded and the settlement spread out to the present village of Wynberg. The proportion of men who took their discharge and succeeded in making a living on their own account was, however, always very small. It was probably not ten per cent. of the whole. The

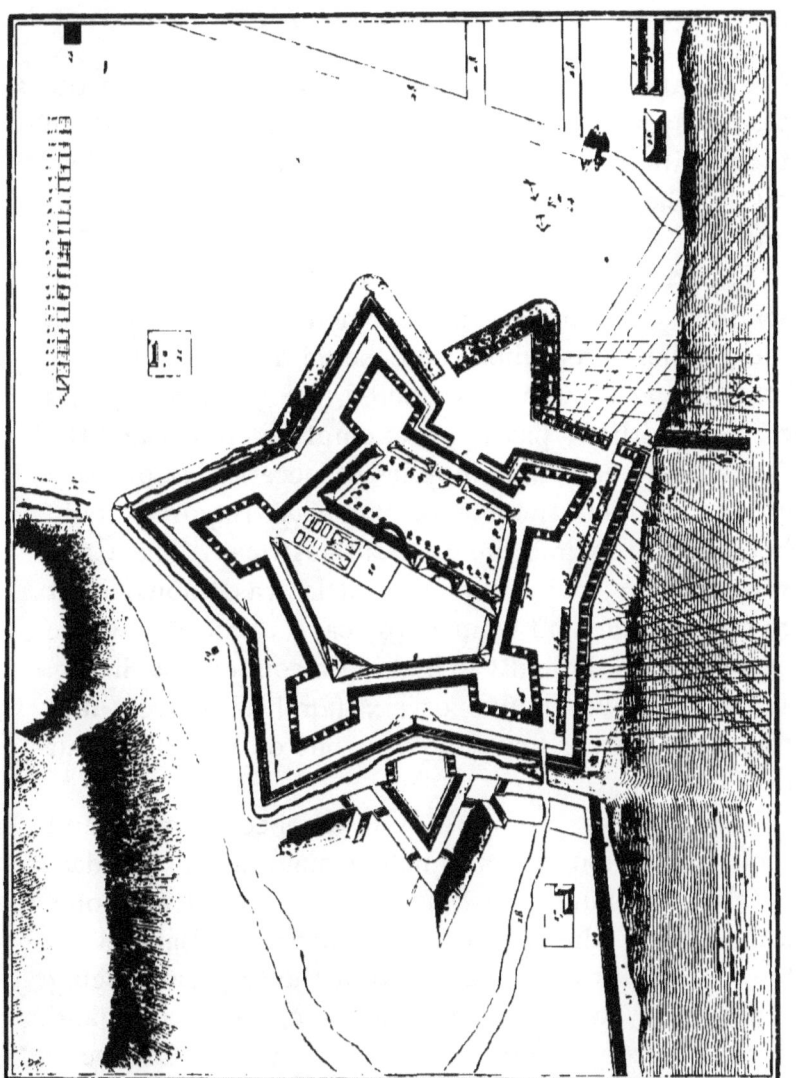

PLAN OF THE CASTLE OF GOOD HOPE.

others after a trial had to be taken back into the Company's service as soldiers or sailors, most of them with debts that they could never wholly clear off. The system was thus a very unsatisfactory one.

The directors thought of improving upon it by sending out families accustomed to agriculture in the Netherlands, who would serve as models for the others; but though they offered free passages, grants of land without payment, exemption from the tithe for twelve years, and supplies of necessaries on easy credit, very few people of the class required could be induced to migrate to South Africa. The Cape was too far away and too little was known of it to tempt men and women to leave a country where there was no difficulty in making a comfortable living. In 1671, however, five or six families arrived, and thereafter during several years one or two came out occasionally.

Twenty years after Mr. Van Riebeek landed and took possession of as much ground as he needed, without thinking of asking the consent of any one, a member of the high court of justice at Batavia on his way back to Europe called at the Cape, and being superior in rank to any one here, took command during his stay. This officer—Arnout van Overbeke by name—considered it advisable to make a formal purchase of territory from the nearest Hottentot chiefs, and these petty potentates, on being applied to, very readily gave their consent. If they reasoned at all about the matter, they probably thought that the price offered was clear gain, for the white people would certainly take as much ground as they needed, whether sold to them or not.

At any rate the principal chief of one tribe and the regents of another affixed their marks to documents that are still in existence, in which they ceded to the East India Company the whole territory from Saldanha Bay to False Bay, reserving to themselves and their people, however, the right to move freely about and make use of any part of it not occupied by Europeans. They received nominally in return goods to the value of £1,600, actually—according to the accounts furnished to the directors—the articles transferred cost £9 12s. 9d.

A few months after this transaction an outpost was formed at Hottentots-Holland, near the head of False Bay, on the eastern side of the isthmus. One of the objects in view was to raise a large quantity of wheat, for which purpose the ground at that place appeared specially suitable, but the chief design was to provide a retreat for the garrison in case it should be needed. The Free Netherlands were then engaged in the most unequal struggle that modern Europe has witnessed, for Louis XIV of France, Charles II of England, and the ecclesiastical princes of Cologne and Munster were united against them. On two occasions shortly before the war broke out the admirals of French fleets had taken possession of Saldanha Bay, though without leaving any men there to guard it, and it was believed that the French king might make an effort to seize the Cape peninsula. An attack by the English was equally probable. As events turned out, the Dutch got the better of their opponents in Europe, and the Cape settlement was not molested, so that the outpost at Hottentots-Holland became simply a farming establishment where the wheat needed by the Company was grown.

By this time the belt of land along the sea coast as far eastward as Mossel Bay had been thoroughly explored by parties sent out to obtain cattle. In 1658 some members of a trading expedition climbed to the top of the mountain barrier near the ravine through which the Little Berg river flows; but the land as far as they could see appeared to be uninhabited, so there was nothing to induce further search in that direction. Nine years later another way over the barrier was found at the place now known as Sir Lowry's pass, sixty miles south of the ravine of the Little Berg river. The Hottentot tribes termed the Hessequa, Gauriqua, Attaqua, and Outeniqua were then successfully reached and traded with. Those previously known along the western coast were the Chainouqua, the Goringhaiqua (or Kaapmans), the Cochoqua, the Grigriqua, and the Namaqua.

Bushmen had been met on several occasions, and their manner of living was pretty well known. Some of these wild people had once attempted to seize the merchandise belonging to a European trading party, when a number of them were shot down, greatly to the satisfaction of the Hessequa and other Hottentots who lived in the neighbourhood of the place where the event occurred.

VI.

THE SECOND HOTTENTOT WAR AND ITS CONSEQUENCES.

ONE of the most powerful of the Hottentot tribes near the Cape peninsula was called the Cochoqua, or by some name which the Europeans wrote in that form, for probably it had clicks in it. This tribe was composed of two great clans, the larger of which was under a chief named Gonnema. Gonnema had an evil reputation among all the other Hottentots with whom the Dutch were acquainted, for he was in the habit of swooping down upon them unawares and helping himself to their daughters and their cattle, and they were too weak to resist him. He had sold a good many oxen to the white people, but they did not like him either, for his bearing was never very friendly. They usually termed him the black captain, on account of his habit of using soot instead of clay to paint himself with.

In 1673 a war broke out between Gonnema and the Europeans, the only war that has ever taken place between white people and natives in South Africa of which we have not the versions of both parties to form a judgment from. The Cochoqua clan has left no story, nor is there a plea on its behalf on record. But the Dutch accounts are full of details, and it is easy from them to ascertain how Gonnema came to feel himself aggrieved.

The country was teeming with game, antelopes of many kinds, elephants, rhinoceroses, and hippopotami. Hunters were sent out from the fort, and brought back waggons laden with dried meat, which was supplied to the garrison instead of beef. The hippopotamus, or sea-cow as it was called, was specially sought after, for its flesh was regarded as equal to pork, and whips made of its hide commanded a very high price everywhere. Parties of burghers were in the habit of getting leave from the government and going out hunting elands and sea-cows, sometimes being away from home three or four weeks together. It never seems to have occurred to the white people that the Hottentots might object to the destruction of so much game, but very likely that was the cause of Gonnema's hostility.

In 1672 he came upon some hunters at Riebeek's Kasteel, and took their waggons and other property, but allowed them to escape with their lives. In the following year he made prisoners of eight burghers and a slave who were hunting near the same place, and after detaining them some days murdered them all. At the same time one of his sub-captains surprised a little trading outpost of the Company at Saldanha Bay, plundered it, and murdered four Europeans.

A mixed force of soldiers and burghers was then

sent against the Cochoqua clan, and as it was partly composed of horsemen it had the good fortune to cut off Gonnema's people from a strong position to which they tried to retreat and to seize eight hundred of their horned cattle and nine hundred sheep. The Hottentots followed the expedition when returning to the fort, but did not succeed in recovering their stock. Ten or twelve of them were shot, and on the other side one burgher was wounded.

Various clans now offered their aid against Gonnema, and were accepted as allies by the Europeans. For several months the Cochoqua kept out of the way, but at length they were so nearly surrounded that they barely managed to escape, leaving all their cattle behind. The spoil was much greater than on the first occasion, and was divided between the Europeans and the Hottentot allies.

Gonnema after this loss kept to the mountains for nearly two years, avoiding his enemies, but preventing all intercourse between them and the tribes beyond. Then he pounced suddenly upon some of the Hottentot allies of the Europeans, and with the loss of only fifteen of his own men killed a good many of them and swept off the greater part of their herds. He was pursued by all the soldiers and burghers that could be mustered, but he got safely away to his mountain fastnesses. No expedition sent against him after that time managed to surprise him, for his scouts were always on the alert. The Europeans found that they were wearying themselves to no purpose in trying to find him, so they desisted from the fruitless task.

For four years the settlement was kept practically in a condition of blockade on the land side, when Gonnema sent to ask for peace, as he was tired of living like a Bushman in the mountains. His messengers were well received, and were followed by three of his chief men, who agreed in his name to the terms proposed. They were that there should be peace and friendship between all the parties engaged in the war, and that Gonnema should pay to the Company a yearly tribute of thirty head of cattle. Presents were then exchanged, and the land was once more at rest.

Perhaps it was never intended that tribute should really be paid, at any rate it was considered prudent not to refer to the subject again, and the Cochoqua clan was left untroubled about it.

This was the last war with Hottentots during the rule of the Dutch East India Company in South Africa. It was a trifling affair if considered by the number of combatants or the quantity of spoil, and not a single hand-to-hand engagement had taken place; but it had very important consequences. During four years Gonnema had cut off the cattle trade, so there was no fresh beef or mutton for the crews of the fleets that called, and even the hospital could not be supplied, as the oxen and sheep that were captured and that the clans in alliance with the Europeans were able to furnish were soon exhausted. The Company was not disposed to run the risk of a second experience of this kind. The expense of the station had grown very far beyond original expectations, there was now a huge fortress to be kept up and a large garrison to be maintained in addition to victualling charges properly so called; and such an outlay could only be justified by the perfect efficiency of the establishment. If a supply of fresh meat could not be depended upon, one of the main objects of its existence was a failure. And as trade with the Hottentots might at any time be cut off again, European cattle-breeders must be introduced.

The great difficulty in the way was the scarcity of Europeans with the habits needed. They would be obliged to live far apart, and would be exposed to plunder by the natives and losses from the ravages of wild animals. The country was swarming with lions, leopards, hyenas, and jackals; and with the clumsy firelocks of those days it was a risky matter to go out alone into the wilds. As a commencement the Company established several cattle posts on its own account on the eastern side of the isthmus, to which cows and ewes were sent as they could be procured in barter, and at each a corporal was stationed with a few soldiers to guard the stock.

Then offers were made to the gardeners at Rondebosch and Wynberg to improve their prospects by turning cattle breeders. They could select land near the Company's posts, so that they would not be altogether without companionship, no taxes of any kind would be demanded from them till they were in a good position, and breeding cattle would be lent to them to take care of, half the increase of which would be their own. The view of the government was that if gardeners and small farmers could not be procured as emigrants from Europe, they must be trained in the old way of selection to take the place of those who should become stock-breeders.

The prospect, however, did not appear very attractive, for before the close of 1679 only eight burghers accepted the Company's offer, and took up their residence beyond the isthmus.

At this time a very energetic man, named Simon van der Stel, arrived from Amsterdam as commander. No one could have been better qualified to carry out the new project, and he threw himself heart and soul into it. He had, however, a particular desire that only Netherlanders should settle in the country, for he believed that whatever was Dutch was good, and whatever was not Dutch was not worth bothering about. But the directors in Holland were not of this opinion. They were very glad to obtain the services of competent men of all nationalities, and provided the majority of the settlers were Dutch they were quite willing to give equal privileges to others.

Except in this respect Simon van der Stel was allowed to carry out the plan in his own way. He began by inducing a party of eight families to remove from Rondebosch to a fertile and beautiful valley beyond the isthmus, where he gave them large plots of ground in freehold, with extensive grazing rights beyond. This settlement, which was named Stellenbosch, he intended to be the centre of a district in which all kinds of farming pursuits should be carried on, where vineyards should be planted and wine be made, where wheat should be grown and cattle be reared. When the fleets from India put into Table Bay on their way home, the commander's agents ingratiated themselves with the people on board, and whenever a man likely to make a good colonist was discovered, inducements were held out to him to remain in the country. In this way the vacancies were filled up in the Cape peninsula as fast as they arose, and many new-comers could be located beside experienced men at Stellenbosch.

A few years later a settlement was formed in a similar manner at Drakenstein, in the valley of the Berg river, one of the most charming situations in South Africa.

The directors were doing all that was in their power to get suitable people to migrate from the Netherlands. Among others they sent out a few young women from the orphan asylums in Amsterdam and Rotterdam, who were carefully protected and provided for until they found husbands in the colony.

And now an event took place in Europe which enabled them to secure over a hundred families of the very best stamp. This was the revocation by Louis XIV of the edict of Nantes, which drove many thousands of Protestant refugees from France into Holland. Their presence in some of the provinces so greatly reduced the demand for labour that industrious Dutch families were more willing to remove than they had previously been, and the Company was able to send to South Africa nearly two hundred Huguenots and about the same number of Dutch people of both sexes and all ages. Upon their arrival they were scattered over the country between the Groenberg, the Koeberg, and Hottentots-Holland, the larger number of the French being located in the valley of the Berg river. Care was taken, however, to mix them together, so that the nationalities would speedily become blended.

Having now a base to fall back upon if necessary, a few stragglers began to push their way in one direction down the Berg river, and in another beyond the Koeberg. Still, at the close of the seventeenth century there was no white man living more than forty-five miles from the castle, and the whole territory occupied by Europeans was within the range of mountains visible from ships at anchor in Table Bay.

The colonists, with their wives and children, were then some fourteen hundred in number. The French Huguenots were about one-sixth of the whole, a rather larger proportion consisted of Germans from the borderland between the high and low Teutons, and nearly two-thirds were Dutch from the different Netherland provinces. The Germans were, almost without exception, men who were married to Dutch women. Intermarriages between the Huguenots and other colonists were common, and in another generation distinctions of nationality were entirely lost.

The language used in common conversation was Dutch made as simple and expressive as possible, so as to be understood by slaves with only the mental capacities of children. Grammatical rules were disregarded. In the pulpit and in family devotions, however, correct Dutch was used, as it is very generally to the present day.

There were three churches provided with clergymen: in Capetown, at Stellenbosch, and at Drakenstein. At each of these places there was also a public school, in which children were taught to read the bible, to cast up simple accounts, to repeat the Heidelberg catechism, and to sing the psalms. The Dutch reformed was the state church, and no other public services were allowed, but in their own houses people might hold any kind of worship that they pleased.

The head of the settlement was now termed the governor. Public matters of all kinds were regulated by a council of eight individuals, who were the highest officials in rank in the country. In this council the governor sat as president. In Capetown there was a court for the trial of petty cases, and a high court of justice, from whose decisions there was an appeal to the supreme court at Batavia. Three burghers had seats in the high court of justice whenever cases affecting colonists were tried. They were the spokesmen between the colonists and the government, and were consulted upon all matters affecting the settlement, but they had no votes outside the court of justice. They were called burgher councillors.

At Stellenbosch there was a court which had cognisance of all petty cases beyond the Cape peninsula. It was presided over by an official termed a landdrost, who also collected the revenue and looked after the Company's interests generally. Eight burghers—termed heemraden—had seats and votes. This court acted further as a district council, in which capacity it saw to the repair of roads, the distribution of water, the destruction of noxious animals, and various other matters. It raised a revenue by erecting a mill to grind corn and leasing it to the highest bidder, by collecting a yearly tax of one shilling and fourpence for every hundred sheep or twenty head of horned cattle owned by the farmers, and by sundry other small imposts. Further, it had power to compel the inhabitants to supply waggons, cattle, slaves, and their own labour for public purposes.

In Capetown there was an orphan chamber, which acted as trustee of property belonging to children when a parent died. There was also a matrimonial court, before which every person in the settlement—male and female—who wished to be married had to appear and show that there were no legal impediments to the union.

All these bodies—burgher councillors, petty court of justice, heemraden, orphan chamber, and matrimonial court—as also the consistories of the churches, were in a manner self-perpetuating corporations. Every year some of their members retired, but before doing so double lists of names were sent by the boards to the government, and from these lists their successors were appointed. Such a thing as popular election to any office was unknown. The system worked well on the whole, and the people were satisfied with it.

The burghers were required to meet at stated periods for drill and practice in the use of arms, and all were held liable for service in case of the appearance of an enemy. They were formed into companies of cavalry and infantry, each with its standard of a particular colour. Most of them were excellent marksmen, owing to their habits of frequently hunting game; but their firearms were very clumsy weapons compared with those of our day. To reduce the cost of the garrison, numbers of soldiers were permitted to engage as servants to burghers, on condition that they could be called back to their colours at any time.

Capetown at the close of the century contained about eighty private houses. The great garden of the Company, which Simon van der Stel had partly converted into a nursery for European, Indian, and native plants, was regarded as something marvellous by visitors of all nations, so great a variety of vegetation was to be seen and admired there. This governor, upon his retirement in 1699, went to live upon a beautiful estate which the Company gave him a little beyond Wynberg, where he planted the vineyards that in later years produced the celebrated Constantia wines. He was an enthusiast in the matter of cultivating oak trees, and during the twenty years of his government many scores of thousands were planted by his orders all over the settlement.

The system of taxation was as bad as could be devised, so far as effect upon the character of the people was concerned. The exclusive right to sell various articles—among others spirituous liquors—was sold by auction as a monopoly to the highest bidder. Upon anything that the government required—such as beef and mutton—a price per pound was fixed to the residents in Capetown, and a much higher price to foreigners; the monopoly was then put up for sale, and whoever offered to supply the Company at the lowest rate became the purchaser. Thus beef might be a penny a pound to a mechanic in Capetown, twopence a pound to the captain of an English ship, and a halfpenny a pound to the Company's hospital. The tithe of grain and the district tax upon cattle were both paid upon returns made by the farmers themselves, so that a premium was offered for falsehood. This system was soon discovered to be vicious, but it was continued without modification until towards the close of the next century.

The government exercised the right of fixing the price of anything that it needed, and prohibiting the sale of the article to any one else until its own wants were supplied. Thus, if half-a-dozen Dutch ships and two or three English Indiamen were lying at anchor in Table Bay at a time when the meal in the Company's stores was exhausted, the Englishmen would certainly get no bread until the Hollanders' tables were covered. But, upon the whole, strangers were much better treated here than the Dutch were treated in foreign ports, and it was only in times of scarcity that they had cause to complain of anything except high prices.

The Company was supposed to be the only wholesale merchant in the country. From its stores in Capetown shopkeepers were supplied with imported goods, and everything that was exported in bulk passed through its hands. But in point of fact a large proportion of the trade of the country was carried on with ships' people, Dutch and foreign. From the captain of an Indiaman of any nationality down to the youngest midshipman, every one had some little venture of his own that he was always ready to trade with. It might be a bale of calico, or it might be a slave, for many bondsmen were brought to South Africa in this way. Even among the foremast hands the spirit of commerce was strong. A sailor when homeward bound was commonly accompanied by monkeys and parrots and cockatoos and various descriptions of birds and beasts till the forecastle was often like a menagerie, in his chest he had fancy articles from Japan, silk handkerchiefs from China, or perhaps some curiosities picked up at an Indian isle. This kind of commerce was very petty, but in the aggregate it must have amounted to something considerable, for the inhabitants of Capetown during more than a hundred years lived and throve upon it. Nowhere in the world, we read again and again in accounts of travellers of many nationalities, could a greater variety of goods be purchased and sold. The traffic was carried on openly, for though there was a law that goods should not be imported by foreigners, it was not applied to ventures by ships' people—English, French, or Danish—on their own account.

By this time the knowledge of South African geography had very greatly increased. Simon van der Stel himself with a large party of attendants had visited the copper mountain of Little Namaqualand, and had received information from the natives there of the great river now known as the Orange. Some Dutch and English sailors, shipwrecked on the eastern coast, before they were rescued had travelled in one

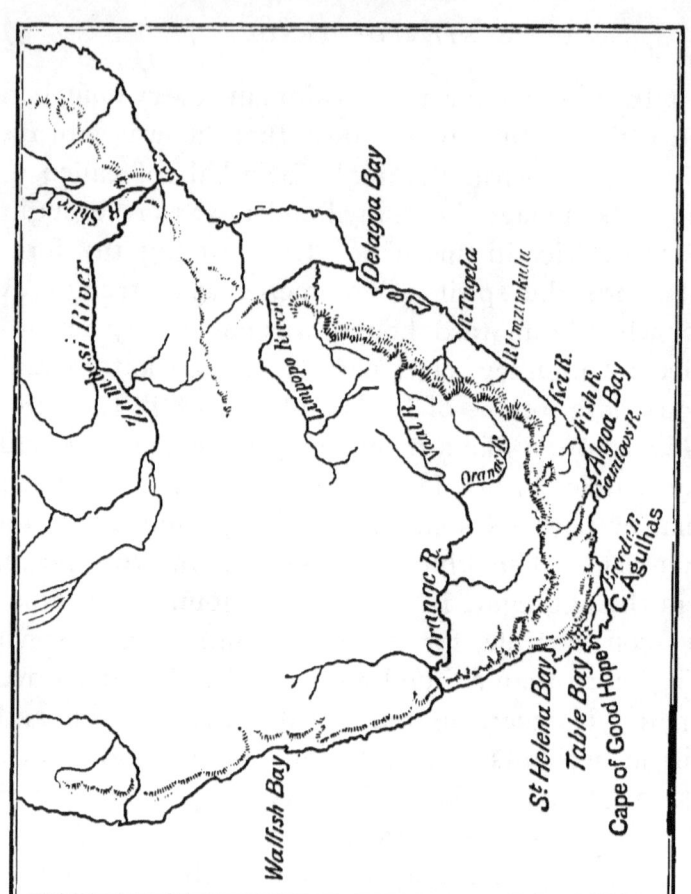

EXTENT OF THE SETTLEMENT IN 1700

direction to Delagoa Bay, and in the other to the Buffalo river. From them as accurate an account of the southern Bantu tribes was obtained as any we have at the present day. Parties of cattle traders had brought back information of every Hottentot tribe in existence except the Korana. But as yet no white man had set foot upon the plain of the Karoo, and consequently nothing was known of the far interior.

VII.

PROGRESS OF THE CAPE COLONY FROM 1700 TO 1750.

In the first year of the eighteenth century the second terrace upward from the sea began to be occupied by Europeans. Wilhem Adrian van der Stel, eldest son of Simon van der Stel, was then governor. He made a tour of inspection through the settlement, and afterwards crossed the mountain range close to the ravine of the Little Berg river, for the purpose of examining the country beyond. It was the beautiful tract of land now called the Tulbagh basin which the governor and his party entered, and it seemed to them to invite human occupation.

The settlement on the coast belt had been a success, but it had not been able to supply many cattle. The land was adapted for cultivation, there was a market within easy reach, and the ideas of the people favoured the plough. To this day the inhabitants of that part of the country depend upon their crops of wheat, their fruit, and their wine, and keep no more oxen and sheep than are required for their own use.

LIFE OF THE EARLY SETTLERS. 61

On the other side of the mountain range agriculture was not then possible. The Tulbagh basin is fertile ; its extensive corn lands, its vineyards, and the gardens and orchards round its homesteads form now a pleasant sight in the early summer ; but in those days, when there was no other way of access to it than over a mountain that could only be crossed with the greatest difficulty, no man would think of making a living by the plough. Cattle breeding alone could be depended upon there.

A small military outpost was formed in the basin to protect the settlers from the Bushmen who had their haunts in the surrounding mountains, and then several families were induced to try their fortune in the lonely vale. A few individuals were still being sent out from Europe every year, and the old system of discharging servants of the Company continued in practice, so that settlers were obtainable. But as a rule new-comers were located near the Cape peninsula, and young people born in the country commenced life for themselves beyond the mountain range.

Gradually they spread beyond the Tulbagh basin, down the valley of the Breede river, and over the Witsenberg to the high plateau called the Warm Bokkeveld. Others crossed the range at Hottentots-Holland, and pushed their way along the banks of the Zonderend and down towards the sea at Cape Agulhas. Others again kept up the western coast belt, passed the Piketberg, and in course of time reached the mouth of the Elephant river.

The life led by these pioneers of civilisation was

SOUTH AFRICAN TENT WAGGON.

rough and wild, but it had its own peculiar charm. Cattle breeding was found to pay fairly well. Sometimes Bushmen would drive off oxen or sheep, and a little excitement was caused by the pursuit of the marauders, but otherwise the time passed away quietly. The best of health was commonly enjoyed, and there was the most perfect freedom. The only direct tax towards the general revenue was £5 a year, which each grazier was required to pay, and for which he had a legal right to the use of six thousand acres of ground, with the privilege of moving into the Karoo for a couple of months every year to give his stock a change of pasture. During these migrations he and his family slept in a great tent waggon, and passed the day in the open air, usually selecting a patch of trees on the bank of a stream for a camping place. A distaste for town life, with its restraints and all the nameless annoyances to which simple people are exposed when in contact with men of sharper intellect, soon became part of the nature of a cattle breeder, and grew stronger with each succeeding generation. The children and grandchildren of Dutch gardeners, German mechanics, and Huguenot tradesmen by force of circumstances reverted in habits and in thought to the condition of semi-nomads. In the language of South Africa these people were called trekboeren, that is wandering farmers. Many of them became expert elephant hunters, and travelled great distances in search of ivory.

Behind them, as they moved onward, a more settled class of people occupied the country, though very thinly. These built better houses than the others, as soon as rough roads were made they combined agriculture with cattle breeding, and generally they led more stable lives. In this manner hardly a year passed by without an expansion of the settlement.

Wilhem Adrian van der Stel, who was governor when the colonists crossed the first mountain range, was a man of culture and ability, but he had an inordinate passion for making money, a fault that was common to many of the Company's servants. To get together a fortune with which to return to the Netherlands was an object ever before the eyes of these men, and the system under which they served favoured the accomplishment of their plans. The Company paid its officers the smallest of salaries, but allowed them perquisites of various kinds. In the preceding chapter mention has been made of the trade carried on under its sanction by the people of its fleets. Its officials on shore had even greater privileges. Some of them received commissions on sales and purchases of goods, others held monopolies of lucrative duties, others again were allowed to trade in specified articles on their own account. Spices only were guarded with the most extreme jealousy, and if any one had ventured to buy or sell a pound of pepper or a dozen nutmegs except at the Company's stores, dismissal from the service would have been the lightest part of his punishment.

It followed from this system that in the early days of the settlement the officials in South Africa were in general exceedingly anxious to get on to India, because there was little or nothing to be made here. Some of them had been allowed to carry on farming on their own account, the landdrost of Stellenbosch had a monopoly as an auctioneer, the secretary of the council had a monopoly of making out certain legal documents, and several others had exclusive privileges; but what were these petty gains, they thought, to the wealth that was gathered by others in the Indian isles.

Wilhem Adrian van der Stel looked about for some means to fill his purse, but could devise nothing else than a farm. Of course he could not take ground for himself; but an officer of higher rank who called was obliging enough to give him a tract of land at Hottentots-Holland, to which he afterwards added by granting a plot of the adjoining ground to one of his dependents, and then purchasing it from the grantee at a nominal price. At this place he erected extensive buildings, planted nearly half a million vines, and laid out groves, orchards, and corn lands to a corresponding extent. In the open country beyond the mountain he kept from six to eight hundred breeding cattle and eight or ten thousand sheep. Of this extensive establishment the directors were kept in entire ignorance, and there is no mention whatever of it in any official document until complaints against the governor reached Holland.

The burghers looked upon the big farm with very lively indignation. Their principal gains were derived from the sale of produce to foreigners, and they saw that market being practically closed to them. The governor, they believed, would manage to secure the larger part of any profitable business for himself, and whatever escaped him would fall to his father, who

HOUSE ON W. A. VAN DER STEL'S ESTATE.
(From a Sketch by W. A. van der Stel.)

was farming at Constantia, or to his younger brother, who was farming below Stellenbosch.

There have never been people less willing to submit silently to grievances, real or imaginary, than the colonists of South Africa. In 1705 some of them sent a complaint of what was going on to the governor-general and council of India, but at Batavia nothing was done in the matter. Probably they did not expect redress from that quarter, for before there was time to receive a reply, a memorial to the directors was drawn up and signed by sixty-three of the best men in the settlement. In this document Wilhem Adrian van der Stel was accused of misconduct and corrupt practices tending to the serious loss and oppression of the colonists. Similar charges, but in a lower degree, were made against the officer next in rank to the governor and against the clergyman of Capetown. These persons also had been neglecting their public duties, and devoting their attention to farming.

With the arrival of the homeward-bound fleet at the beginning of 1706 the governor learnt of the complaint sent to Batavia, and immediately suspected that a similar charge would be forwarded to Holland. The danger of his position now drove him to acts of extreme folly as well as of tyranny. He caused a certificate to be drawn up, in which he was credited with the highest virtues and the utmost satisfaction was expressed with his manner of ruling the colony. The residents in the Cape peninsula were invited to the castle, and were then requested to sign this certificate. The landdrost of Stellenbosch was directed to proceed with an armed party from house to house in the country, and get the residents there to sign it also. By these means two hundred and forty names in all were obtained, including those of a few Asiatics and free blacks. Many, however, refused to affix their signatures, even under the landdrost's threat that they would be marked men if they did not.

The governor suspected that a farmer at Stellenbosch named Adam Tas was the secretary of the disaffected party, and the landdrost was directed to have him arrested. Early one morning his house was surrounded by an armed party, he was seized and sent to the castle, his premises were searched, and his writing-desk was carried away. There could be no truce after this between the governor and his opponents, for if a burgher could be treated in this manner, upon mere suspicion of having drawn up a memorial to the high authorities, no man's liberty would be safe. Bail was at once offered for the appearance of Tas before a court of justice, but was refused. He was committed to prison, where he was kept nearly fourteen months.

In his desk was found the draft from which the memorial to the directors had been copied. It was unsigned, but papers attached to it indicated several of those who had taken part in the matter. Within the next few days seven of these were arrested, two of whom were committed to prison, one was sent to Batavia, and four were put on board a ship bound to Amsterdam. The governor hoped to terrify them into signing the certificate in his favour and denying the truth of the charges against him, but not one of them faltered for a moment. Their wives petitioned that the prisoners might be brought to trial at once before a proper court of justice, and when it was hinted that if they would induce their husbands to do what was desired, release would follow, these true-hearted women indignantly refused. In the meantime the memorial had been committed to the care of a physician in the return fleet, and after the ships sailed he gave it to one of the burghers who were banished.

The governor continued to act as if his will was above the law of the land. Further arrests of burghers were made by his direction, the properly constituted courts were abolished, and in their stead his creatures were appointed to office. The people of Stellenbosch, men and women, announced their determination to maintain their rights, upon which a body of soldiers was sent to support the landdrost.

Meantime three of the burghers sent to Europe arrived at Amsterdam, the other having died on the passage, and they lost not a day before presenting the memorial to the directors and making their own complaint. In a matter of this kind it was necessary to act with promptitude as well as with justice. The Company had numerous and powerful enemies always watching for a chance to attack it before the states-general, and a charge of oppression of free Netherlanders in one of its colonies would be a weapon of which they would not fail to make good use. A commission was therefore appointed to investigate the matter, and a report was presently sent in by it that the charges were very grave. In consequence the governor, the officer next in rank, the clergyman of Capetown, and the landdrost of Stellenbosch were suspended from duty and ordered to return to Europe to undergo a trial. The colonists sent delegates home to maintain their charges, and the result was that the offending officials were all dismissed from the service and Wilhem Adrian van der Stel's farm was confiscated.

From the documents connected with this case the views of the directors and of the colonists concerning the government of the country and the rights of its people can be gathered with great precision. The directors desired to have a large body of freemen living in comfort, loyal to the fatherland, ready and willing to assist in the defence of the colony if attacked, enjoying the same rights as their equals in Europe, and not differing much from each other in rank or position. They issued orders that no official, from the highest to the lowest, was to own or lease a tract of land larger than a garden, or to trade in any way in corn, wine, or cattle. The burghers were to be governed in accordance with law and justice.

On their part, the colonists claimed exactly the same rights as if they were still living in the Netherlands. They expressed no wish for a change in the form of government, what they desired being merely that the control of affairs should be placed in honest hands. In their opinion they forfeited nothing by removal to South Africa, and the violence displayed by the governor towards Adam Tas and his associates was as outrageous as if it had taken place in the city of Amsterdam. They asserted their undoubted right to personal liberty, to exemption from arrest unless under reasonable suspicion of crime, to admission to bail, to speedy trial before a proper court of justice, to freedom to sell to any one, burgher or foreigner, except under special circumstances when restriction was needed for the good of the community, whatever their land produced, after the tithes had been paid and the Company's needs had been supplied. And these claims, made in as explicit terms as they could be to-day by an Englishman living in a crown colony, were not challenged by the directors or even the partisans of the late governor, but were accepted by every one as unquestioned.

In 1710 the island of Mauritius was abandoned by the Dutch East India Company, the directors having come to the conclusion that it was not worth the cost of maintaining a large garrison, and that with a small garrison it was not secure. A few colonists who were there had the choice of removal to South Africa or to Java, and nine families elected to come to this country. A few months later the French took possession of the island, and under them it soon became a place of importance.

In 1713 a terrible evil came upon the country. In March of that year the small-pox made its first appearance in South Africa. It was introduced by means of some clothing belonging to ships' people who had been ill on the passage from India, but who had recovered before they reached Table Bay. This clothing was sent to be washed at the Company's slave lodge, and the women who handled it were the first to be smitten. The Company had at the time about five hundred and seventy slaves of both sexes and all ages, nearly two hundred of whom were carried off within the next six months.

From the slaves the disease spread to the Europeans and the natives. In May and June there was hardly a family in the town that had not some one sick or dead. Traffic in the streets was suspended, and even the children ceased to play their usual games in the squares and open places. At last it was impossible to obtain nurses, though slave women were being paid at the rate of four and five shillings a day. All the planks in the stores were used, and in July it became necessary to bury the dead without coffins. During that dreadful winter nearly one-fourth of the European inhabitants of the town perished, and only when the hot weather set in did the plague cease.

The disease spread into the country, but there the proportion of white people that perished was not so large as in the town. It was easier to keep from contact with sick persons. Some families living in secluded places were quite shut off from the rest of the colony, and the farmers in general avoided moving about.

The death rate among the free blacks was very high, but it was among the Hottentots that it reached its maximum. Whole kraals in the neighbourhood of the Cape peninsula disappeared without leaving a single representative. The unfortunate clans when attacked, believing that they were bewitched, gave way to despair, and made no effort to save themselves. The beachrangers in Table Valley did not even remove the dead from their huts, but sat down and awaited their own turn without a gleam of hope.

When the disease ceased there were only dejected remnants left of the old tribes of the Hessequa, Chainouqua, Goringhaiqua, Cochoqua, and Grigriqua. Beyond them it had not spread. After this date these tribal titles are not found in official records or accounts by travellers, and the Hottentot clans that remained within a hundred miles of the castle ceased to be regarded as of any importance. They continued as before to be governed by their own chiefs without interference from the European authorities except when they committed crimes against white people or slaves, there were reserves specially set apart for their use, and they were at liberty to roam over any land not occupied by colonists; but they were without influence or power, and their friendship was no longer courted nor their enmity feared.

It does not appear that the Bushmen suffered from the small-pox, for by some chance they did not come into contact with other people while it was prevalent. In general there was war between them and the colonists. As the game was destroyed or retreated, they turned to the oxen and sheep of the graziers for sustenance, and it was then a matter of necessity to expel them from their haunts. They would not, or could not, accommodate themselves to the new order of things that was growing up around them, and therefore they were doomed to perish. But the struggle was a severe one, and there were times when it almost seemed as if the wild people would be able to turn back the wave of colonisation that was spreading over the country. They managed to inflict heavy losses upon the Europeans by burning houses and driving off cattle, and occasionally a man or a woman died from the poison of their arrows; but in the long run the combined action of the farmers and the superiority of the flintlock over the bow decided the question against them.

In 1721 the Company established a station at Delagoa Bay, with the object of opening up a trade along the eastern coast. This station was a dependency of the Cape government, just as Mauritius had been. But the place proved exceedingly unhealthy, and the trade in gold, ivory, copper, and slaves was very much smaller than had been anticipated. On one occasion also the factory was surprised and plundered by pirates. Attempts were repeatedly made to explore the country and find the place from which a little alluvial gold was brought by occasional black visitors, but the parties sent out never succeeded in getting beyond the Lebombo mountains, as either fever attacked them or hostile natives barred the way. In every respect the station was a failure, and, therefore, after maintaining it for nearly ten years at a great sacrifice of life and money, the Company abandoned it.

After the punishment inflicted upon Wilhem Adrian van der Stel and his associates, the government of the Cape Colony was conducted for nearly three-quarters of a century in a fairly honest manner, and no complaint of tyranny or oppression was made by the people. The system of administration, indeed, opened a door to abuses that in the same form would not be tolerated now, and they were certainly of a grave nature. Thus a perquisite of the storekeeper was to buy at one rate of exchange of silver money and to sell at another rate, by which he gained a commission of nearly eightpence in the pound. The victualler was allowed to require a few pounds overweight in every bag of grain that the Company purchased from a farmer, and to place the surplus to his own credit. The police magistrate, as his perquisite, kept half the fines which he inflicted for contravention of simple regulations as well as for crimes. The governor himself and the officer second in rank had as perquisites a fixed sum deducted from the purchase amount of every cask of wine brought to the Company's stores.

But as this was the established order of things, the colonists submitted to it without complaint. Sometimes they grumbled about bad seasons, or the destruction of their crops by locusts, or the low prices given for farm produce; and cattle diseases of one kind or other often caused them much loss. When foreign vessels were in Table Bay, too, there was always much dissatisfaction if the Company required anything that was saleable at a large profit. There was never any distress, however, through want of the necessaries of life, nor was there any interference by the government with the recognised rights of the people.

Experiments in the cultivation of various plants

were frequently made by order of the directors, in the hope of finding something beside wheat and wine that would pay the farmers to grow and the Company to export. The olive was tried again and again, but always without success. Tobacco, indigo, and flax were also fruitlessly experimented with. Great expectations were once raised by the production of eight pounds of raw silk, but that also proved a failure, as the returns were so trifling that people would have nothing to do with it.

In the winter season Table Bay was unsafe, being exposed to the fury of north-west gales, and the Company had often sustained heavy losses by shipwreck there. Thus, in a terrible gale during the night of the 16th of June 1722 seven Dutch and three English vessels were driven ashore, and six hundred and sixty men were drowned. On this occasion property valued at nearly £250,000 was destroyed. And on the 21st of May 1737 nine vessels belonging to the Company were wrecked, and two hundred and eight lives were lost. The cost price of the cargo alone which was strewn on the beach was £160,000.

These and many other disasters caused the directors to issue orders that a mole should be constructed in Table Bay, so as to form a safe harbour, and in the meantime their ships were to refresh at Simon's Bay from the 15th of May to the 15th of August, the season when gales from the north-west are common. Simon's Bay offered secure shelter during the winter season, but there was a drawback to its use in difficulty of access by land, which made the supplying a ship with fresh provisions very expensive. In 1742 it was first used as a port of call. A village then sprang up on its southern shore, which received the name Simonstown.

The mole in Table Bay was commenced in February 1743. As it was held to be a work of importance to the colony as well as to the Company, a tax was levied upon all the white people in the settlement. Those in the Cape peninsula were assessed at the labour of one hundred and fifty-three stout slaves for two months in the year, and those in the country at £293 in money or provisions. All the Company's slaves and all the waggons and cattle that could be spared from other work were employed upon the mole. A strong gang of convicts was sent from Batavia to assist in its construction. By the close of 1746 it was three hundred and fifty-one feet in length from the shore, but the work was then stopped. The convicts from Java had nearly all died from change of climate and excessive fatigue, and the burghers declared that they could not pay their quota any longer. The expense was found to be beyond the means of the Company, though it was believed that if the work could be completed Table Bay would be a perfectly safe harbour. The base of the mole is still to be seen like a reef running out from the shore, and its site is called Mouille Point on that account to the present day.

By this time the settlement extended so far that it was considered necessary to provide two more churches in the parts most thickly populated and a court of justice for the colonists on the frontier. In

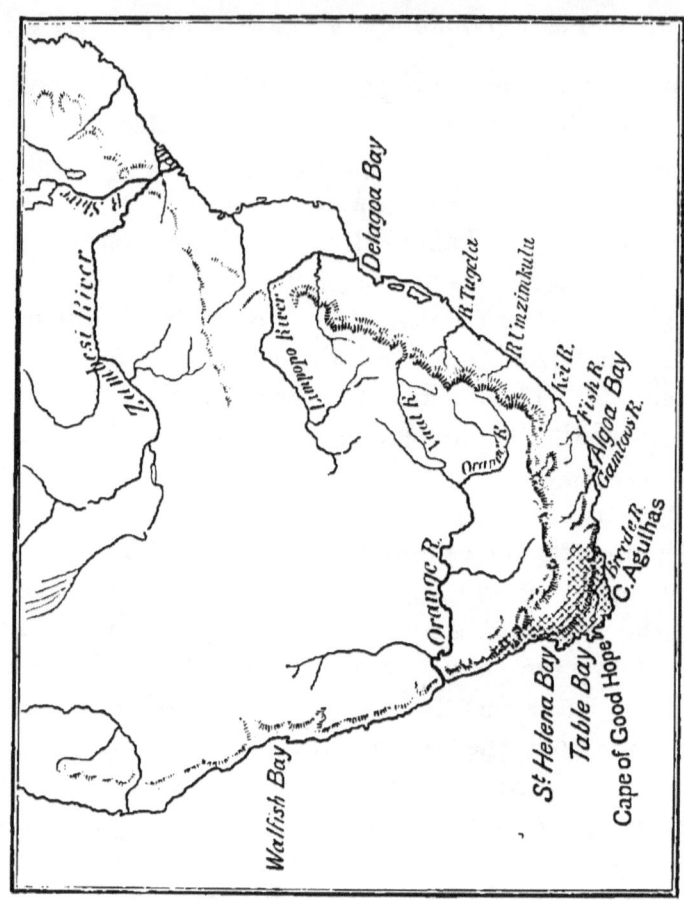

EXTENT OF THE CAPE COLONY IN 1750

1743 a clergyman was stationed at Roodezand, now the village of Tulbagh, and a church was established there. Two years later a clergyman and a schoolmaster were appointed to Zwartland, and went to reside at the warm bath, the site of the present village of Malmesbury. In 1745 a landdrost was stationed at a place thereafter known as the village of Swellendam, and a board of heemraden was appointed, just as at Stellenbosch. A dividing line was laid down between the districts of Stellenbosch and Swellendam, and also between the Cape and Stellenbosch, but on the north and the east the boundary was declared to be "where the power of the honourable Company ends."

VIII.

COURSE OF EVENTS IN THE CAPE COLONY FROM 1750 TO 1785.

From 1751 to 1771 the colony was governed by Ryk Tulbagh, a man of very high moral character and considerable ability, who had risen by merit alone from the humblest position in the Company's service. Though two great troubles fell upon the country within this period, it was always regarded by the old colonists as the brightest time during Dutch rule in South Africa. The governor was firm, but just and benevolent, and was so beloved that he was commonly called Father Tulbagh.

One of the troubles referred to was an outbreak of small-pox, that terrible scourge having been introduced at the beginning of the winter of 1755 by a homeward-bound fleet from Ceylon. At first it was supposed to be a kind of fever, but after a few days there were cases that admitted of no doubt. It assumed, however, various forms, and among some of the distant Hottentot tribes differed in appearance so much from what was held to be true small-pox that the Europeans termed it gall sickness.

In Capetown hardly a single adult who was attacked recovered. In July the weather was colder than usual, and during that month over eleven hundred persons perished. If that death rate had continued, before the close of the year there would have been no one left, but as soon as the warm weather set in the disease became milder. Two great hospitals were opened: one for poor Europeans, supported by church funds, the other for blacks. To the latter all slaves who were attacked were sent, the expense being borne by their owners. Those who recovered were employed as nurses. In Capetown from the beginning of May to the end of October nine hundred and sixty-three Europeans and eleven hundred and nine blacks died.

In the country the white people did not suffer very severely, as they kept so secluded on their farms that for several months hardly a waggon load of produce was taken to town for sale. The government excused the muster of the burghers for drill, and even the services in the churches were not attended by people from a distance.

With the Hottentot tribes that escaped on the former occasion the disease created fearful havoc. Not one was left unscathed, except the Korana along the Orange and its branches. On the coast northward to Walfish Bay and eastward until Bantu were reached, the tribes as such were utterly destroyed. The individuals that remained were thereafter blended together under the general name of Hottentots, and their old distinguishing titles became lost even among themselves.

How far the disease extended among the Bantu cannot be stated with certainty. These people had pushed their outposts as far westward as the Keiskama, and at least one Hottentot tribe—the Damaqua—had been incorporated by them, while another—the Gonaqua—was beginning to be assimilated. According to Tembu traditions the territory between the Kei and the Bashee was almost depopulated by the small-pox, and the clans between the Kei and the Keiskama must have suffered severely, but to what extent those beyond the Bashee were affected is not known.

The other trouble was a depression in the price of agricultural produce, especially of wine, that brought the colonists to the verge of bankruptcy. The Company had been in the habit of purchasing a considerable quantity of wine for sale and consumption in India, where it was served out instead of spirits to the soldiers and sailors, but so many complaints were made about its quality that in 1755 its use there was nearly abandoned. By some chance just at this time very few foreign ships put into Table Bay, so that the market was glutted with produce for which there was no demand. Prices fell lower than had ever been known before, and the farmers saw nothing but ruin before them.

But South Africa has always been a country of sudden reversions from adversity. In this instance matters were at their worst when in December 1758 a large fleet of French men-of-war and transports with troops arrived from Mauritius, purposely to refresh and lay in a supply of provisions. At once the price of produce doubled or trebled, and all the surplus stock was disposed of. There was then war between Great Britain and France, and the representatives of both nations in India soon came to look upon the Cape Colony as a convenient source of supply. The officers of French packets from Mauritius and of English packets from St. Helena bid against each other in Capetown for cattle and meal and wine, so that until March 1763, when tidings of the conclusion of peace were received, the farmers enjoyed unusual prosperity.

During Mr. Tulbagh's administration some previously unexplored parts of the country were carefully examined. One expedition travelled along the coast eastward to the Kei, and in returning kept as close as possible to the foot of the Amatola mountains and the Winterberg. West of the Tyumie river this party found no inhabitants except Bushmen. A botanist who was with the expedition brought back many specimens of plants then strange to Europeans, which he afterwards cultivated in the garden in Capetown. Another exploring party made its way far into Great Namaqualand. Among its spoils was the skin of a giraffe, an animal that never roamed south of the Orange river, and consequently was unknown to the colonists. The skin was sent by Governor Tulbagh to the museum of Leiden, together with many specimens of the animals and plants of South Africa.

Capetown at this time contained six or seven thousand inhabitants, rather more than half of whom were slaves. It had but one church building, but

THE OLD BURGHER WATCH-HOUSE, CAPETOWN.

there were three clergymen. The houses were commodious, though commonly but one story in height. In front of each was an elevated terrace, called a stoep, on which the inhabitants lounged in the evenings. In the principal streets were miniature canals, that served for drainage purposes, and along which were rows of trees as in the Netherlands. The town was patrolled at night by a burgher watch. The watchhouse, built while Mr. Tulbagh was governor, is still standing, and now serves as municipal offices.

The village of Stellenbosch had grown to be a very pretty place, and was quite embowered with oak trees and rose hedges. It was a custom for old people to live there, so as to be near the church and to provide homes for their grandchildren attending school, while men and women in the prime of life were occupied in their vineyards or on their farms.

Simonstown contained several large buildings belonging to the Company, but had not many private residences of much importance. Most of the families, indeed, moved to Capetown for the summer, and the place was then almost deserted.

Swellendam and Paarl were mere hamlets, consisting of large gardens, orchards, and vineyards along a single street. Both were in charming situations as far as scenery was concerned, and their beauty was increased by a row of oak trees on each side of the road. Swellendam had no clergyman, but was provided with a school, and the teacher conducted religious services. Its most prominent building was the drostdy, as the courthouse and residence of the landdrost was termed. The clergyman of the Drakenstein congregation resided at Paarl, and the church building was there. The hamlet had a school, but no courthouse, as it was within the magistracy of Stellenbosch.

While Mr. Tulbagh was governor the colonists spread out eastward to the Little Fish river and northward to the head waters of many of the streams that flow into the Orange. They did not indeed occupy one-tenth of all the land embraced within these limits, but they took possession of the choicest spots for grazing cattle, and went beyond extensive tracts that were less suited to their needs.

Governor Tulbagh died in 1771. His successor, Mr. Joachim van Plettenberg, was a man of very different character. He was not devoted to money making like Wilhem Adrian van der Stel, but he allowed his subordinates to do what they pleased, and many of them were not ashamed to resort to nefarious practices to increase their possessions. In consequence the residents in Capetown and the burghers who lived by agriculture were soon in a state of unrest. The graziers, who seldom came in contact with an official, were much less subject to oppressive treatment, and in general did not concern themselves much with what went on at the seat of government.

In 1778 the governor made a tour through the colony. On the Zeekoe river, near the present village of Colesberg, he set up a beacon to mark the extent of his journey and the north-eastern limit of the colony. When returning to Capetown by another route, he inspected the bay which still bears his name, and caused another beacon to be erected there. At Willem Prinsloo's farm on the Little Fish river, the site of the present village of Somerset East, the governor stayed several days. There the frontier graziers and hunters assembled to meet him and make him acquainted with their condition and wants. Their principal requests were very commendable, for what they desired most earnestly was that a magistrate and a clergyman might be stationed with them. The governor forwarded a report of this interview to the directors, with a recommendation that the desires of the frontiersmen should be complied with. The result was that in 1786 a landdrost—as head of a new district—was stationed at a place which received the name Graaff-Reinet, and soon afterwards a clergyman went to reside there.

From Prinsloo's farm Governor Van Plettenberg sent messengers to invite the nearest Bantu chiefs to visit him. The Bantu tribe farthest in advance was the Kosa, and some of its clans were then living on the Tyumie and Kat rivers, while nearer the sea the remnant of the Gonaqua tribe of Hottentots, whose territory was between the Fish river and the Keiskama, had by mixture of blood become practically incorporated with it. Several of the chiefs accepted the governor's invitation, and a friendly conference took place, at which it was arranged that the lower course of the Fish river should be a dividing line between the Bantu and the Europeans. In November 1780 this agreement was formally sanctioned by the council, and thereafter for many years the lower

Fish river was regarded as the eastern boundary of the colony.

On the northern border the struggle between the colonists and the Bushmen was incessant. The wild people had been obliged to retire before the advancing wave of colonisation, and they seemed now to be massed in the mountains bordering the great plain south of the Orange river, while the graziers were scattered over the choicest pastures along the same range. Horned cattle, sheep, and goats were driven off in hundreds together, the herdsmen were murdered, and from several places the Europeans were obliged to retire. In May 1774 a commandant was appointed for the northern border, and a plan was made to eject the Bushmen from their strongholds and restore the farmers to the places from which they had been driven.

At the beginning of summer a combined force of burghers, half-breeds, and Hottentots, in three divisions acting in concert, took the field. The country for more than three hundred miles along the great mountain range was scoured, and all the Bushmen found who would not surrender were shot. According to the reports furnished to the government, five hundred and three were killed and two hundred and thirty-nine taken prisoners. Some of these were afterwards released, and others were bound to the farmers for a term of years.

It was hoped that this punishment would deter the Bushmen from thieving, but it had no such effect. They became even more troublesome than before, and it was with difficulty that the graziers held their own.

Another enemy also had now to be reckoned with, for the extension of the settlement had brought the Europeans face to face with the Kosas, a people who might be called civilised when compared with Bushmen, but who were almost as expert stock-lifters. The arrangement made by Governor Van Plettenberg and the chiefs who met him at Prinsloo's farm was not observed for a single year. In 1779 several Kosa clans crossed the Fish river and spread themselves over the present districts of Albany and Bathurst. They said they did not want to quarrel with the Europeans, and to prove the truth of their assertions they murdered a number of Hottentots and took their cattle, without molesting the colonists. But shortly they began to drive off the herds of the white people also, and in September 1779 the farmers of the invaded districts, together with those along the right bank of the Bushman's river, were obliged to withdraw to a place of safety.

Two commandos took the field against the intruders. The Kosas were attacked and defeated on several occasions, but they were not entirely driven to their own side of the Fish river. In the winter those who were supposed to have been subdued crossed again into the colony, together with many others, and it became evident that a grand effort must be made to expel them.

The government then appointed a farmer named Adrian van Jaarsveld commandant of the eastern frontier. He gave the Kosas notice that they must retire at once, or he would shoot them. One of the clans thought it prudent to remove, and was therefore not molested, but the others remained where they were.

The commandant thereupon collected all the European and Hottentot families of the frontier in a couple of lagers formed by drawing up waggons in a circle and filling the spaces between the wheels with thorn trees. Leaving a few men to defend these camps, with ninety-two burghers and forty Hottentots, all mounted and well armed, he fell upon the Kosas and smote them hip and thigh. He was in the field less than two months, and when he disbanded his force there was not a Kosa west of the Fish river, and the first Kaffir war was over.

While the colony was in a state of disaffection and confusion, owing to misgovernment and strife with barbarians, tidings were received—March 1781—that Great Britain had declared war against the Netherlands, and that the republic was in alliance with France. The East India Company at this time was declining in prosperity, and was unable to maintain a large garrison in this country, where its yearly outlay was greater by about £25,000 than its income. Practically, therefore, Capetown was almost defenceless, and Great Britain had cast a covetous eye upon it as a half-way station to the great empire she was building up in Hindostan.

As soon as war was proclaimed, an English fleet with a strong body of troops was despatched under Commodore George Johnstone to seize the colony, but the object of the expedition was made known to the French government by a spy, and a squadron was hastily fitted out to thwart it. Pierre André de

Suffren, in later years vice-admiral of France, was in command of the French ships.

Commodore Johnstone put into Porto Praya to take in a supply of fresh water, and anchored without any arrangements for defence, as he believed his destination was unknown to every one except the British government and himself. One of Suffren's ships was also in want of water, so he too steered for Porto Praya, and not expecting to find the English fleet there, made no preparations for action. Upon rounding a point of land he caught sight of his opponent, and in his ardour pressed on with only half his ships to secure the advantage of surprise.

A sharp action followed, which ended by the French being beaten off, but some of the English ships were badly damaged. Suffren now pressed on under all the sail his vessels could carry, and upon his arrival at the Cape landed a strong body of French troops, who speedily made the peninsula secure against attack.

As soon as his fleet was refitted Johnstone followed, but learning the condition of things from the crew of a prize, he made no attempt upon the colony. He inflicted great damage upon the East India Company, however, by seizing several richly-laden Indiamen that were waiting in Saldanha Bay for men-of-war to escort them homeward.

To the great losses sustained during this war the bankruptcy of the Company has usually been attributed, but it may be doubted whether the corruption of its officials in the Indian islands had not as much to do with its downfall. As far as South African history is concerned, the cause is immaterial, the fact remains that the government of the Cape Colony now found itself unable to meet the calls upon it. It tried to borrow money on interest, but did not succeed in getting as much as it needed, and it then issued paper notes without any security excepting a promise to pay when possible, at the same time declaring these notes a legal tender for payment of debts. Some of them were redeemed a few years later, but others were afterwards issued, and then gold and silver disappeared from circulation and unsecured paper took their place.

The disaffection of the colonists in the vicinity of Capetown towards the government of Mr. Van Plettenberg was openly and fearlessly shown. In 1779 they sent four delegates to Holland to represent their grievances and endeavour to obtain redress. And now for the first time the burghers asked to be represented in the government, for they had been told by travellers of the events that had taken place on the other side of the Atlantic, and had begun to apply to themselves the political doctrines which the young republic was teaching. They asked also for free trade with the mother country and its eastern dependencies, and liberty to sell their produce to foreigners without a license from the fiscal, as the chief law officer of the colony was termed. The practice of requiring a license had grown from a simple quarantine regulation to a source of great oppression, as the fiscal would do nothing unless he was heavily bribed. Many of the officials were openly keeping shops, and the burghers asked that this should be prohibited. Besides these they had several other grievances, most of which, however, can be summed up that they desired closer connection with Holland and less dependence upon Batavia.

But matters in the Netherlands were not as they had been in the time of Wilhem Adrian van der Stel. Then the East India Company was prosperous, and had many enemies always attacking it and bringing its transactions to light, so that there was a guarantee for the good government of its possessions. Now the Company was tottering to its fall, and men of all shades of opinion were doing their utmost to prop it up, as its crash might ruin the state. The directors, therefore, did not enter with alacrity into the unpleasant matter brought before them, though they appointed a committee to investigate the complaints. This committee sent copies of all the documents received from the delegates to the officials in the colony to report upon, and awaited the replies without doing anything further. The officials naturally tried to put their case in as good a light as possible, and the war gave them ample time for consideration.

Thus four full years elapsed before the committee sent in a report, and then it was to the effect that the charges had not been proved. Almost the only relief recommended was that the high court of justice should consist of an equal number of officials and of burghers. The directors adopted this report, and thus the efforts of the burghers to obtain redress were so far a failure.

At this time the colonists were thriving, and it was

supposed by the directors that they would not make much effort to disturb an order of things in which money was easily made. There had never before been such a demand for produce as that created by the large garrison and the French forces in the East. The Company's needs were very small during the war and for some time afterwards, so that little was taken at low prices. Many new trading houses had been opened by burghers. In Capetown there was a display of prosperity which astonished strangers. European and Indian wares in the greatest variety were introduced in large quantities by Danish ships, and though the prices asked were very high, they commanded a ready sale.

But the burghers of South Africa, though relishing keenly the pleasure of making money, have at every period of their history shown a firmer attachment to what they hold to be their political rights and liberties. If at times a few men have been found to waver between money and freedom from misrule, the women have never hesitated to reject wealth at the price of submission to wrong. On this occasion neither men nor women were disposed to let the question rest. The government resorted to various petty acts of tyranny, but the party opposed to it grew in strength, and resolved now to appeal to the states-general.

The delegates were still in Holland, so documents were sent to them from the colony to be laid before the supreme authority of the republic. But as the directors now announced that they intended to replace the principal officials with other men, and to make a few small changes in the system of government and of carrying on trade, the states-general declined to take up the cause of the burghers until the effect could be seen. The colonists sent home other delegates to push their case, but these quarrelled with each other, and could therefore effect nothing. The agitation in South Africa did not cease, however, until the rule of the East India Company came to an end.

IX.

THE END OF THE EAST INDIA COMPANY'S RULE IN SOUTH AFRICA.

Though the condition of the East India Company was that of hopeless insolvency, as was afterwards seen, the directors managed to obtain large sums of money on loan, and among other expensive projects they resolved to fortify the Cape peninsula so that it should not again tempt an invader. With the consent of the states-general they sent out as governor an engineer officer named Cornelis Jacob van de Graaff, in order that he might direct the work, and they stationed here a large body of mercenary troops, chiefly German and Swiss regiments in their pay.

Colonel Van de Graaff took as little trouble to restrain the officials from acting unjustly as his predecessor had taken, and the new men were soon as corrupt as the old. They all knew that the end of the Company was at hand. Most of them were trying to make as much money as they could before the final crash, no matter by what means, and the governor, though free of that vice, had no scruple in squandering the property entrusted to his care. No one at the Cape had ever before lived in such style. The horses, carriages, and servants at his town and country houses would have sufficed for the governor-general of India. There was reckless waste in everything that he took in hand. The public expenditure was made to exceed the revenue by nearly £92,000 a year, and though much of this was expended on military works, more was utterly thrown away.

In 1790 the money borrowed by the Company was exhausted, and as it was impossible to raise another loan, an immediate and great reduction of expenditure was unavoidable. The spendthrift governor was recalled, military works of every kind were stopped, and nearly the whole of the troops were sent to India.

The states-general now appointed a commission to examine the Company's affairs and report upon them, with the result that a supreme effort was made to prevent a collapse. Two men of ability—Messrs. Nederburgh and Frykenius—were sent to South Africa and India with power to reform abuses, increase revenue, and reduce expenditure. In June 1792 they arrived at the Cape and assumed control of affairs.

By increasing some of the old taxes and imposing new ones, the commissioners raised the revenue to rather over £30,000 a year. The white people in South Africa of all ages at this time were about fifteen thousand in number, so that on an average each paid £2 a year to the government. With this increase of revenue, and by reducing expenses in every way that seemed possible, the balance of loss to the Company was brought down to £27,000 a year.

Distress, consequent upon the reduction of the garrison and an almost total cessation of trade, was now general. Professedly to relieve it, and at the same time to increase the revenue, the commissioners established a loan bank in connection with the government. Paper was stamped to represent different sums, amounting in all to £135,000, was declared a legal tender, and was issued through the bank to applicants at six per cent. interest on good security. By this means relief from pressure of debt was obtained by many landowners; but the effect of adding such an amount to the cartoon money already in circulation, with no gold to redeem it, was highly disastrous.

The commissioners redressed a few of the grievances of which the burghers complained, but they made no change in the form of government. They fixed the price at which the Company could demand as much wheat as it needed at about five shillings the hundred pounds, and gave the colonists permission to export the surplus to India or the Netherlands, provided it was sent in Dutch ships. They also threw open the trade in slaves with Madagascar and the east coast of Africa. At the same time they forbade the landing of any goods whatever from foreign vessels. Trade with strangers was restricted to the sale of provisions for money, unless special permission was first obtained from the government.

Against this order the residents in Capetown protested in the strongest language. "We live from God and the foreigners," they said, "and if the trade is stopped we must perish." The commissioners declined to cancel the regulation, but they were at length induced to suspend it for three years, which, as events turned out, amounted to the same thing.

The graziers on the eastern frontier were in as great trouble as the residents of Capetown. A powerful Kosa chief had recently died, leaving as his heir a boy of tender years, named Gaika. The councillors of the tribe selected Ndlambe, an uncle of the lad, as regent, but some of the clans refused to submit to him, and in March 1789 they suddenly crossed the Fish river into the colony. The farmers fled before them, but were unable to save the whole of their cattle. The landdrost of Graaff-Reinet then called the burghers of the district to arms, and sent an express to Capetown with a request that the government would assist him with a hundred soldiers.

The government decided that war with the Kosas must be avoided at any cost. A commission was appointed to induce them to make peace, and was plainly instructed to purchase their good will. In the meantime the burghers had taken the field, when the Kosa clans, without waiting to be attacked, fell back to the Fish river. They were lying on the western bank, and the burghers were approaching, when the instructions of the government were received by the landdrost. The commando was at once discharged. Not a shot had been fired, nor a single head of cattle recovered, so the burghers were indignant and almost mutinuous when they were required to disband.

The commission then sought an interview with the Kosa chiefs, and tried by means of large presents and smooth words to induce them to retire to their own country; but as this did not succeed, an arrangement was made that they might occupy the land between the Fish river and the Kowie during good behaviour. Of course they attributed such a concession to the weakness of the white people, and in a short time they sent out parties to steal cattle far and wide. This condition of things lasted four years, until May 1793, when a reprisal was made upon a kraal by a party of farmers. The clans in the colony were then joined by many of their tribe beyond the Fish river, all eager for plunder, and in a very short time they spread over the whole of the coast lands as far as the Zwartkops river, burning the houses, driving off the cattle, and murdering all the farmers that fell in their way.

There were fully six thousand warriors west of the Fish river, and over sixty-five thousand head of cattle, taken from colonists, had been driven across that stream. The government therefore had no option, but was obliged to call out the burghers of Swellendam, and attempt to drive the intruders back and recover the booty. The control of operations, however, was entrusted to a man who professed to believe in the guilelessness of children of nature and who had more sympathy with the Kosas than with the Europeans, so that the campaign ended in utter failure. The commandant then managed to get the chiefs to promise that they would live in peace with the white people, and upon this the government declared the second Kaffir war at an end.

The burghers were naturally dissatisfied, but the government took no notice of their request that some one in whom they could have confidence should be placed in command, and the war be prosecuted until the intruders were expelled from the colony. They were obliged to disperse, and they did so in a spirit which needed very little provocation to induce a revolt against the East India Company.

The Dutch reformed still continued to be the state church, but it was not now the only one in the colony. In 1780 the Lutherans were permitted to have a clergyman in Capetown, and in 1792 the Moravians founded the mission station Genadendal for the benefit of the Hottentots. This society had sent an evangelist to South Africa many years before, and he had met with nothing but kindness until he baptized some converts, when the government interfered, as in its opinion religious strife would follow the creation of a rival church. Now, however, more liberal views were entertained, and the Moravian clergymen met with hearty encouragement.

A great change was taking place in the Dutch reformed church itself, by the introduction of the teaching usually termed evangelical. The reverend Helperus Ritzema van Lier, a correspondent of the reverend John Newton, of Olney, who was imbued with the same spirit as that celebrated clergyman, created almost a revolution in Capetown.

For the cold formal services of two or three hours' length, which constituted the principal duty of the earlier ministers, he substituted shorter sermons and prayers, more visitation of parishioners, frequent meetings for religious purposes, and incitement to acts of benevolence and charity. At this date mission work among the heathen was commenced by

CHURCH OF LAST CENTURY IN CAPETOWN.
(*From a Sketch by G. Thompson.*)

the colonial church, and it has ever since gone on increasing in volume. At this time also the philanthropic labours of a band of ladies in Capetown began, which resulted a few years later in the establishment of an orphan asylum, a mission chapel and school, and a fund from which to the present day aged women in poor circumstances draw weekly allowances. The reverend Mr. Vos, of Tulbagh, belonged to the same school of thought as Mr. Van Lier, and his congregation set an example in mission work, which was shortly followed by others in the country.

Western Europe was now in the throes of the mightiest convulsion of modern times. France had become a republic. The people of the Netherlands were divided into two parties, one of which was in sympathy with the French, while the other favoured a stadtholderate with very large powers and the continuance of the alliance with England which had existed since 1788. The first was termed the patriot, the second the Orange party. An appeal to arms was unavoidable, and on the 1st of February 1793 a declaration of war with Great Britain and the stadtholder's government was issued at Paris.

Upon tidings of the outbreak of hostilities reaching South Africa, the commissioners formed all the clerks and junior officers in the civil service into a military company, which they termed the pennist corps, and they raised a company of half-breeds and Hottentots, put them in uniform, and set them to learn to be soldiers. This corps was termed the pandours. No other means could be devised of strengthening the colony.

Messrs. Nederburgh and Frykenins then appointed an old Indian official, named Abraham Josias Sluysken, head of the Cape government, and as soon as he took over the duty they proceeded to Java.

During 1794 the complaints of the burghers of

Graaff-Reinet were unceasing with regard to the paper money, the stagnation of trade, the new taxes, and, above all, the arrangement with the Kosas which the authorities termed peace. The landdrost took no notice of their statements, so they requested the government to recall him, but Mr. Sluysken would not even listen to them. By this treatment their patience was at length exhausted.

In February 1795 they expelled the landdrost, and set up a republic of their own. No more absurd form of government than that which they established has ever existed, but it served their purpose. Adrian van Jaarsveld was appointed military commander of the new state. The burghers declared that they were not in rebellion against the Netherlands, but that they would be governed by the East India Company no longer. Mr. Sluysken had no force to send against them, so they had everything their own way.

In June the people of Swellendam followed the example of those of Graaff-Reinet. They too expelled their landdrost, declared themselves a free republic, and elected a governing body which they termed a national assembly. In Stellenbosch and in Capetown there were many persons who sympathised with these movements, though they themselves did not proceed to the length of open rebellion. It is highly improbable that the puny states thus called into existence could have held their own for any length of time, as their commerce could easily be cut off; but, on the other hand, the East India Company could not establish its authority over the distant colonists again. The country was really in a state of anarchy.

The troops in the Cape peninsula consisted of six hundred and twenty-eight infantry, four hundred and thirty engineers, and two hundred and ten pandours. The head of the whole force was Colonel Robert Jacob Gordon. The infantry regiment was termed the national battalion, though it was composed of men of various countries. It was commanded by Lieutenant-Colonel De Lille.

While matters in South Africa were in this condition, the French were meeting with astonishing success in Europe. The winter of 1794-5 was so severe that towards the end of January the rivers were frozen hard, and their armies crossed into Utrecht and Gelderland, compelling the English forces to retire to Germany. The patriot party in the Netherlands gave them an enthusiastic welcome. The government was changed in form, the stadtholder made his escape to England in a fishing boat, and the Batavian Republic, as the country was now named, entered into close alliance with France.

The British government immediately fitted out an expedition to seize the Cape Colony, and in hope of facilitating the conquest a mandate was obtained from the fugitive stadtholder requiring the authorities in Capetown to admit English troops into the castle and forts. In June 1795 the expedition arrived in Simon's Bay. Admiral Elphinstone and Major-General Craig, who were in command respectively of the sea and land forces, presented the mandate to Mr. Sluysken and the

SIMONSTOWN IN 1795.
(From a Sketch by C. de Jong.)

council, who were in entire ignorance of recent events in Europe.

With hardly an exception the officials in South Africa sympathised with the Orange party, but they could not in decency openly obey an order issued in a foreign country by a fugitive prince. They therefore made many protestations of their duty to their country and of their determination to resist an invading force to the utmost, but their actions did not correspond with their words. There was but one way in which they could oppose the British forces with any hope of success, and that was by repudiating the East India Company and declaring for the patriot faction. The colonists, almost to a man, favoured that faction, as did the engineer corps and the few Dutch soldiers in the national battalion. The foreign soldiers in that battalion were disaffected, owing to being paid in paper money, and would not fight under any circumstances. But, with the engineers, from five to six hundred trained men were available, and at least two thousand burghers would have responded to an appeal to aid the patriot cause. Rather than this, however, Sluysken, Gordon, and De Lille were willing to let the English get possession of the country.

A long correspondence with the British officers followed, but it ended in nothing. Eighteen days after the arrival of the fleet in Simon's Bay the Dutch abandoned Simonstown, and concentrated their force at Muizenburg, a very strong natural position on the road to Capetown. A fortnight later eight hundred English soldiers were landed, and were quartered in deserted buildings.

On the 7th of August General Craig, at the head of sixteen hundred men, marched from Simonstown to attack the Dutch camp at Muizenburg. That position could easily have been made impregnable, but little or nothing had been done to strengthen it. De Lille, who was in command, did not even attempt to defend it, but fell back towards Capetown as the English approached. He would not resist the friends of the prince of Orange, and indeed, shortly afterwards entered the English service. Some artillerymen, under Lieutenant Marnitz and some burghers made a brief stand, but being abandoned by their commander and the national battalion, they were driven from the post. Besides securing the only obstacle to an advance upon Capetown, General Craig thus got possession of the greater part of the Dutch military stores and of a quantity of provisions, which he much needed. Two days later three hundred and fifty soldiers arrived from St. Helena to strengthen the force under his command.

Up to this time the burghers believed that the government was in earnest in opposing the English, and though they had little confidence in the military leaders and none at all in the national battalion, nearly fifteen hundred of them assembled in arms and were eager to defend the country. Even Swellendam sent a contingent, for the people there knew very well that if the English were masters of Capetown their republic would not last long. But now a belief began to spread that they were being betrayed, and in consequence every day some of those in arms left their colours and returned home.

On the 4th of September a fleet of English ships entered Simon's Bay with three thousand soldiers on board, under command of General Sir Alured Clarke. Some of them were destined for India, but as matters stood, they were all landed and sent on to Muizenburg. On the 14th two columns were formed, together between four and five thousand strong, and marched towards Capetown, sixteen miles distant by the road to be followed.

The Dutch forces, military and burgher, under Captain Van Baalen, were stationed at Wynberg, half way between Muizenburg and Capetown. Some burgher cavalry tried to harass the English troops on the march, and succeeded in killing one man and wounding seventeen, but the force to which they were opposed was too strong to be checked by any efforts that they could make.

Van Baalen drew up his troops as if he meant to stand firm, but as soon as the English were within range of his guns he retreated with the greater part of the national battalion. The burghers cried out that they were being betrayed and sold. It was a scene of confusion. One company of infantry and most of the engineers made a stand for a few minutes, and then fled towards Capetown, abandoning the camp with everything in it. The burghers, strongly impressed with the idea that Mr. Sluysken and Colonel Gordon, as well as the officers of the national battalion, were traitors at heart, and considering that if they fell back to Capetown they would be in a trap and must become prisoners of war, dispersed and returned to their homes.

The council then sent a messenger to the British officers, requesting a suspension of arms in order to arrange conditions of surrender, and at midnight General Clarke consented to an armistice for twenty-four hours. Next morning General Craig met the Dutch commissioners—Messrs. Van Ryneveld and Le Sueur—at Rondebosch, and after some discussion articles of capitulation were agreed to. These provided for the surrender of the Dutch troops, but the officers were to be at liberty either to remain in Capetown or to return to Europe, upon giving their word of honour not to serve against England while the war lasted. The colonists were to retain all their rights, including the existing form of religion. No new taxes were to be levied, but the old imposts were to be reduced as much as possible. Everything belonging to the East India Company was to be handed over to the English officers, but all other property was to be respected. The lands and buildings belonging to the East India Company were to be considered as security for the paper money in circulation.

At three o'clock in the afternoon of Wednesday, the 16th of September 1795, fourteen hundred British soldiers under General Craig arrived at the castle and drew up on the open ground in front. The Dutch troops marched out with colours flying and drums beating, passed by the English, and laid down their arms, surrendering as prisoners of war. In the evening General Clarke arrived with two thousand infantry and a train of artillery.

Thus ended the rule of the Dutch East India Company in South Africa, after an occupation of a little over a hundred and forty-three years. The Company itself had ceased to exist before the symbol of its authority disappeared from the castle of Good Hope. Its administration until a quarter of a century before its fall, though by no means admirable, was as just and honest as that of any English foreign possession at the same time, because it had powerful opponents who kept a vigilant eye upon its proceedings; but when that wholesome restraint was removed, its rule became corrupt and ruinous. Yet none of its acts even then were so unjust as prejudice has made them appear. Thus one English writer of eminence —Sir John Barrow—represented a regulation concerning the apprenticeship of children of slaves and Hottentot women living on farms as if it applied to the whole Hottentot race, and succeeding compilers copied his statement without question or doubt. Worse still, two English commissioners of inquiry, without taking the trouble to investigate the matter, reported upon a law concerning degraded Hottentot women and vagrants in Capetown as if the Hottentots everywhere had been made subject to its provisions; and their report has been quoted again and again as proof of the merciless misgovernment of the East India Company. Now that its records are open to inspection, such charges are known to be incorrect. It governed South Africa with a view to its own interests, its method of paying its officials was bad, its system of taxation was worse, in the decline of its prosperity it tolerated many gross abuses; but it cannot in fairness be accused of overbearing tyranny or cruelty towards either Europeans or Hottentots.

X.

THE FIRST BRITISH OCCUPATION.

The surrender of the Cape Colony to the British forces brought together two branches of the same race, for conquerors and conquered were of one stock. Of all the nations of Europe the inhabitants of the northern Netherlands are the closest in blood to the people of England and Scotland. During the centuries that they had been separated, however, their training had been different, so that many slight variations had arisen. Though in the most important features their characters were the same, each regarded the variations in the other as blemishes, and often made more of them than was fair or honest. If this can be said of Englishmen and Dutchmen in Europe, it can be asserted more strongly of Englishmen and Dutchmen when they first came in contact in South Africa, for in this country circumstances had tended greatly to develop a few traits.

The system of taxation had been pernicious in its effects upon the character of the people. There were exceptions, but in general the farmers had come to regard very lightly the giving in the number of their cattle and the produce of their lands at less than a third of the true quantity. A man, whose word under other circumstances might be depended upon, in this matter would utter deliberate falsehoods without any twinges of conscience, and even thought he was justified in doing so because the returns he was supplying were for taxation purposes. This trait in the character of the burghers was at once detected by the Englishmen with whom they came in contact, and made a very bad impression.

On the other hand, the habit of most Englishmen of that time of distorting accounts of national events made an equally bad impression upon the South African burghers, and thus each regarded the other as untruthful.

The system of perquisites by which the East India Company's officials were paid had caused another ugly trait to be unduly developed in the character of many of the colonists. Accustomed to be mulcted of petty amounts in every transaction, they had come to consider it rather a proof of cleverness than an immoral act to get the better of those with whom they were bargaining. It was regarded as nothing more than fair retaliation to cheat the government and its officers whenever and by whatever means it could be done. The tendency to dishonest and deceitful practices was made much of by unfriendly critics, though it was far from general, and at its worst was not greater than that of traders elsewhere who sell a bad article at the price of a good one.

The burghers were charged with being very igno-

SOUTH AFRICAN FARMHOUSE OF THE BETTER CLASS IN 1795.

rant. Excepting those in Capetown, they had hardly any education from books, and knew nothing more than how to read, write, and compute a little. All had bibles, the psalms in metre, and the Heidelberg catechism; but few possessed any books on secular subjects. Yet no people on earth were less stupid. They filled the offices of elders and deacons in the churches, of heemraden in the courts of law, of commandants and fieldcornets in war, with as much ability as educated people in Europe could have shown.

The colonists at a distance from Capetown were described as living in a very rough style. Their houses were small, poorly furnished, and untidy, said English visitors. It was true that the frontier farmers did not build large houses, for they were constantly liable to be plundered and driven away by savages. As soon as a district became tolerably safe, however, comfortable dwellings were put up by all who had means. The untidiness complained of was the result of the employment of coloured servants. The ancestors of the colonists brought to South Africa the cleanly and orderly habits of the people of the Netherlands; but in many instances families had been unable to sustain the effort of compelling their servants to be neat and clean, and had fallen into the way of letting things take their course. But this was not peculiar to the Cape Colony: it was the case wherever coloured people were employed as domestics. Mrs. Stowe's picture of Aunt Dinah's kitchen is just as faithful with the scene laid in Louisiana as if it had been laid in South Africa.

The other faults attributed to the colonists were those of country people all the world over. They were inclined to bigotry in religious matters, were very plain in their language, and loved to impose marvellous tales upon credulous listeners. They were accused of indolence by some English visitors, but that was not a charge that could fairly be made. The man who managed either a grain or wine or cattle farm so as to make it pay had sufficient occupation without doing much manual labour.

On their side, the colonists found just as great faults in the English character. They pictured Englishmen as arrogant above all other mortals, as insatiable in the pursuit of wealth, as regardless of the rights of others, and as viewing everything with an eye jaundiced by national prejudice.

And yet, with all these harsh opinions of each other, there was really so little difference between English people and South Africans that as soon as they came together matrimonial connections began to be formed. The attractions of blood were stronger after all than prejudices born of strife and want of knowledge.

In the blemishes of the colonial character that have been described, there was nothing that education of a healthy kind would not rectify, and against them could be set several virtues possessed in a very high degree. The colonists were an eminently self-reliant people, and seldom lost heart under difficulties. In tenacity of purpose they were without equals. Their hospitality was admitted even by those who were determined to see in them nothing else that was praiseworthy, and their benevolence towards persons in distress was very highly developed. There was no part of the world where a well-behaved and trustworthy stranger more readily met with assistance and genuine friendship.

Though the British troops were in possession of Capetown, the people of the country districts were not disposed to acknowledge the new authorities. The greater number of the farmers retired to their homes, declaring that they did not consider themselves bound by the acts of the late government. Under these circumstances every possible effort to soothe the colonists was made by the English commanders. The people of Capetown were treated in such a manner as to dispel their anxiety, and they were assured that they would presently be in the enjoyment of such liberty and good fortune as they had never known before. Many of the old servants of the East India Company, who were willing to take an oath to be faithful to the king of England as long as he should hold the colony, were retained in employment, and most of the clerks in the different offices were allowed to keep their situations.

The paper money in circulation amounted to rather more than a quarter of a million pounds sterling, and was a source of much anxiety to its holders. The British commanders announced that it would be received at the public offices at its full nominal value. They also abolished a very obnoxious tax on auction accounts, and substituted for the old burgher councillors a popular board termed the burgher senate. Two days after the capitulation they sent a document over the country, in which a promise was made that every one might buy from whom he would, sell to whom he would, employ whom he would, and come and go whenever or wherever he chose, by land or by water. The farmers were invited to send their cattle and produce to Capetown, where they could sell whatever they wished in the manner most profitable for themselves, and the English would pay for anything purchased in hard coin. They were also invited to send persons to confer with the British commanders, if there was any matter upon which they wished for explanation.

These measures had the desired effect in the Cape and Stellenbosch districts, and no opposition was made there to the new authorities. In Swellendam also, after a short time, the people decided to abolish the republic, and to submit to the English. An attempt to hold out was, however, made by the burghers of Graaff-Reinet, acting chiefly under guidance of a man named Jan Pieter Woyer. Supplies of ammunition and goods of every kind were therefore cut off from them, with the result that before the close of 1796 they too were obliged to tender a nominal submission, though they were in hope that before long aid from abroad would enable them to recover their independence.

Woyer had left the country in a Danish ship bound to Java, that put into Algoa Bay, where vessels were then very rarely seen. Six French frigates happened to be at anchor in Batavia Roads when he arrived there. The admiral sent one with a supply of powder and lead for the Graaff-Reinet farmers, but when she reached Algoa Bay an English ship of war happened to be there, and after a short action the frigate was obliged to retire. The government of Java also sent a vessel laden with munitions of war, clothing, sugar, and coffee, for the use of the farmers. It was intended that her cargo should be landed at Algoa Bay, but in a storm the vessel was so much damaged that she put into Delagoa Bay to be repaired, and in that port was seized by the crew of an English whaler aided by a few Portuguese.

A fleet of nine ships, sent from Holland under command of Admiral Lucas, also failed in the object of aiding the colonists against the English. The admiral put into Saldanha Bay, and was there caught as in a trap between a much stronger British fleet on one side and a large British army on the other. On the 17th of August 1796 he was obliged to surrender his ships and nearly two thousand soldiers and sailors, without even an attempt to resist.

Admiral Elphinstone and General Clarke only remained in South Africa a few weeks after the capitulation. They then went on to India, leaving General Craig at the head of the Cape government. This officer did his utmost to place English rule before the colonists in as favourable a light as possible, and though as a conqueror he could not be loved, as a man he was highly respected.

When tidings of the conquest reached England, the high authorities resolved that the Cape Colony should be ruled by a man of rank, who should have all the power held by the governor and the council under the Dutch East India Company. A very strong garrison was to be maintained in Capetown, and the officer in command was to act as administrator in case of the governor's death or absence.

Accordingly the earl of Macartney, an old Irish nobleman who had done good service in India, was sent out as governor, and took over the duty in May 1797. His administration was free of the slightest taint of corruption, but was conducted on very strict lines. Those colonists who professed to be attached to Great Britain were treated with favour, while those who preferred a republic to a monarchy were obliged to conceal their opinions, or they were promptly treated as guilty of sedition. There never was a period in the history of the country when there was less freedom of speech than at this time. All the important offices were given to men who could not speak the Dutch language, and who drew such large salaries from the colonial treasury that there was little left for other purposes. An oath of allegiance to the king of England was demanded from all the burghers. Many objected, and a few did not appear when summoned to take it. The governor was firm, dragoons were quartered upon several of those who were reluctant, and others were banished from the country.

The free trade promised in 1795 also came to an end. Commerce with places to the east of the Cape of Good Hope was restricted to the English East India Company, and heavy duties were placed upon goods from the westward brought in any but English ships. British goods brought from British ports in British ships were admitted free of duty. The government resumed the power to put its own prices upon farm produce, and to compel delivery at those rates of all that was needed for the garrison and the ships of war frequenting Simon's Bay. The prices fixed, however, were fair and reasonable, and the burghers did not object to sell at such rates, though among themselves they spoke very bitterly of the arbitrary rule to which they were subjected.

In November 1798 the earl of Macartney returned to Europe on account of his health. Major-General Francis Dundas then acted as administrator until December 1799, when Sir George Yonge arrived from England as governor.

During this interval there was a petty insurrection by a party of farmers in Graaff-Reinet. The arrest of Adrian van Jaarsveld on a charge of forgery and setting a summons of the high court of justice at defiance was the immediate cause of the outbreak. The old commandant was being conveyed to Capetown for trial when he was rescued by a band of frontiersmen, the same who had been the last to submit to British authority. A strong military force, consisting of a squadron of dragoons, a regiment of infantry, and a Hottentot corps, was at once sent to quell the disturbance. This was an easy matter, as the great majority of the people of the district of Graaff-Reinet declined to aid the insurgents, who thereupon sent in a petition for pardon. The officer in command of the troops replied in writing that they must lay down their arms before he would have any dealings with them, and named a place where they could do so.

One hundred and thirteen men appeared at the place appointed, and gave up their arms to the troops. There was no promise of any kind in the document sent to them, but they were under the impression that pardon was implied in its terms, and therefore protested when they were made prisoners. Ninety-three were released upon payment of fines, and the remaining twenty were sent to Capetown, where they were placed in close confinement. Forty-two others afterwards gave themselves up, and were pardoned; but seven of the most violent fled into Kaffirland, where they were joined by a band of deserters from the British army, and lived for several years under protection of a powerful chief. Those who were sent to Capetown were brought to trial before the high court of justice, when two were condemned to death and the others to various kinds of punishment; but with the exception of one who was flogged and banished and two who died in confinement, they were all released by the high commissioner De Mist in 1803.

The appearance of the pandours on the frontier gave rise to a disturbance of another kind. Some of the Hottentots of that part of the country, seeing men of their own class in arms against colonists, very naturally felt an inclination to aid them, and began to plunder the farmhouses of guns, powder, and clothing. They shed no blood, however, and when they had secured what appeared to them to be sufficient booty, they repaired to the British camp with their wives and children, in the belief that they would be regarded as having acted in a praiseworthy manner. General Vandeleur, the officer in command, did not know what to do with them. He allowed a hundred of the young men to enlist in the Hottentot regiment, and the others—about six hundred of both sexes and all ages—he sent to Algoa Bay with an escort to wait there until he could receive instructions concerning them from the government in Capetown.

A matter of much greater importance than either of these petty insurrections had unexpectedly arisen, and was claiming all his attention. Gaika, who was a boy at the time of the second Kaffir war, had recently attained manhood, and had then claimed the chieftainship to which he was by birth the heir. His uncle, the regent Ndlambe, was unwilling to resign, and a large party in the tribe declared its readiness to support him. Gaika appealed to arms, and a battle was fought, in which he was not only victorious but had the good fortune to take his uncle prisoner. Ndlambe was carelessly guarded, however, and in February 1799 he managed to escape, when with a great number of followers he crossed the Fish river into the colony. All the clans that had been living between the Fish river and the Kowie since the previous war, except one, joined the powerful refugee. The white people who were in or near the line of his march took to flight, some losing all they had, others who could collect their cattle in time driving them off and leaving everything else behind. In a few days the invaders were in full possession of the whole country along the coast to the Sunday river.

General Vandeleur had no intention of employing British soldiers against the Kosas, but as he was marching towards Algoa Bay, with a view of returning to Capetown, he was attacked by them in a thicket on the bank of the Sunday river. He beat them off, and then fell back a little and formed a camp to enable a patrol of twenty men to join him. But this patrol had already been surrounded, and after a gallant defence all were killed except four men who managed to escape. The camp was hardly formed when it was attacked by the Kosas, who rushed on in masses with their assagai shafts broken short so that they could be used as stabbing weapons. These charges were met with volleys of musket balls and grape shot, that covered the ground with bodies, until at length the Kosas turned and fled.

The general then marched to Algoa Bay. After fortifying a camp on the Zwartkops river, he sent some of his soldiers to Capetown by sea, and called out a burgher commando to expel the invaders. The Hottentots who had plundered the frontier farmhouses were still at the bay drawing rations, and he thought it prudent to disarm them; but upon the attempt being made they fled in a body and joined the Kosas.

At the beginning of June a burgher commando assembled at the Bushman's river, but instead of attacking the intruders, General Vandeleur tried to persuade them to retire. Thus the farmers lost heart by being kept waiting, and many dispersed, while the Kosas came to believe that the white men were afraid of them. They and the insurgent Hottentots then overran and pillaged the country far and wide. By the close of July twenty-nine white people had lost their lives, there was hardly a house left standing east of the Gamtoos, and nearly all the cattle were in the hands of the marauders.

In August a large burgher force was got together, and five hundred soldiers were sent to Algoa Bay. General Dundas, however, was determined to make another attempt to come to a friendly arrangement, so he proceeded to the disturbed district himself, and sent a confidential agent named Maynier to parley with the hostile chiefs. Six or seven hundred soldiers and three strong divisions of burghers were in the field. There was nothing left within reach to plunder. So when Maynier offered not to molest the Kosas in the coast belt east of the Bushman's river, if they would promise not to trespass beyond that territory, they readily pledged their word, and accepted as a mark of friendship the presents which he offered them. To get a parallel to either this transaction or the dealings of the East India Company with the Kosas in the previous war, we must go back in English history to the time of the heathen Danes. The hearts of the farmers sank within them when peace was proclaimed, but they were obliged to abide by the decision of their rulers, and thus for a short time there was a kind of truce which was observed in an indifferent manner.

Things remained in this state for nearly three years, during which time the farmers of Graaff-Reinet were in a condition of great poverty and distress. The depredations of the Kosas and Hottentots were then carried so far that for very shame's sake it was necessary to renew hostilities. A burgher force was called out, and placed under a very brave and highly respected farmer named Tjaart van der Walt. Some success attended the early operations of this force, but in August 1802 the commandant was killed in action, and the burghers then dispersed. Five months later they were brought together again, but as the Kosas now asked for peace and promised to return to their own country as soon as possible, terms were concluded with them. They and the Hottentots engaged not to roam about and plunder, and the Europeans engaged to give them time to remove without disturbing them.

The government of Sir George Yonge was thoroughly corrupt. It could not indeed be proved that he received bribes for his own benefit, but he could only be approached through his favourites, and they were unscrupulous to the last degree. In a short time so many complaints reached England from people of every nationality at the Cape that he was recalled. He left the colony in April 1801, and upon his arrival in London was tried by a special commission and disgraced. Major-General Dundas for the second time acted as administrator, and held that office until the restoration of the colony to Holland.

In 1799 the first agents of the London missionary society arrived in South Africa. Unfortunately almost from the day of their landing some of them took a more prominent part in politics than in elevating the heathen, and as they advocated social equality between barbarians and civilised people, they were speedily at feud with the colonists.

Terms of peace between Great Britain, France,

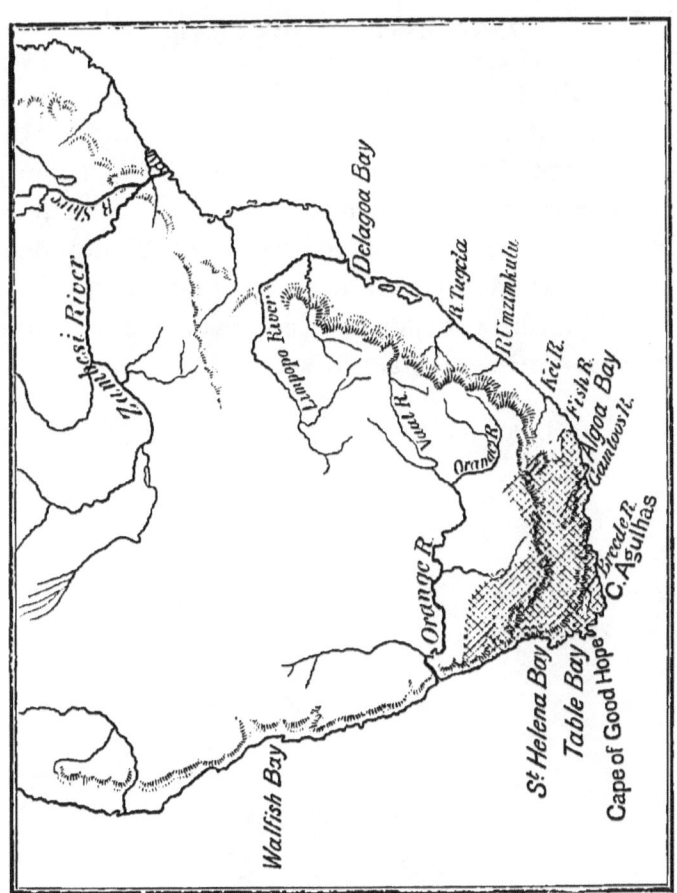

EXTENT OF TERRITORY UNDER EUROPEAN RULE IN 1800

and the Netherlands—then the Batavian Republic—were signed at Amiens on the 27th of March 1802, one of the conditions being that the Cape Colony should be restored to its former owners. Accordingly in February 1803 a Dutch garrison of rather over three thousand men replaced the British troops, and General Dundas transferred the government to the Batavian commissioner De Mist.

XI.

THE COLONY UNDER THE BATAVIAN REPUBLIC.

THE Cape settlement was now a direct dependency of the states-general as the governing body of the Batavian Republic, and liberal measures were adopted regarding it. The executive power was entrusted to a governor, who was also commander-in-chief of the garrison. For this office Lieutenant-General Jan Willem Janssens—an able military officer and a man of high moral worth—was selected. A legislative and executive council was provided, consisting of four members and the governor as president. The high court of justice was made independent of the other branches of the government, and consisted of a president and six members, all versed in law. Trade with the possessions of the republic everywhere was allowed on payment of a small duty for revenue purposes. An advocate of good standing—Mr. Jacob Abraham de Mist—was sent out as high commissioner, to receive the colony from the English, to instal the new officials, and to draw up such regulations as he might find necessary, which, after approval by the states-general, were to be embodied in a charter.

The 1st of March 1803 was observed as a day of thanksgiving to Almighty God for the restoration of the colony to its ancient owners. In the morning service was held in all the churches, and at noon the commissioner De Mist installed Lieutenant-General Janssens as governor. The other officials also who had arrived from Europe had their duties formally assigned to them. The landdrosts and most of the clerks under the English rule retained their posts.

In April the governor left Capetown to visit the eastern part of the colony, and ascertain how matters were standing with the white people, the Kosas, and the Hottentots. At Algoa Bay he found a party of Hottentots under the guidance of Dr. Vanderkemp, a missionary of the London society; and for their use he assigned a tract of land in the neighbourhood, ever since known as Bethelsdorp. Locations of ample size were also assigned to the Hottentot captains who had recently been in arms against the colonists, but with the improvidence of their race most of them with their people soon wandered away to other parts of the country, and the land set apart for their benefit was regarded as waste by succeeding governors. For the time being, however, matters were placed on a satisfactory footing with the people of this race who had lately been hostile.

The governor then proceeded to the Sunday river, where he had a conference with Ndlambe and the other Kosa chiefs who were living in the colony. The chiefs, who of course knew nothing of the relative strength of England and Holland, were under the impression that the Dutch government must be much more powerful than the other, because it was apparent to them that it had supplanted its opponent, and they knew that the colonists were supporting it with enthusiasm. The farmers were in high spirits, and had sent them word that they must not think the old times had come back again, for the great person called the Batavian Republic was immeasurably superior to the poor creature John Company, who had been ill a long time and was now dead. They therefore expressed a desire for peace and friendship with the white people, and there was no difficulty in settling minor matters with them. But the all-important question of their return to their own country could not be arranged so easily, for though they admitted the Fish river as the boundary, they declared they could not cross it through fear of Gaika.

Shortly after this the intruding clans began to quarrel among themselves. Two of them joined Gaika in an attack upon Ndlambe, but the old chief succeeded in beating them back. The Kosas thus remained in occupation of the belt of land along the coast east of the Bushman's river. The other parts of the district of Graaff-Reinet, however, enjoyed for a season a fair amount of tranquillity, so that the farmers were able to carry on their usual occupations.

Mr. De Mist also, like the governor, made a tour through the colony, in order to become acquainted with the condition and wants of the people. The settlement was previously divided for magisterial and fiscal purposes into four districts—the Cape, Stellenbosch, Swellendam, and Graaff-Reinet,—he now divided it into six of smaller size, and stationed landdrosts at Tulbagh and Uitenhage.

Among the many regulations which he made was one giving full political equality to persons of every creed who acknowledged and worshipped a Supreme Being. Another provided for the creation of state schools, but this was an idea in advance of the times in South Africa, for the great majority of the colonists objected to schools that were not in connection with the church. The country did not remain long enough under the Batavian flag to test this question, but the probability is that state schools could not have succeeded, as the antipathy to them was so strong. Yet another regulation permitted marriages to take place before the landdrosts, and required them to be registered in the district courts.

In 1805 the European population of the colony consisted of between twenty-five and twenty-six thousand individuals, exclusive of soldiers. They owned nearly thirty thousand slaves, and had in their service about twenty thousand free coloured people. It is impossible to say how many Hottentots were living at kraals, or Bushmen roaming about on the border, for these people paid no taxes, and therefore no notice was taken of them by the census framers. Capetown had a population of rather over six thousand Europeans and nearly eleven thousand persons of colour.

In May 1803, less than three months after the restoration of the colony, war broke out again between Great Britain and the Batavian Republic. On receiving this intelligence, General Janssens devoted all his attention to putting the Cape peninsula in a condition for defence. But soon instructions were received from Holland that he must send his best regiment to Batavia, as the mother country was unable to furnish more men, and troops were urgently needed in Java. All that the governor could do to make up for its loss was to increase the Hottentot corps, which had been transferred to him by General Dundas, to six hundred rank and file, and to form the Asiatics in and about Capetown into a volunteer corps, termed the Malay artillery.

No one doubted that the English would attempt to seize the colony again, but a state of suspense continued until the last week of 1805, when tidings were received that a great fleet was approaching. Signals were at once made to the different drostdies, summoning the burghers to arms, and though the heat was so intense that they could only ride at night, hundreds came trooping to Capetown. But there were no means of feeding them long after they arrived, for the two previous seasons had been exceptionally bad, and it had not been possible to lay up a store of grain. At this time, though the government made desperate exertions to obtain corn, there was never more than sufficient flour in Capetown for two days' consumption of the garrison and the inhabitants. Under these circumstances a large force, however devoted to the cause it was striving for, could not be kept together long.

In the evening of the 4th of January 1806 the fleet—which consisted of sixty-three ships—came to anchor west of Robben Island, at the entrance of

Table Bay. There were on board nearly seven thousand soldiers, under command of Major-General David Baird, an officer who was well acquainted with the Cape and its fortifications, having served here in 1798. On the 6th and 7th six regiments were landed, with some artillery and provisions, at a little cove about eighteen miles by road from Capetown.

As soon as it was known that the English were landing on the Blueberg beach, General Janssens marched to meet them, leaving in Capetown a considerable burgher force and a few soldiers under Lieutenant-Colonel Von Prophalow to guard the forts. He had an army rather over two thousand strong, but composed of a strange mixture of men. There were mounted burghers, Dutch soldiers, a German mercenary regiment, the crews of two wrecked French ships, Malays, Hottentots, and even slaves. He had sixteen field-guns.

At three o'clock in the morning of the 8th this motley force was under arms, when the scouts brought word that the English were approaching. Two hours later the British troops came in sight on the side of the Blueberg. General Baird had with him about four thousand infantry, besides artillerymen and five or six hundred sailors armed with pikes and drawing eight field-guns.

As soon as the armies were within range, the artillery on both sides opened fire. A few balls from the English guns fell among the German mercenary troops, who at once began to retreat. The burghers, the French corps, the remainder of the troops, and the coloured auxiliaries behaved well receiving and returning a heavy fire of artillery and musketry. But the flight of the main body of regular troops made it impossible for the mixed force left on the field to stand a charge which was made by three Highland regiments, and by order of General Janssens the remnant of the army fell back.

The loss on the English side in the battle of Blueberg was fifteen killed, one hundred and eighty-nine wounded, and eight missing. The roll-call of the Dutch forces when the fugitives were rallied shows the killed, wounded, and missing together. When it was made that afternoon three hundred and thirty-seven men did not answer to their names. General Janssens after his defeat sent the foreigners in his army to Capetown, and with the burghers and Dutch troops retired to the mountains of Hottentots-Holland.

In the morning of the 9th General Baird resumed his march towards Capetown. It was not in Colonel Von Prophalow's power to resist with any prospect of success, so he sent a flag of truce to request a suspension of arms in order to arrange terms of capitulation. General Baird granted thirty-six hours, but required immediate possession of the outer line of defence, including the fort Knokke at its extremity on the shore. His demand could not be refused, and that evening an English regiment was quartered in Fort Knokke.

In the afternoon of the 10th articles of capitulation were signed. The regular troops and the Frenchmen of the wrecked ships were to become prisoners of war. Colonists in arms were to return to their former occupations. Private property of all kinds was to be respected, but everything belonging to the Batavian government was to be given up. The inhabitants were to preserve all their rights and privileges, and public worship as then existing was to be maintained. The paper money was to continue current until the pleasure of the king could be known, and the public lands and buildings were to be regarded as security for its redemption. The inhabitants of Capetown were to be exempt from having troops quartered on them.

The force opposed to General Janssens was so great that he could not hope to make a long resistance, but his position in the mountains of Hottentots-Holland was more favourable for obtaining terms than if he had fallen back upon Capetown after the defeat at Blueberg. General Baird proposed that he should capitulate on honourable conditions, and on the 18th arrangements to that effect were made. They provided that the troops should not be considered prisoners of war, but be sent to Holland at the expense of the British government, and that the inhabitants of the colony were to enjoy the same rights and privileges as had been granted to those of Capetown, except that the right of quartering troops upon them was reserved, as the country had not the same resources as the town.

Seven transports were prepared, and the troops—ninety-four officers and five hundred and seventy-three rank and file—were embarked in them. One of the best was placed at the disposal of General Janssens, who had liberty to select such persons as he wished to accompany him. Thirty-one of the civil servants under the Batavian administration desired to return to Europe, and were allowed passages. Fifty-three women and the same number of children also embarked. All being ready, on the 6th of March 1806 the squadron, bearing the last representative of the dominion of the Netherlands over the Cape Colony, set sail for Holland.

XII.

EARLY YEARS OF ENGLISH RULE IN SOUTH AFRICA.

Conquest is a grievous thing for any people, no matter how lightly the conqueror imposes his rule. Apart from all other considerations, it wounds their pride and reduces their energy, for it is everywhere seen that a man of a leading race will do without second thought what one of subject nationality will never do at all.

It was thus only natural that the colonists should feel dejected when the English flag was again the symbol of authority in South Africa. They had been ardently attached to the Batavian Republic, and had enjoyed three years of good government combined with ample liberty: now all they had cherished was gone. General Baird, indeed, used the most consoling language; but they remembered that General Craig had done the same, and a hard unsympathetic rule had followed. They saw all authority again centred in one man, for the council was abolished, and the independence of the high court of justice was destroyed. The members of that court—the president only excepted—were now ordinary civil servants who were appointed by the governor and held office during his pleasure. Even religious freedom came to an end, for a Roman catholic clergyman who had been chaplain to some of the foreign troops in the Dutch service was not permitted to remain in the colony. *His* expulsion, however, was not felt as a grievance, for, in truth, the great majority of the burghers desired his presence less even than General Baird.

There was one hope left, and that rested on the chance of war. If Napoleon should succeed in the struggle with England, which seemed very probable in 1806, they would once more be connected with their fatherland. And so in a spirit of despondency, but not of absolute despair, they submitted to the power that they could not resist.

For some time there was fear of actual famine in Capetown. The inhabitants were restricted to a small daily allowance of bread, but with all haste wheat and rice were imported from India, and as the crops of the following season were remarkably good, the danger passed away.

As soon as possible the colony was again placed under the same form of government as during the first British occupation, and under the same commercial regulations. The earl of Caledon, an Irish nobleman only twenty-nine years of age, was sent out as governor with very great authority, though in matters of primary importance he was to act under instructions from the secretary of state in London. He could fix prices for any produce required by the army, and assess the quantity each farmer was compelled to deliver. He directed and controlled the different departments. His proclamations and notices had the force of law. With the lieutenant-governor he formed a court of appeal in civil cases of over £200 value, and with two assessors he decided appeals in criminal cases. He had also power to mitigate or suspend sentences passed by the inferior courts.

Some of the orders of the earl of Caledon, such as forbidding the farmers of certain districts to keep African sheep, read strangely to-day; but though he was very strict, he was an amiable and upright man, and was guided in all his doings by a desire to improve the country. His benevolence was almost unbounded, and, indeed, his last act when leaving South Africa was to present a thousand pounds in currency to the orphan asylum.

The most important measure of his administration had reference to the Hottentots. These people had always in theory been regarded as independent of the European government, and subject to chiefs of their own race. Only in cases where white people or slaves were concerned were they liable to be tried before courts of justice, and they were neither taxed nor called upon to perform public services except when of their own accord they enlisted as pandours. In reality they lived in a state of anarchy. Whoever believed that men of all colours and conditions were equal, the Hottentots certainly did not. They respected the poorest and weakest white man far more than they did their own nominal chiefs, for whose authority they cared nothing at all. Many of their women formed connections with slaves, and the farmers were obliged to maintain them, or the slaves would run away. Children born of such connections could be apprenticed to the farmers for a certain number of years, when through their mothers' rights they became free to go where they chose. With this exception, all but those who lived in Capetown or one of the villages or mission stations could assault or plunder one another without fear of punishment.

As far as land was concerned, there were reserves set apart for their benefit in the long-settled parts of the country, and they could use ground not occupied by farmers anywhere. But many of them preferred to live as dependents of a white man, though they seldom remained long in the service of the same person. To obtain brandy and tobacco they were willing to perform light labour occasionally, but nothing could induce them to adopt a life of regular industry. In short, they had become rovers and vagrants.

The earl of Caledon issued a proclamation which removed all vestiges of chieftainship from the Hottentots in the colony, made them subject to European law, and restrained them from wandering over the country at will. Any one found without a pass from a landdrost or an employer was to be treated as a vagabond.

Certain missionaries of the London society raised a great outcry in England against this proclamation and another giving the landdros's power to apprentice children of destitute Hottentots, which was issued by Sir John Cradock ; but no measures could be devised of greater benefit to the people affected. It is true that some small bands, rather than submit to control, moved over the Orange river into Great Namaqualand; but the vast majority of the Hottentots were rescued by these apparently harsh proceedings from utter ruin, if not from extinction.

In 1811 Sir John Cradock succeeded the earl of Caledon as governor. He too was a man of very high principle, so that autocratic rule at this period was presented to the colonists in its best form.

Ever since the return of the English the Kosa clans within the colony had been restless, probably because they saw that the burghers were not attached to the new rulers, and in consequence were less capable of resistance. They not only sent out plundering parties to drive off cattle, but they were constantly taking more territory, and only laughed at the remonstrances of the white people. When Sir John Cradock reached South Africa, he found reports awaiting him from the landdrost of Uitenhage, in which he was informed that there was only one farm still occupied east of the drostdy, and that no other choice was left than the expulsion of the Kosas by force or the abandonment of the remainder of the district.

A strong body of burghers was therefore called out, and some European soldiers with the Hottentot regiment were sent to the front. Lieutenant-Colonel John Graham was placed in command of the whole force. He was instructed to try to persuade the Kosas to retire peacefully; but if they would not do so he was to take the most effectual measures to compel them to return to their own country. Major

Cuyler with an escort of twenty-five farmers and an interpreter was therefore sent to the most advanced kraal to hold a parley with the chiefs. Close to the kraal some men were observed, and the major tried to speak to them, but the old chief Ndlambe advanced a few paces from the others, and, stamping his foot on the ground, shouted : " This country is mine ; I won it in war, and intend to keep it." Then shaking an assagai with one hand, with the other he raised a horn to his mouth. Upon blowing it, two or three hundred men rushed from a thicket towards Major Cuyler's party, who owed their escape solely to the fleetness of their horses.

There was thus no alternative to the employment of force. Everything was arranged for an attack upon the Kosas, but before it was made the landdrost of Graaff-Reinet and eight farmers were treacherously murdered during a conference with a party of warriors. In January 1812 an advance was made by the burghers and Hottentots in six divisions, that swept the country before them, while the European soldiers occupied strong positions in the rear. This plan succeeded admirably, for the Kosas, about twenty thousand in number, after a brief resistance fled to their own country. Some women who were made prisoners were then sent to inform them that on their own side of the boundary they would not be molested, but if they returned to the colony they would be shot. By the beginning of March the fourth Kaffir war was over, and it had ended—as neither the second nor the third had—favourably for the Europeans.

VIEW IN THE KOWIE VALLEY, BELOW GRAHAMSTOWN.
(*From a Sketch by Rev. W. Shaw.*)

A line of military posts, garrisoned partly by European soldiers, partly by the Hottentot regiment—which was shortly afterwards raised to eight hundred men,—and partly by burghers, was now formed from the sea to the second chain of mountains, to prevent the return of the people expelled. The principal post in the line, where the head-quarters of the troops on the frontier were stationed, was named Grahamstown, in honour of the officer in command.

During recent years several governors had thought of establishing a circuit court, but the various changes which had taken place prevented the completion of the design until 1811. Three members of the high court of justice then left Capetown on the first circuit, with instructions to try important cases, to ascertain whether the landdrosts performed their duties correctly and impartially, to inspect the district chests and buildings, and to report upon the condition of the people and all matters affecting public interests. Their proceedings were conducted with open doors, and no distinction was made between persons of different races or colour, either as accusers, accused, or witnesses. Throughout South Africa satisfaction was expressed with the establishment of a circuit court of this kind, and everywhere the judges were received with the greatest respect.

Unfortunately, however, the reverend Messrs. Vanderkemp and Read, missionaries of the London society, had given credence to a number of stories of murder of Hottentots and other outrages said to have been committed by colonists, and their reports—in which these tales appeared as facts—were published in England. By order of the British government, the charges thus made were brought before the second circuit court, which held its sessions in the last months of 1812.

In this, the black circuit as it has since been called, no fewer than fifty-eight white men and women were put upon their trial for crimes alleged to have been committed against Hottentots or slaves, and over a thousand witnesses—European, black, and Hottentot —were summoned to give evidence. The whole country was in a state of commotion. The serious charges were nearly all proved to be without foundation; but several individuals were found guilty of assault, and were punished. The irritation of the relatives and friends of those who were accused without sufficient cause was excessive; and this event, more than anything that preceded it, caused a lasting unfriendly feeling between the colonists and the missionaries of the London society.

In 1813 the French met with great reverses in Europe, and one of the first results was that the prince of Orange, who had been in exile in England since 1795, returned to the Netherlands and was received by the people as their ruler. To this time the British government regarded the Cape Colony not as a national possession, but as a conquest that might be restored to its original owner on the conclusion of peace. But now an agreement was made with the sovereign prince of the Netherlands that for a sum of six million pounds sterling he should cede to Great Britain the Cape Colony and some Dutch provinces in South America. This agreement was embodied in a convention signed at London in August 1814, when the claim of the Netherlands to South Africa was extinguished for ever.

And so the hopes that the colonists entertained of coming again under the flag of Holland were dissipated, but time had done much to soften their regret. To say that they were reconciled to English rule would be incorrect. They were, however, becoming accustomed to it, and as yet, excepting the statements of the London missionaries, nothing had occurred to cause any friction. Their language was still used in the courts of law and the public offices. Their churches had been increased to nine, and their clergymen were paid by the state. Six new magistracies—George, Clanwilliam, Caledon, Grahamstown, Cradock, and Simonstown—had been established. The financial condition of the government, bad as it subsequently proved to be, was not yet causing much alarm. In the Cape peninsula, where alone Englishmen were met in considerable numbers, intermarriages were already so common that race antipathies were rapidly dying out. After the absorption of Holland by France, also, the colonists lost the enthusiastic attachment which they had felt for the Batavian Republic, so that altogether the prospect was fair that in course of time the Europeans in South Africa would forget their old aversion to British rule, unless something untoward happened to revive it.

XIII.

THE ADMINISTRATION OF LORD CHARLES SOMERSET.

Though the colony had now become a permanent British possession, no change in the form of its government was made, nor was there any reduction of the excessively high salaries paid to the officials sent from England. Lord Charles Somerset, who succeeded Sir John Cradock in 1814, drew a salary of £10,000 a year, and was provided at the public expense with a residence in town, a country house at Newlands, a marine villa at Camp's Bay, and a shooting lodge at Groeneklool. He and the heads of departments among them absorbed more than one-fourth of the entire revenue of the country. Buildings needed for landdrosts' offices in the country districts and for various purposes in Capetown had been provided during recent years, but the cost had been defrayed by the creation of paper money, not from surplus funds in the treasury. Such a system could only end in disaster, but apparently no one saw trouble ahead, and the secretary of state took no steps to correct it.

Lord Charles Somerset had been in the colony a

little longer than a year when an event took place which stirred the smouldering fire of disaffection to British rule.

There was a farmer named Frederik Bezuidenhout living on the eastern frontier, in a secluded dell in the valley now called Glen Lynden. This man was summoned to appear before a court of justice on a charge of ill-treatment of a servant, but did not attend, so a company of pandours was sent to arrest him. When they were seen approaching he fired upon them, and then took shelter in a cavern close by, where, as he refused to surrender, he was shot dead.

On the following day his relatives and friends assembled for the funeral, when one of his brothers declared that he would never rest until the Hottentot regiment was driven from the frontier. The others present expressed themselves of the same mind, and a plan of insurrection was made. An attempt to induce others to join them failed, however, and they were never able to muster more than fifty men.

Within a very short time the government became acquainted with what was taking place, and as a strong force of burghers who had no sympathy with lawlessness assisted the troops sent to restore order, the revolt was suppressed without difficulty. Most of those who had taken part in it surrendered, but a few tried to escape to Kaffirland. These were followed by a party of pandours, and all were captured except Jan Bezuidenhout, who would not surrender, and, with his wife and little son helping him, stood at bay till he was shot dead.

The prisoners—thirty-nine in number—were tried

by a special commission of the high court of justice, and six were sentenced to death, the others to various kinds of punishment. Lord Charles Somerset would only mitigate one of the death sentences, and five of the insurgents were hanged in presence of their companions. The burghers who had assisted the government were greatly shocked by this severe punishment, for they had not thought they were helping to bring their misguided countrymen to death. By them, as well as by the families of those who took part in the disturbance, the event was long remembered with very bitter feelings towards the British authorities.

It is now necessary to cast a glance at the clans east of the Fish river, for movements were taking place among them that brought on another war with the white people, apparently a most unjustifiable war on the part of the European government, but really one for which a good reason was not wanting.

After Ndlambe's expulsion from the colony, bands of his followers found means to get through the line of military posts and plunder the farmers beyond. His young athletes, good-natured when not in a state of excitement, fleet of foot, daring, and capable of long abstinence from food, made their way from thicket to thicket through the country they had lived in nearly thirteen years, and the first notice of their presence in any locality was an empty fold from which the cattle had been driven at night. The more expert the robber, the greater hero was he among his companions, and the prouder were his relatives of him. It was their way of earning glory and gain at the same time.

Occasionally a band of soldiers would appear at one of their kraals and take compensation for the losses of the farmers, and then another account would be run up in the same way. Thus there was a feeling of hostility on both sides, with no prospect of a change for the better.

Ndlambe and Gaika were all the time quarrelling with each other, and in 1818 the elder chief suddenly became the stronger of the two. A large and important clan, previously neutral, went over to his side, and a famous seer, named Makana, declared in his favour. This Makana was a man of conspicuous ability among his countrymen. If he had been of chieftain's blood, there is little doubt that he would have made a great position for himself, but his parents were commoners, and therefore in Kaffirland he could never be the head of a tribe. He took the only way to power open to him, and became a religious teacher. The people believed that he was in communication with the spirits of the mighty dead, and that his visions and dreams were inspired. His precepts were of a highly moral nature, for he had learned a good deal of Christianity from missionaries, and adapted it to his own ideas.

In time Makana acquired enormous influence, which he used in an attempt to solidify the western section of the Kosa tribe, by bringing the half-independent clans of which it was composed into complete subjection to one head. Gaika, sunk in drunkenness and sensuality, was incapable even of comprehending such a purpose; so he declared for the manly and clear-headed Ndlambe, though that chief must then have been nearly eighty years of age. The nominal head of the tribe, who was named Hintsa, resided far away beyond the Kei, and usually troubled himself very little about the western clans, over whom he had hardly any authority. But on this occasion he too pronounced in favour of the old chief, and sent a band of warriors to aid him.

By a stratagem of Makana, the greater number of Gaika's adherents were drawn into an ambush on the Debe flats, where after a desperate battle they were driven from the field with frightful slaughter. The defeated chief fled to the Winterberg, and sent to the colony to beg for aid.

Now comes the question: Was Lord Charles Somerset justified in assisting him? The quarrel was between two rivals in a tribe over which he had no right of control, what business had he to interfere in it? The answer is that the governor could not permit a formidable hostile power to grow up on the border of the colony. To those who do not consider that reason sufficient, his action must appear unjustifiable.

Regarding Ndlambe as an implacable and dangerous enemy, he issued instructions to Lieutenant-Colonel Brereton to proceed to Gaika's assistance with a combined force of burghers and soldiers. In December 1818 Colonel Brereton crossed the Fish river, and being joined by Gaika's adherents, attacked Ndlambe, who was believed to be at the head of eighteen thousand men.

Ndlambe and his followers, however, did not venture to make a stand on open ground, but retired to dense thickets, which afforded them shelter. Their kraals were destroyed, and twenty-three thousand head of cattle were seized. The British commander found it impossible to restrain the savage passions of Gaika's followers, who were mad with excitement and joy at being able to take revenge, and were unwilling to show mercy when any of their enemies fell into their hands. He withdrew, therefore, before Ndlambe was thoroughly humbled, and on reaching Grahamstown the burghers were disbanded and permitted to return to their homes.

Ndlambe at once took advantage of the opportunity. Falling upon Gaika, he put that chief to flight, and then he poured his warriors into the colony. The inhabitants of the district between the Fish and Sunday rivers, unless in the neighbourhood of military posts, were compelled hastily to retire to lagers, and lost nearly all their property. Seventeen white people and thirteen Hottentots were murdered.

A burgher force was called out, but before the farmers could take the field Grahamstown was attacked. In the early morning of the 22nd of April 1819 between nine and ten thousand warriors, led by Makana, made a sudden rush upon that post, which had then a garrison of only three hundred and thirty-three men. They were met with a deadly fire of musketry and artillery, and after a short struggle were driven back with heavy loss.

Three months later a strong army of colonists and soldiers crossed the Fish river, drove Ndlambe's adherents eastward to the bank of the Kei, killed many of them, seized all their cattle, and burned their kraals. The old chief's power was completely broken. The fifth Kaffir war ended by the surrender of Makana, who gave himself up in the hope that his friends would then be spared. He was sent a prisoner to Robben Island, and three years afterwards was drowned when trying to escape.

Though there was no more fighting, the forces were kept in the field for several months. The governor then resolved to try to prevent the Kosas from entering the colony again by keeping a belt

FORT WILLSHIRE. BUILT 1820; ABANDONED 1837.
(*From a Sketch by A. Steedman.*)

of land beyond the border unoccupied except by soldiers, who were to patrol constantly up and down it. The military officers recommended that the Keiskama and Tyumie, as being a better line of defence than the Fish river, should be made the limit of Kaffirland, and the governor accepted their advice. In October he met Gaika, who depended upon his good will so completely that when he proposed his scheme the chief at once agreed to it.

On the right bank of the Keiskama a defensible

barrack was then built, which was named Fort Willshire, and there a body of European troops was stationed. A little later another barrack was built on the Kat river, and was named Fort Beaufort. The territory between the Fish river and the new line was kept without inhabitants, but it was easily traversed by the Kosas, who knew every thicket and jungle in it. In 1820 it was ceded by Gaika to the colony.

We have now arrived at an important period in the history of South Africa. To this time the colonists outside of Capetown were almost entirely Dutch-speaking, henceforward the English language is to be heard in many farmhouses as well as in the villages and towns throughout the country, and English customs and ideas are to come into rivalry with the customs and ideas of the earlier settlers.

For several years after the general peace which followed the fall of Napoleon much distress was felt by the labouring classes in Great Britain, and emigration was commonly spoken of as the only effectual remedy. In the Cape Colony in 1819, according to the census, there were only forty-two thousand white people; so it seemed to the imperial government that the country invited settlers, and parliament without demur granted £50,000 to defray the cost of sending out a large party.

Heads of families representing nearly ninety thousand persons applied for passages, and from these a selection was made of the number required. The ships in which they left England and Ireland, with one exception, reached South Africa safely, and in

April 1820 the immigrants commenced to land on the sandy beach of Algoa Bay. A few hundred who arrived a little later were located first at Clanwilliam, but in a short time most of them abandoned that part of the colony and followed the others to the eastern frontier. Several were people of some means, who brought out a number of servants and apprentices, the others were of various callings, a large proportion being artisans, men who had worked in factories in England, clerks, and storemen. There were nearly twice as many male as female adults.

The imperial government defrayed the cost of ocean transit, and each head of a family was promised a plot of ground one hundred acres in extent, on condition of occupying it for three years. Those who brought out servants were to have an additional hundred acres for each. Nothing more than this was promised, but means of transport to the land on which they were located were provided by the government, and for more than eighteen months rations of food were supplied to all who needed them. With few exceptions, the immigrants were located between the Bushman's and Fish rivers, the Zuurberg and the sea, a pleasant land to look upon, with its waving grass and many streamlets and patches of dark evergreen forest in the recesses of the mountains. It was part of the territory that Ndlambe had occupied for thirteen years, and that he had vainly tried to hold in 1812.

At the same time that these people were being sent from Great Britain at the expense of the government, a few came to South Africa without any aid, on the assurance of the secretary of state that they would receive larger grants of land if they paid for their passages. Altogether, nearly five thousand individuals of British birth settled in the colony between March 1820 and May 1821.

For several years the immigrants were subject to much distress. Most of them knew nothing about tilling ground, but they tried to live upon their little farms until they could get title-deeds, in order to be able to sell. Season after season their wheat crops were destroyed by rust. Then there was a great flood, which washed away many cottages and gardens. In addition to other troubles, roving Kosas made their way into the district, and robbed the poor people of many of the cattle that they had purchased.

At the end of 1821 the artisans began to disperse. In different villages throughout the colony they obtained plenty of work, at prices that soon placed them in a good position. They were followed from the locations by many others, who were not qualified to make farmers, but who easily found openings in other pursuits. The government then enlarged the farms of those who knew how to make use of them, and better times for all set in. It was about five years after their arrival before each one found himself in the sphere for which he was best adapted, and in another five years it began to be questioned whether a similar party had ever succeeded so well in any other country.

Grahamstown and Port Elizabeth owe their importance to these British immigrants. In 1820 neither of these places was more than a hamlet attached to a military post, but a few years later both were flourishing towns.

About one-eighth of the European inhabitants of the colony were now English-speaking, and theirs was a language which quickly spreads. When a man from the British Islands and one from any other country live together, their intercourse is conducted in the language of the Briton, for he refuses to learn a speech that was strange to him in youth. In South Africa this matter might with great advantage have been left to settle itself. But the deepest feelings of the old colonists were stirred by an order of the imperial government that after the 1st of January 1825 all official documents, and after the 1st of January 1828 all proceedings in courts of law should be in English. In Simonstown, Grahamstown, and Port Elizabeth, the exclusive use of the English language in the courts of law was not objected to; but in other places, where Dutch was spoken by nearly the whole people, the order was regarded as a very serious grievance. Many requests were made to the government to annul it, but to no purpose, and upon the dates named English became the official language of the country. It would have been difficult to devise a measure more calculated to irritate the Dutch inhabitants.

Just at this time also great distress was caused to many people by an order concerning the paper money. There were in circulation notes to the nominal value of a little over £700,000, of which about one-third had been created by the English government, one-seventh had been forged so cleverly that they could not be separated from those that were genuine, and the remainder were of Dutch origin. The existence of this paper was certainly a very great drawback to commerce, and it was necessary for the advancement of the country that it should be got rid of. But when an order came from England reducing it to three-eighths of its nominal value, and making British silver money a legal tender at that rate of exchange, it was felt as a crushing blow by many people. Not a few were entirely ruined. But commerce was placed on a safe footing, for the old rixdollar notes were replaced by others at the reduced rate, on which the value was marked in pounds sterling, and the imperial treasury was responsible for their redemption at any time in gold.

Notwithstanding the widespread discontent and the drawbacks to prosperity which have been mentioned, the colony showed many signs of progress during the administration of Lord Charles Somerset. The villages of Beaufort West, Bathurst, Worcester, Somerset East, and Somerset West were founded, the first lighthouse on the coast was built, a good waggon road was opened through a cleft in the mountain range behind French Hoek, and the South African public library was established. The breed of cattle, and especially of horses, was greatly improved, mainly through the importation of thoroughbred stock by the governor himself. Wine was the principal article of export, but mules were now sent to Mauritius and horses to India in considerable numbers.

The clergymen of the Dutch church were increased

to sixteen, and of the English church to five. A Wesleyan clergyman who was sent out from England in 1814 was not permitted by the governor to conduct services publicly, so his society appealed to the secretary of state, with the result that religious liberty was secured for the colony. A Roman catholic clergyman was now resident in Capetown, and Protestant clergymen of various denominations were scattered over the country and carrying on mission work beyond the borders. At each drostdy a high-class government school was established, to which parents were invited to send their children free of charge. In the eastern part of the colony these schools were of the utmost service, but as instruction was given through the medium of the English language only, they were regarded with much antipathy in the western districts, and were not there as useful as they might otherwise have been.

In 1825 a council was established to advise the governor in such affairs of importance as he might choose to submit to it for discussion. It consisted of six officials appointed by the secretary of state, and was intended to modify the despotic power of the governor; but practically it was a very slight check upon the authority of a man of strong will like Lord Charles Somerset, who treated in a most arbitrary manner all who professed democratic principles or who ventured to oppose him in any way. Among other acts which caused much clamour was the suppression by his order of a liberal newspaper called the *Commercial Advertiser*, and the virtual confiscation of the press with which it was printed.

RESIGNATION OF THE GOVERNOR.

The later years of his administration were marked by distress among the farmers—owing to bad seasons,—by a decreasing revenue, by much grumbling about the burden of taxation and the excessive cost of government, and by numerous complaints of his tyranny made to the secretary of state and to the imperial parliament. But he had influential friends, for he was a brother of the duke of Beaufort and of that Lord Fitzroy Somerset who afterwards became Lord Raglan, and his party was then in power. In 1826, however, he was obliged to return to England to defend his conduct against charges by the liberal leaders in the house of commons, who were making capital of him in their attacks upon the treasury benches, and as there was a change of ministry shortly afterwards, he considered it prudent to resign the government of the Cape Colony, a course of action that prevented his case coming on for hearing.

XIV.

THE WARS AND DEVASTATIONS OF TSHAKA.

At this period nearly the whole of South Africa beyond the borders of the Cape Colony was in a state of violent disturbance, owing to wars among different Bantu tribes.

About the year 1783, or perhaps a little later, one of the wives of the chief of a small tribe living on the banks of the river Umvolosi gave birth to a son, who was named Tshaka. Before he was fully grown the boy excited the jealousy of his father, and was obliged to flee for his life. He took refuge with Dingiswayo, head of a powerful tribe, who in his early years had gone through many strange adventures, and had by some means come to hear of the European military system. When Tshaka fled to him, Dingiswayo was carrying on war with his neighbours, and had his followers regularly drilled and formed into regiments. The young refugee became a soldier in one of these regiments, and by his bravery and address rapidly rose to a high position. Time passed on, Dingiswayo died, and the army raised Tshaka, then its favourite general, to supreme command. This was the origin of the terrible Zulu power.

Tshaka was a man of great bodily strength and of unusual vigour of mind, but he was utterly merciless.

A ZULU WARRIOR IN UNIFORM.
(*Sketch by Captain Gardiner.*)

He set himself the task not merely of conquering but of exterminating the tribes as far as he could reach. With this object he greatly improved the discipline of the army, and substituted for the light assagai a short-handled long-bladed spear formed either to cut or to stab. With this weapon in his hand, the highly trained Zulu soldier, proud of his fame and his ornaments, and knowing that death was the penalty of cowardice or disobedience, was really invincible.

Tribe after tribe passed out of sight under the Zulu spear, none of the members remaining but a few of the handsomest girls and some boys reserved to carry burdens. These boys, with only the choice before them of abject slavery or becoming soldiers, always begged to be allowed to enter the army, and were soon known as the fiercest of the warriors.

The territory that is now the colony of Natal was densely peopled before the time of Tshaka. But soon after the commencement of his career, various tribes that were trying to escape from his armies fell upon the inhabitants of that fair land, and drove before them those whom they did not destroy. As far as the Umzimvubu river the whole population was in motion, slaughtering and being slaughtered.

One large horde of fugitives made its way as far as the river Umgwali, and was there attacked and beaten by a combined force of Tembus and Kosas. After the battle the horde dispersed, and its fragments settled down in a condition of vassalage among the clans between the Kei and the Umtata. So also at a little later date did other remnants of various tribes from the north, all of the refugees taking the common name of Fingos, or wanderers. By the beginning of 1824, between the rivers Tugela and Umzimvubu there were not left more than five or six thousand wretched starvelings, who hid themselves in thickets, and some of whom became cannibals as the only means of sustaining life.

On the other side of the great mountain range known as the Kathlamba or Drakensberg, the destruction of human beings was even greater. Before the rise of the Zulu power, Bantu tribes peopled densely the northern part of the territory now termed Basutoland, the north-eastern portion of the present Orange Free State, and the whole area of the South African Republic of our days. During the winter of the year 1822 a tribe fleeing from the Zulus crossed the mountains and fell upon the people residing about the sources of the Caledon. They, in their turn, fell upon others in advance, until the whole of the inhabitants of the country as far as the Vaal in one great horde crossed the river and began to devastate the region beyond. Among their leaders was a woman named Ma Ntatisi, from whom the horde received the name Mantatis.

After crossing the Vaal, the Mantatis turned to the north-west, and created awful havoc with the tribes in their line of march. As each was overcome, its cattle and grain were devoured, and then the murderous host passed on to the next. Their strength was partly kept up by incorporating captives, but vast numbers of the invaders, especially of women and children, left their bones mingled with those of the people they destroyed. Twenty-eight distinct tribes are believed to have disappeared before the Mantatis received a check. Then Makaba, chief of the Bangwaketsi, fell upon them unawares, defeated them, and compelled them to turn to the south. In June 1823 they sustained another defeat from a party of Griqua horsemen, and then the great horde broke into fragments.

One section—the Makololo—went northward, destroying the tribes in its course, and years afterwards was found by Dr. Livingstone on a branch of the Zambesi. Another section, under Ma Ntatisi, returned to its old home, and took part in the devastation of the country along the Caledon. And various little bands wandered about destroying until they were themselves destroyed. Several thousand refugees from the wasted country found their way into the Cape Colony, where they were apprenticed by the government to such persons as were not slaveholders.

In the winter of 1828 a Zulu army penetrated the country as far south as the Bashee. Tshaka himself with a body-guard remained at the Umzimkulu, and sent one of his regiments to destroy the Pondos, while another division of his force proceeded to deal in the same manner with the Tembus and Kosas. The Pondos were plundered of everything they possessed, but the chief and most of his people managed to hide themselves until the Zulus retired. The Tembus and Kosas fared better. There was an Englishman, named Henry Fynn, with Tshaka, and he succeeded in inducing the chief to recall the army before there was much destruction of life or property.

The Tembus and Kosas, however, were greatly alarmed. They sent to beg help from the Europeans, and to prevent them from being driven into the colony a commando of a thousand men, under Lieutenant-Colonel Somerset, marched to their aid. This commando encountered a large body of fierce warriors, who were believed to be Zulus, and an engagement followed which lasted several hours. Afterwards it was discovered that the men whom the Europeans were fighting with were some of those who had fled from Tshaka, and whose course was marked by fire and blood. They were defeated with heavy loss, and as soon as they were scattered the Kosas and Tembus fell upon them and nearly exterminated them.

In September 1828 Tshaka was murdered by two of his brothers, one of whom—Dingan by name—succeeded as chief of the Zulus. The new ruler was equally as cruel, but not so able as his predecessor. Under his government the military system was kept up, though the only people left within reach that he could exercise his arms upon were the Swazis. War with them was almost constant, but their country contained natural strongholds which enabled them to set Dingan, as they had set Tshaka, at defiance. Various armies, however, that had been put in motion at an earlier date were still moving on, some at a great distance from their starting places.

One of these was under a chief named Moselekatse, whose reputation as a shedder of human blood is second only to that of Tshaka himself. He was in command of a division of the Zulu army, and had acquired the devoted attachment of the soldiers, when a circumstance occurred which left him no choice but flight. After a successful onslaught upon a tribe which he was sent to exterminate, he neglected to

168 WARS AND DEVASTATIONS OF TSHAKA.

forward the whole of the booty to his master, and Tshaka, enraged by such conduct, despatched a great army with orders to put him and all his adherents to death. These, receiving intimation of their danger in

PORTRAIT OF DINGAN.
(*From a Sketch by Captain Gardiner.*)

time, immediately crossed the mountains and began to lay waste the central zone of the country that is now the South African Republic.

The numerous tribes whose remnants form the

Bapedi of our times looked with dismay upon the athletic forms of the Matabele, as they termed the invaders. They had never before seen discipline so perfect as that of these naked braves, or weapon so deadly as the Zulu stabbing spear. All who could not make their escape were exterminated, except the comeliest girls and some of the young men who were kept as carriers. These last were led to hope that by faithful service they might attain the position of soldiers, and from them Moselekatse filled up the gaps that occurred in his ranks. The country over which he marched was covered with skeletons, and literally no human beings were left in it, for his object was to place a desert between Tshaka and himself. When he considered himself at a safe distance from his old home he halted, erected military kraals after the Zulu pattern, and from them as a centre his regiments traversed the land north, south, and west in search of spoil.

It is impossible to give the number of Moselekatse's warriors, but it was probably not greater than ten thousand. Fifty of them were a match for more than five hundred Betshuana. They pursued these wretched creatures even when there was no plunder to be had, and slew many thousands in mere wantonness, in exactly the same spirit and with as little compunction as a sportsman shoots snipe.

While the Matabele were engaged in their career of destruction, other bands were similarly employed farther north, so that by 1828 there was not a single Betshuana tribe left intact between the Magalisberg and the Limpopo. On the margin of the Kalahari desert several were still unbroken, though they had suffered severely. In 1830 Moselekatse moved against these tribes, and dispersed them. They were not exterminated, because they took refuge in the desert, where they found sustenance in places to which the Matabele could not pursue them; but they were reduced to a very wretched state.

After this Moselekatse built his military kraals on the banks of the Marikwa, and was lord of the country far and wide.

Only one tribe escaped, and that the weakest and most degraded of all the southern Betshuana. The principal Batlapin kraal was then at the source of the Kuruman river, where missionaries resided for a short time at the beginning of the century. The station was soon abandoned, but was occupied again in 1817 by agents of the London society, and four years later the reverend Robert Moffat went to live there. Towards the close of 1829 Mr. Moffat visited Moselekatse, whose kraals were then about a hundred miles east of the Marikwa. The chief could not comprehend the character or the work of the missionary, but he was flattered by the friendship of such a man, and conceived a great respect for one who could weld two thick pieces of iron. He believed Mr. Moffat to be lord of the people at the Kuruman, and, to show his regard, he abstained from sending his warriors there. Thus the Batlapin, who would have fled from the smallest division of the Matabele army, were saved by the presence among them of a courageous and able European.

Meantime in one corner of the vast waste that had

been created the process of reconstruction was going on. In the territory that is now called Basutoland a young man named Moshesh was collecting together dispersed people of various tribes, and forming them into a compact political body. He was only in rank the son of a petty captain, and his father was still living, so that under ordinary circumstances he would have had little chance of raising himself to power. But Moshesh possessed abilities of a very high order as a military strategist, a diplomatist, an organiser of society, and a ruler of men. His seat of government was Thaba Bosigo, an impregnable mountain stronghold. He prevented attacks of the Zulus by professing himself the humblest vassal of Tshaka and Dingan, and by frequently sending tribute of furs and feathers. All who submitted to him were treated alike, no matter to what tribe they originally belonged, and as much assistance as possible was given to those who needed it. Even bands of cannibals were provided with grain and gardens, that they might become agriculturists once more. Men of tribes that had recently been destroying each other were induced to live side by side in friendship and peace. Thus a new community was forming under Moshesh, by far the ablest black ruler known in South Africa since the arrival of Europeans in the country.

Moselekatse sent plundering parties against him, but his scouts gave warning in time, so that the raiders were not able to do much harm. In 1831 a Matabele army laid siege to Thaba Bosigo, but could not take the stronghold. When the besiegers were

THABA BOSIGO.
(*From a Sketch by Rev. E. Casalis.*)

compelled by want of food to retreat, Moshesh provided them with provisions sufficient for their homeward journey, and a friendly message accompanied the gift. He was never again attacked by them.

In 1833 missionaries of the Paris evangelical society went to reside with Moshesh, from whom they received a hearty welcome, as he recognised that their assistance in temporal matters would be of great service. In the same year a number of wandering bands—Bantu, Hottentots, and half-breeds—were persuaded by Wesleyan missionaries to settle on the right bank of the Caledon, not very far from Thaba Bosigo.

In 1836 a vast portion of the territory east and north of the Cape Colony was lying waste. Between the Keiskama and Umzimvubu rivers were the Kosa, Tembu, and Pondo tribes, with the Fingos, and various clans driven down from the north. Missionaries of the London, Glasgow, and Wesleyan societies were endeavouring to christianise and civilise these people. Between the Umzimvubu and Tugela rivers there were only five or six thousand inhabitants. North of the Tugela were the Zulus, under the chief Dingan, who had twenty-five or thirty thousand highly-trained soldiers at his command.

Within the western border of the present South African Republic, along the Marikwa river, were the Matabele military kraals; but the greater portion of that vast territory was unoccupied, except in the most rugged places, where the broken remnants of former tribes were lurking. The present Orange Free State contained a few hundred Griquas or people of mixed Hottentot, negro, and European blood, who had emigrated from the Cape Colony, a few hundred Hottentots of the Korana tribe, the remnant of the horde under Ma Ntatisi around Lishuane, and some Bantu clans at Mekuatling, Thaba Ntshu, and Bethulie. In the territory now called British Betshuanaland the population consisted of the Batlapin tribe, some roving Koranas, and a few stragglers on the border of the desert. And in Basutoland there were the people collected by Moshesh. American missionaries were attempting to settle in Natal and with the Matabele on the Marikwa, a clergyman of the church of England had just gone to reside with Dingan, and missionaries of the Paris, London, Berlin, and Wesleyan societies were busy wherever there were inhabitants between the Kathlamba mountains and the desert.

XV.

EVENTS IN THE CAPE COLONY FROM 1826 TO 1835.

IT is not a pleasant admission for an Englishman to make, but it is the truth, that it would be difficult to find in any part of the world a people with so much cause to be discontented as the old inhabitants of the Cape Colony for many years after the fall of the ministry of the earl of Liverpool. There was no sympathy whatever shown towards them by the authorities in England, in fact there was a decided antipathy, which was fostered by the so-called philanthropic societies, then at the height of their power. The most outrageous stories concerning the colonists were circulated by men who bore the title of Christian teachers—and nothing was too gross to be believed in England,—until the word Boer (Dutch for Farmer) came to be regarded as a synonym for an ignorant and heartless oppressor of coloured people. It was useless for the governors to report differently, or for the courts of law to pronounce the stories libellous: the great societies condemned "the Boers," and the great societies represented and led public opinion in England.

Something, however, must be said on the other side. The inhabitants of the Cape Colony were not all white people, and the British government tried to do what it held to be justice to the blacks. Then the whole number of Dutch colonists was only equal to the population of a third-class English town, and their sentiments must have been regarded as of little importance by those who were guiding the destinies of a mighty empire. To make them fall into line with the notions of the day in Great Britain seemed not only easy, but the correct policy to carry out. No one imagined that they were capable of making any effectual opposition.

In 1828 the whole of the courts of justice in the Cape Colony were remodelled after the English pattern. In the country districts the landdrosts and heemraden were done away with, and in their stead civil commissioners, resident magistrates, and justices of the peace were created. A supreme court was established, with judges appointed by the crown and independent of the governor, and though the Dutch code of law was retained, the forms of procedure were assimilated to those customary in England. Since that time criminal cases have been tried by a single judge and a jury of nine men, whose verdict must be unanimous in order to convict.

At the same time the burgher senate was abolished, and the government took upon itself the municipal and other duties previously performed by that body. As if these sweeping changes were not sufficient irritation for the old colonists, a notice was issued that all documents addressed to the government must be written in English or have a translation attached, otherwise they would be returned to those who sent them.

A little later one of the judges removed the criminal cases from the circuit court at Worcester to Capetown for trial, on the ground that there was not a sufficient number of English-speaking men to form a jury at Worcester, though the prisoners and the witnesses spoke Dutch only, and every word that they said had to be translated to the court. The judges were divided in opinion whether it was necessary for jurymen in every case to understand English, and the question remained open until 1831, when an ordinance was issued defining their qualifications, among which a knowledge of English was not included. In the interval, however, the burghers, who regarded their exclusion from the jury-box as an insult, were deeply incensed. But they sent in no memorials, because they would not be driven to have them written in English, and there was little hope of success had they even done so.

And now was heard the first murmuring of a cry that a few years later resounded through the colony, and men and women began to talk of the regions laid waste by the Zulu wars, if it might not be possible to find there a refuge from British rule.

One measure, however, was carried out at this time which gave general satisfaction. The salaries of the officials sent from England had been far beyond the means of the colony, and they were now greatly reduced.

The condition of the Hottentots and other free

coloured people had long been a subject of discussion in England, where it was commonly believed that they were treated with much injustice. In reality it was not so, though there certainly were instances of ill usage, just as there are outrages in all countries of the world.

After November 1809 Hottentots were not allowed to wander over the country without passes, and after April 1812 Hottentot children born while their parents were in service, and maintained for eight years by the employers of their parents, were bound as apprentices for ten years longer. In the opinion of the governor who made this law it was better for the children that they should acquire industrious habits, even if restraint had to be used, than that they should become vagrants. The reverend Dr. Philip, however, who was superintendent of the London society's missions in South Africa, claimed for people of all colours and conditions exactly the same treatment; and as the great philanthropical societies of England supported him, he was virtually master of the position.

In July 1828 an ordinance was issued which relieved the Hottentots and other free coloured people from the laws concerning passes and the apprenticeship of children, and placed them in all respects on a political level with Europeans. From that time the colony was overrun by idle wanderers to such an extent that farming could hardly be made to pay, and the coloured people were falling back in the scale of civilisation; but when an attempt was made a few years later to get a vagrant act proclaimed,

Dr. Philip and his party opposed the measure so strenuously that it had to be abandoned.

Sir Lowry Cole, who became governor in 1828, caused between two and three thousand Hottentots and people of mixed blood to be located at the Kat river, in the territory ceded by Gaika to the colony. Several small streams unite to form this river, and in their valleys the land is easily irrigated and is of great fertility. In the best places settlements were formed, each divided into plots of from four to six acres in extent, upon which a family was placed. The ground between the settlements was to remain as a commonage, each family having the right to graze cattle on it. The settlers were to remain five years on trial, at the end of which period those who had built cottages and tilled the ground were to receive grants in freehold, but every plot not improved within that time was to revert to government. For a while the settlement appeared to flourish. The government supplied seed corn, furrows for leading out water were made, and a large extent of ground was brought under cultivation. In the course of a few years, however, it was seen that the pure Hottentots could not sustain such efforts beyond two or three seasons, but there were many halfbreeds among those to whom plots of ground were assigned, and they formed a more stable class.

Early in 1834 Sir Benjamin D'Urban arrived as governor, with instructions from the secretary of state to carry out several important measures. The first was retrenchment of expenditure on a very extensive scale, as the colonial revenue was less than the outlay, and the public debt was increasing. Various offices were now combined, so that one man had to do the work previously performed by two, and all salaries were greatly reduced. The outlay on roads, buildings, and, indeed, everything maintained by the government, was cut down as much as possible.

The second measure was a slight change in the form of government, caused by the creation of distinct legislative and executive councils. The colonists had often sent petitions to England to be allowed to have a representative assembly, but these had always failed. At length, however, the imperial authorities resolved to make the government of the Cape appear a little less despotic, and for this purpose a legislative council was created. It consisted of the governor, as president, five of the highest officials, and five colonists selected by the governor. Its power can be inferred from a remark of Sir George Napier to one of the unofficial members who was combating the government view of a question: "You may spare your breath in this matter, everything of importance is settled before it comes here." Still it was a step—though a very short one—in the right direction.

The council of advice previously existing now became an executive council, and was made to consist of four high officials.

The third special object which Sir Benjamin D'Urban was instructed to carry into effect was the emancipation of the slaves.

As long as the Dutch East India Company held

the colony slaves were brought into it, but not in very large numbers, for their services were only needed to a limited extent. During the first British occupation a great many were imported, as the trade was then profitable, and English energy was employed in it. The Batavian government, being opposed to the system, allowed very few to be landed, and had it lasted a couple of years longer, every child born thereafter would have been declared free.

The suppression of the foreign slave trade by the British government followed so closely upon the second conquest of the colony, that there was only time in the interval for five hundred negroes to be imported. From that date the increase in the number of slaves was due to the large excess of births over deaths.

There never was an attempt in South Africa to defend the system in theory. Indeed, it was a common remark that it was worse for the white man, who had all the care and anxiety, than for the negro, who had only manual labour to perform. But it is not easy to disturb any system, good or bad, upon which the habits of a people have been formed, and in the Cape Colony money to the amount of over three million pounds sterling was invested in slaves.

The testimony of every one competent to form a correct opinion concurred that in no other part of the world was bondage so light. Except in planting and harvesting the labour of the negroes was easy, and they certainly did not feel themselves degraded by compulsory service. They were the most lighthearted of mortals. The English governors were of opinion that they enjoyed more comfort than labourers in Great Britain, and that the Dutch laws gave them sufficient protection against ill-usage. To judge of their condition by imagining what a European would feel in a similar state leads to a false conclusion, for their hereditary training and line of thought were entirely different.

In 1816 laws began to be made for reducing the power of the masters and conferring rights upon the slaves, and almost every year they increased in stringency. For some time the colonists made no objection to them, but at length control over dependents was so limited that many negroes became insubordinate. Public meetings were then held, at which the opinion was maintained that the ties between master and slave were too weakened to bear further straining. A resolution was passed with one voice at a meeting of slaveholders at Graaff-Reinet, and was generally agreed to in the other districts, that if the English government would stop irritating legislation they would consent that from the date of the arrangement all female children should be free at birth, in order that slavery might gradually die out.

Another plan was adopted by a few well-meaning persons in Capetown, who formed a society for aiding deserving slaves and slave children to purchase their freedom. The society collected subscriptions, and turned its attention chiefly to the emancipation of young girls. It hoped to receive aid in money from the British treasury and from benevolent persons in England, but was disappointed in both. With means limited almost entirely to colonial subscriptions, however, it was able to purchase the freedom of about twenty-five girls yearly.

In England neither of these plans met with favour.

In 1830 an order in council was issued prescribing the quantity and quality of food to be given to slaves, the clothing that should be provided for them, the hours during which they should not be obliged to work, and many other matters. It was followed in 1831 by another order in council, limiting the hours of slave labour to nine daily, and nearly destroying the owners' authority. The excitement was now so great that the governor thought it necessary to prohibit public meetings and to threaten to banish any one who should attempt to disturb the peace.

As soon as the clamour subsided, however, he gave his consent to a public meeting being held, and about two thousand slaveholders came together in Capetown. The utmost order was observed, though resolutions were carried that the lately made laws were highly unjust. The whole assembly then marched to the open space in front of government house, when two gentlemen were deputed to inform the governor that the slaveholders were prepared to suffer the penalties of the orders in council, but could not obey them.

The strain upon the colonists was so great that it was felt as a relief when in August 1833 an emancipation act, to have force in all the British possessions, was passed by the imperial parliament. For the Cape Colony it provided that on the 1st of December 1834 slavery was to cease, and after a short term of apprenticeship the negroes were to have exactly the same civil rights as white people. The sum of twenty million pounds sterling was voted to compensate the owners in the nineteen slave colonies of Great Britain, and the share of each colony was to be determined by the appraised value of its slaves.

There was a general impression that this money would suffice to meet the whole, or nearly the whole, value of the slaves, and as most people believed that a vagrant act would be passed before the day of emancipation, they were disposed to accept the new condition of things without demur or heartburning.

There were then in the colony thirty-nine thousand slaves, of whom between three and four thousand were aged or infirm, and the others were appraised at rather over three million pounds sterling.

The year 1835 was well advanced when intelligence was received from England that the returns for all the colonies were complete, and that of the twenty millions sterling the share awarded to the Cape was a little less than one million and a quarter. The intelligence created a panic greater than any ever known before in South Africa. Many of the late slaves were mortgaged to the various institutions for lending money, and every bond contained a clause covering all other property. At once there was a demand for the redemption of the bonds, and goods and effects were sold at any price that could be obtained. In some instances slaves had been the sole property of widows, or minors, or aged people, and the late owners were at once reduced to indigence.

But the whole loss was not even yet known. Succeeding mails brought information that the imperial government would not send the money to South Africa, but that each claim would have to be proved before commissioners in London, when the amount allowed would be paid in stock, after certain charges were deducted. This decision brought into the country a swarm of petty agents, who purchased claims at perhaps half their real value, so that a colonist, instead of receiving two-fifths of the appraised value of his slaves, often received only one-fifth or one-sixth.

It would be difficult to picture too darkly the misery caused by this confiscation of two millions' worth of the property of a small and not over flourishing community. Some families never recovered from the blow. Aged men and women who had not before known want went down to the grave penniless, and in hundreds of the best households of the country the pinch of poverty was sorely felt. Emancipation in itself assuredly was a righteous act, for there can be nothing more abominable than one man holding another as property; but a vast amount of distress might have been prevented by effecting it in the manner that the colonists proposed.

In addition to the direct loss, the wheat and wine farmers for many years were unable to bring as much produce to market as before, owing to the scarcity of labour. One industry only—but that afterwards a very important one,—the breeding of merino sheep for the sake of wool, received a great impetus from the emancipation of the slaves, for it could be carried on with fewer workmen than were required in agriculture.

The liberated slaves mostly flocked into the towns and villages, where missionary and philanthropic energy in all conceivable forms has ever since been expended upon them and their descendants. In general they can now exist by working perhaps half as many hours as before the emancipation, for much of their time is passed in idleness; but they are neither more comfortably clothed or better fed or housed, nor—with few exceptions—have they made any perceptible intellectual advancement.

On the other hand, they have probably improved in morals, very many of those who attend the mission chapels certainly have. As free agents their pleasures continue to be of a low order. Given any noisy musical instrument, a bright sun, and a gaudy dress, and their mirth is unattainable by Europeans. Without energy, or ambition, or a thought of the responsibility of life, they manage to pass their days in an easy and joyous manner.

Three of the special duties assigned to Sir Benjamin D'Urban have been mentioned: another was to enter into treaties of friendship with the native chiefs beyond the colonial frontier.

Both on the north and the east the border was then in a disturbed condition. There was a band of freebooters—mostly Hottentots—plundering the graziers of the northern districts, and as their haunts were on some islands in the Orange river, which were covered with jungle and very difficult of access to strangers, they were able to set their pursuers at defiance.

Farther up the river a petty Griqua captain, named Andries Waterboer, was living, and through the agency of his missionary a treaty was entered into with him. He was to receive £100 a year as a subsidy for himself and £50 a year for a mission school, he was provided with two hundred muskets and a quantity of ammunition, and he engaged in return to be a faithful friend and ally of the colony and to preserve peace along the border from Kheis to Ramah. This was the first treaty of the kind ever made in South Africa, and it was the only one that answered its purpose. Waterboer kept his engagement, and the freebooters were rooted out.

Sir Benjamin D'Urban intended to visit the eastern frontier to make similar arrangements with the Kosa chiefs, but was detained in Capetown by pressing business, and before he had been a year in the colony the sixth Kaffir war commenced.

The plan of Lord Charles Somerset to keep the tract of land between the Fish and Keiskama rivers unoccupied soon proved a failure, as robbers made their way across it without difficulty. Then clans of Kosas supposed to be friendly—among others those under two sons of Gaika named Makoma and Tyali —were allowed to occupy the ground, in hope that they would prevent cattle-lifters passing through. But they proved to be as expert and unscrupulous robbers as ever the followers of Ndlambe had been, and it became necessary to make reprisals upon them just as upon the others. After a while Ndlambe and one of his sons were recognised by the government as chiefs of the people who through all their troubles had adhered to them, and from that moment the sons of Gaika regarded the Europeans as enemies.

Their conduct now became so bad that the governor was obliged to remove first one and then the other from the ceded territory, and this, of course, created a strong feeling of resentment on their part. In 1829 Gaika died, leaving a young lad named Sandile as his principal heir, when Makoma's power was greatly increased, as he became regent for his half-brother. Ndlambe had died in the preceding year, and quarrels arose among his sons and grandsons, some of whom allied themselves with Makoma to gain support. Thus it happened that the family whose position the government had done so much to build up was now both strong and hostile.

A rupture had long been threatening, when some Kosas, by stealing the horses of the officers at Fort Beaufort, drew a party of soldiers into a quarrel in which a petty captain was slightly wounded and some cattle belonging to Tyali were seized. This was announced by the chiefs to be a declaration of war, and a few days later—21st of December 1834— between twelve and twenty thousand warriors made a sudden rush into the colony, swept off nearly all the cattle east of the Sunday river, burned the houses, and murdered every white man who could not escape. Among others, most of the British settlers of 1820 who were living on farms were reduced to destitution. The unfortunate people had barely time to flee to Grahamstown, Bathurst, or some other place of refuge, and were compelled to abandon everything.

When intelligence of the invasion reached Capetown, Colonel—afterwards Sir Harry—Smith hastened to the frontier, and began to organise a force to operate against the Kosas. The governor followed as speedily as possible. The burghers all over the colony were called out, and as soon as they could muster, an advance was made into Kaffirland, the raiders having in the meantime retired to the fastnesses of their own country, after sending the cattle over the Kei to be guarded by Hintsa.

The Kosas, as is their custom, refused to meet the Europeans on open ground, and it was no easy matter to deprive them of their strongholds. They simply retired from one jungle to another, after resisting as long as they could, and reoccupied every place that was not well guarded after being taken. To meet this difficulty, Sir Benjamin D'Urban formed several camps in commanding positions, from which patrols could be sent out frequently to scour the forests in their neighbourhood. It was the only plan open to him, but the country was too large to be held in subjection in this way by the force at his disposal.

As soon as this arrangement was completed, the governor crossed the Kei with a considerable army to recover the cattle. Messages were sent to Hintsa offering peace if he would give them up, but for some time he made no reply. Colonel Smith was then directed to scour his country, and met with such success that the chief himself came to the British camp and agreed to the terms demanded. He left his son Kreli and one of his brothers as hostages with

Sir Benjamin D'Urban, and volunteered to guide a detachment of troops and burghers under Colonel Smith to the place where the cattle were kept; but on the way he attempted to escape, and was shot dead by a colonist who pursued him.

Kreli succeeded his father as paramount chief of

PORTRAIT OF HINTSA.
(*From a Sketch by Captain Michell.*)

the Kosa tribe, and peace was concluded with him upon his undertaking to restore the cattle in instalments. The clans west of the Kei were still holding out, but in September 1835 they tendered their submission, and hostilities came to an end.

The arrangements made by Sir Benjamin D'Urban

for the preservation of peace were such as every one approves of at the present day. He brought some eighteen thousand Fingos from beyond the Kei, and gave them ground between the Keiskama and Fish rivers, where they would form a buffer for the colonists. They and the Kosas hated each other bitterly, and this feeling was deepened by their appropriating and taking with them twenty-two thousand head of cattle belonging to Kreli's people. It was thus to their interest to act honestly towards the Europeans, whose support alone could save them from destruction. Between the Keiskama and the Kei the western Kosa clans were located as British subjects, but a great deal of authority was left to the chiefs. The territory was named the Province of Queen Adelaide, and Colonel Smith was stationed at a place in it which was called King-Williamstown, to command the troops and control the chiefs. This plan of settlement commended itself to the great majority of the colonists and of the missionaries, who hoped that under it the Kosas would make rapid advances towards civilisation and that property on the border would be secure.

There was, however, in Capetown—five hundred miles from the Kaffir frontier—a party under the leadership of the reverend Dr. Philip, that entirely disapproved of the governor's plans. It was composed of only a few individuals, but it had powerful support from abroad. This party desired the formation of states ruled by Bantu chiefs under the guidance of missionaries, and from which Europeans not favoured by missionaries should be excluded. It maintained the theory that the Kosas were an eminently docile and peaceably disposed people, who could easily be taught to do what was right, and who must therefore have been provoked to take up arms by great wrongs and cruelties. The utmost fear was expressed by its members that the Bantu tribes would perish if exposed to free intercourse with white people.

To push his views Dr. Philip visited England with a Kosa and a half-breed Hottentot who had been trained by missionaries. A committee of the house of commons was at the time collecting information upon the aborigines in British colonies, and Dr. Philip appeared before it. His evidence was received at great length, and though it consisted largely of opinion, it was allowed to outweigh that of the officers of greatest experience in South African affairs.

Before the committee of the house of commons appeared also a disappointed retired official from the colony, Captain Andries Stockenstrom, who denounced the proceedings of the government on the eastern frontier as unjust and oppressive. He asserted his belief that there were civilised nations in which the proportion of thieves was greater than among the Kosas, and he was of opinion that treaties could be made with the chiefs by which cattle-lifting could be suppressed.

No evidence could have been more gratifying to the earl Glenelg, who in April 1835 became secretary of state for the colonies. He held the same views as Dr. Philip, and here was Captain Stockenstrom, a South African by birth, in full accord with him. The secretary resolved at once to undo all that Sir Benjamin D'Urban had done. In a despatch, dated the 26th of December 1835, he announced that the sovereignty over the country between the Keiskama and the Kei must be withdrawn, because "it rested upon a war in which the original justice was on the side of the conquered, not of the victorious party." He asserted that "the Kosas had an ample justification of the war in the conduct which was pursued towards them by the colonists and the public authorities through a long series of years, they were urged to revenge and desperation by the systematic injustice of which they had been the victims, and they had a perfect right to endeavour to extort by force that redress which they could not expect otherwise to obtain." He added that a lieutenant-governor would immediately be appointed for the eastern districts, who would be entrusted with authority to arrange border affairs in accordance with his views.

The contents of this despatch spread consternation widely over South Africa. Outside of Dr. Philip's little party in Capetown there was but one opinion: that it destroyed all hope of the preservation of order, and placed life and whatever property was left in the eastern districts at the mercy of the Kosas. The next mail brought tidings that Captain Stockenstrom had been appointed lieutenant-governor, and might shortly be expected. The British settlers at once sent an earnest protest to England, with an appeal for a close investigation of all occurrences on the border, but they could obtain no redress. Sir

Benjamin D'Urban wrote, pointing out that the colonists at any rate were free of blame, as they had no voice in devising the various modes of dealing with the Kosas that had been in force, but the only result was his dismissal from office. To the Dutch colonists in the frontier districts who still possessed the means of moving there seemed to be but one course open: to flee from British rule, and to seek a new home somewhere in the vast wilderness left unpeopled by the wars of Tshaka.

XVI.

GREAT EMIGRATION FROM THE CAPE COLONY. EXPULSION OF MOSELEKATSE FROM THE TERRITORY SOUTH OF THE LIMPOPO.

To people in England one of the strangest events of the present century is the abandonment of their homes by thousands of Cape colonists after 1836, and their braving all the hardships of life in the wilderness for no other cause than to be free of British rule. Yet there is nothing to cause surprise in the matter, if the character of the Dutch people is considered. These colonists were of the same blood as the men who withstood the great power of Philip II of Spain, who laid the richest part of their country under water rather than surrender it to Louis XIV of France. They were not the men and women to submit to what they believed to be misrule, if there was a possibility of successful resistance or a chance of making their escape.

Many of them, as we have seen, were accustomed to live in waggons and to subsist to a large extent upon game, so that moving deeper into the continent was in itself no great difficulty. Before them was a great waste swarming with wild animals, what wonder that they should move into it with such powerful motives to urge them on.

Let us look again briefly at the grievances which determined their conduct. First, there was subjection by a foreign and unsympathetic government. Second, there was the prohibition of their language in the public offices and courts of law. Third, there was the superintendent of the London missionary society, their ablest and most relentless opponent, in possession of boundless influence with the British authorities. Fourth, there were the slanderous statements made by the philanthropic societies in England concerning them. Fifth, there was the sudden emancipation of their slaves without adequate compensation. Sixth, there was the whole mass of the coloured people placed upon a political footing with them, and that without a vagrant act being put into force. Seventh, there was no security for life or property in the eastern districts, which were exposed to invasion by the Kosas, as the secretary of state took part with the barbarians. These were the chief causes of the great emigration, and there were many others of less importance.

And now all over the frontier districts the great waggons were laden with household goods and provisions and ammunition, and bands of people set out to seek a new home in the north. Each party was usually made up of families related to each other, and the man of greatest influence in it was elected its leader, with the title of commandant. The horned cattle, horses, sheep, and goats were driven slowly on, and often when the pasture was good the caravans would rest for weeks together. They went up from the grass-covered hills along the coast and the bare Karoo farther inland, till they came to one or other of the steep passes into the elevated basin drained by the Orange and its numerous tributaries. With twenty to thirty oxen before each waggon they struggled up, and then went on without difficulty down the long slope to the river and across the wide plains of the present Orange Free State.

North of the Orange the emigrants regarded themselves as beyond English authority, for over and over again it had been officially announced that Great Britain would not enlarge her possessions in South Africa.

The first party that left the colony made its way northward to the Zoutpansberg, where it divided into two sections of about fifty individuals each. One of these sections was cut off by a band of blacks, and all its members except two children were murdered. The other attempted to explore the country to Delagoa Bay, but lost its cattle by the tsetse, and was then attacked by fever, from which only one man and barely half the women and children recovered. The unfortunate survivors after almost incredible hardships reached Delagoa Bay, where they were very kindly treated by the Portuguese authorities, being provided with food and shelter until their friends could send a vessel from Natal to rescue them.

The second party was much larger, and was under the leadership of a man of considerable ability, named Hendrik Potgieter. It moved slowly on until it reached the banks of the Vet river, a tributary of the Vaal, where it halted. Potgieter found here a native captain in a very wretched condition, who claimed to be the descendant of chiefs that had once ruled over numerous followers in a wide expanse of country. Having lived long in fear of doing anything that might bring him to the knowledge of Moselekatse, he was delighted at the appearance of the white people, especially when he received from them a very liberal offer. Potgieter proposed that he should sell the country which he claimed, except a reserve of ample size for himself and his followers, and receive in exchange protection and a small herd of cattle. The captain at once consented, and then the emigrants took possession of the land between the Vet and Vaal rivers, some of them even moving beyond the Vaal.

After a while Commandant Potgieter and eleven others went out to explore the country northward, and travelled as far as the Zoutpansberg, where they were much pleased with the fertility of the soil and the rich pasture. They believed also that communication with the outer world could be opened through Delagoa Bay, so that the country seemed to offer every advantage that could be desired for a settlement.

In high spirits they set out to return to their families, but on arriving at the place where they had left the last waggons they were struck with horror by finding that many of their friends had been massacred in a dreadful manner not long before. A band of

Moselekatse's warriors, while traversing the country to keep it from being occupied, had suddenly come upon a little party of white people, and murdered all who could not escape. Most of those along the Vaal, however, had notice in time to draw their waggons around them, and, when attacked, were able to beat off their assailants. The Matabele soldiers then returned to the Marikwa for reinforcements.

Potgieter immediately selected a suitable hill, and formed a strong lager on it, by lashing fifty waggons together in a circle and filling all the open spaces except a narrow entrance with thorn trees. He had not long to wait before the Matabele attacked him. They rushed upon the lager with loud hisses, but were received with a deadly fire from the forty men inside, and were obliged to fall back. Again they rushed on regardless of death, and strove to tear the waggons apart, but could not. The forty defenders of the lager were keeping up a rapid fire, for their wives and mothers were loading spare guns for their use. As a last resource the men of one of the Matabele regiments threw their spears over the waggons, where over eleven hundred were afterwards picked up, and when this failed they withdrew, but drove off the whole of the emigrants' cattle. They left a hundred and fifty-five corpses outside the lager.

Potgieter's party was now in great distress. Including servants, forty-six of its members had been murdered, and the survivors were in a solitary waste without the means of moving and with very little food. Fortunately, however, the third band of emigrants, under Commandant Gerrit Maritz, had just encamped at Thaba Ntshu, and learning what had happened, sent oxen to bring away the unfortunate people and their effects.

And now it was to be seen what metal the emigrants were made of. It might be thought that with such experience they would have retreated at once, but the idea of abandoning their project never occurred to one of them. Instead of fleeing from Moselekatse, they resolved to attack him in his own kraal, and punish him severely for what he had done. One hundred and seven farmers mustered for this purpose, and with them went forty half-breeds and a few blacks to look after the horses. A deserter from the Matabele army volunteered to act as guide.

So thoroughly depopulated was the country that not an individual was met between Thaba Ntshu and Mosega, and the commando under Potgieter and Maritz was able to surprise the southernmost military kraal of the Matabele one morning at break of day. Moselekatse himself was not there at the time, and the induna in command of the soldiers happened also to be absent. This was a fortunate circumstance for the farmers. The soldiers grasped their spears and shields, and rushed forward; but volleys of slugs drove them back in confusion, and there was no one of sufficient authority to restore order. They took to flight, and were hunted by the farmers until the sun was high overhead, when it was computed that at least four hundred must have been slain. The commando then set fire to the kraal, and with nearly seven thousand head of cattle returned to Thaba Ntshu.

After this Potgieter's party formed a camp on the Vet river, at a place to which the name Winburg was given in memory of the recent victory. There it was strengthened by the arrival of numerous families from the colony.

At this time also a band reached Thaba Ntshu from the Winterberg with a very able man, named Pieter Retief, as its head.

On the 6th of June 1837 a general assembly of the emigrants was held at Winburg, when a provisional constitution, consisting of nine articles, was adopted. The supreme legislative power was entrusted to a single elective chamber termed the volksraad, the fundamental law was declared to be the Dutch, a court of landdrost and heemraden was created, and the chief executive authority was confided to Mr. Retief with the title of commandant-general. The strong feeling of antagonism that Dr. Philip had roused is shown in one of the articles of the constitution, which provided that every member of the community and all who should thereafter join them must take an oath to have no connection with the London missionary society. That body was regarded by them as purely a political institution, advocating and spreading principles of anarchy; and they regarded it as something like blasphemy to speak of its superintendent in Capetown as a minister of the gospel.

Fresh bands of emigrants were frequently arriving, and some of them thought it would be better to go down into Natal than to remain on the highlands of the interior. Pieter Uys, the leader of one of these bands, had visited Natal a couple of years before, and waxed eloquent when describing its beauty and fertility. Retief himself was inclined to favour a settlement near the sea, but before making up his mind finally, he and some others proceeded to inspect the country below the mountains and ascertain if Dingan would dispose of it.

While they were away the second expedition against the Matabele set out. It consisted of one hundred and thirty-five farmers in two divisions, under Hendrik Potgieter and Pieter Uys. Moselekatse was found on the Marikwa, about fifty miles north of Mosega, and he had with him at least twelve thousand warriors, all splendidly trained and as brave as any troops that ever lived. But the advantage of the farmers in their guns and horses was so great that the hundred and thirty-five did not hesitate to attack a force which was to theirs as ninety to one.

For nine days the Matabele tried to reach their opponents, but all their efforts were in vain. The farmers were more than once nearly surrounded, still their plans were so perfect that they were never quite entrapped. They had little else than dried meat to live upon, and they had no resting-place but the bare ground with a saddle for a pillow. Only the hardiest of men and horses could have carried on aggressive operations so long.

The loss of the Matabele was great, so great that at the end of the nine days Moselekatse gave up the contest and sought only to escape. With his people and his cattle he fled to the north, and in the country beyond the Limpopo commenced to destroy the

Mashona tribes as he had destroyed the southern Betshuana. The farmers were too wearied to follow him, and indeed they could not have continued in the field much longer under any circumstances, so they contented themselves by seizing six or seven thousand head of cattle, with which they returned to Winburg.

After the flight of Moselekatse, Commandant Potgieter issued a proclamation, in which he declared that the whole of the territory which that chief had overrun and now abandoned was forfeited to the emigrants. It included the greater part of the present South African Republic, fully half of the present Orange Free State, and the whole of Southern Betshuanaland to the Kalahari desert, except the district occupied by the Batlapin. This immense tract of country was then almost uninhabited, and must have remained so if the Matabele had not been driven out.

XVII.

DESTRUCTION OF THE ZULU POWER AND FOUNDATION OF THE REPUBLIC OF NATAL.

In all the world there is not a fairer country than the pleasant land of Natal, stretching in steps from the Drakensberg, which bounds it like a mighty wall, downward to the shore of the Indian sea. The coast belt is covered with sub-tropical vegetation, for it is heated by the warm Mozambique current, which runs southward along it, and gives it a higher temperature than is due to its distance from the equator. Each terrace, as the traveller ascends, is cooler than the one below, though it is nowhere cold. It is a well-watered land. Numerous streams, issuing from the Drakensberg and the fronts of the lower terraces, rush along in deep gorges to the sea, and carry off the superabundant moisture, so that it is also well drained. Its soil is rich, its forests yield excellent timber, and the grass in its valleys resembles a meadow. Its climate everywhere is healthy for Europeans.

When Pieter Retief and his companions went down into it by a pass they had discovered, there were between the Tugela and Umzimvubu rivers only from five to ten thousand inhabitants. These acknowledged as their chiefs a few Englishmen whom Tshaka and Dingan permitted to reside at the port, and who carried on trade with the Zulu despot. The present colony of Natal is far short of the Umzimvubu on the south, but it contains in the north the tract of land between the Tugela and Buffalo rivers, which was then partly occupied by Zulu subjects, of whose number it is impossible to give an estimate.

Retief liked the appearance of the country, and the accounts which he received from the Englishmen at the port confirmed his impression. These Englishmen had in vain petitioned the imperial government to declare it a British possession, so now they were only too glad to welcome the emigrant farmers. Two of them, who had been in the country thirteen years and who spoke Zulu as well as English, accompanied Retief to Dingan's residence in the capacity of guides and interpreters.

The Zulu capital was called Umkungunhlovu. It was in the shape of an enormous hollow circle formed by concentric rows of huts that served as barracks for the soldiers. The interior space was the drill ground. An English missionary clergyman, named Owen, was living there at the time, but he had not been able to get any one to listen to his teaching. There was also an English lad named William Wood—son of one of the residents at Port Natal—who was a favourite of Dingan and his confidential interpreter.

The despot received Retief with every show of friendship. There was a grand parade, apparently to please him, and a big dance in which highly trained

UMKUNGUNHLOVU.
(From a Sketch by Captain Gardiner.)

oxen took part with soldiers. Beef in huge pieces was sent to the visitors from the chief's own eating mat, which served as a dish does on a European table, and the best millet beer, such as Dingan himself was used to drink huge draughts of, was supplied in calabashes of the largest size.

When Retief spoke about Natal, the chief said he might have it for his countrymen to live in, but first he must prove his friendship by recovering a herd of about seven hundred cattle that Sikonyela, son of Ma Ntatisi, had recently stolen from a Zulu outpost. Retief accepted the condition, and upon his return to Winburg sent for Sikonyela, whose residence was at Imparani, north of the Caledon, and required him to surrender Dingan's oxen and some horses he had stolen from the emigrants. They were given up without bloodshed, and then nearly a thousand white-tilted waggons in a long line went down the steep pass of the Drakensberg and halted on the banks of the Bluekrans and Bushman's rivers in the uplands of Natal.

Retief now prepared to proceed to Umkungunhlovu with the cattle. There were among the emigrants men who were suspicious of Dingan's good faith, and who thought their leader should not risk a life of such value to the community by going again himself, but he was so confident in the chief's friendly disposition that he would not listen to them. Sixty-five Europeans and about thirty Hottentot servants accompanied him.

They were received, as before, with every outward show of respect and hospitality, and Dingan expressed himself well pleased with the restoration of his cattle. He requested the reverend Mr. Owen to draw up a paper to show that he had given Natal to Retief, and when this was done in the English language and translated to him, he said it was correct and handed it to the emigrant leader. The farmers were so entirely thrown off their guard that when they were ready to leave and were invited to go into the centre of the kraal to partake of some beer and bid adieu to the chief, they left their guns outside. They were seated on the ground without a thought of danger, when Dingan suddenly exclaimed "Seize them!" and immediately a regiment of soldiers rushed upon them, drew them to the place of execution, and broke their skulls with clubs. Not a single emigrant or a Hottentot, not even their English interpreter from Port Natal, was suffered to escape.

A few hours later some ten thousand soldiers left Umkungunhlovu, and, after eleven days' march, at early dawn one morning fell upon the most advanced emigrant encampment, which was near the present village of Weenen. Who can describe in adequate language the horrors that followed? Babes with their brains dashed out against waggon wheels, women ripped up with Zulu spears, girls and boys with their necks twisted, were lying thick on the ground when the sun rose that morning. Forty-one white men, fifty-six white women, one hundred and eighty-five white children, and about two hundred and fifty coloured servants perished in the dreadful massacre. Needless to say, the waggons and their contents were utterly destroyed.

Every emigrant in Natal must have met a similar fate had not, providentially, a young man been awake and close to a cattle kraal when the assault was made. He managed to spring on an unsaddled horse, and rode with all speed to give warning to the parties farther on. These had barely time to draw their waggons around them when the Zulus appeared, but though the most desperate efforts were made by the savage warriors, the simple lagers proved effective, for not one of them was taken. The courage, and skill, and coolness in danger displayed that day by the emigrants, men and women alike, have never been excelled in the world's history. The Zulus, too, were brave, and literally heaps of their dead lay around the lagers before they turned to retreat. At dusk they set out for Umkungunhlovu with as many cattle as they could collect.

The night was spent by the emigrants in watchfulness and prayer, each little party hardly daring to hope that any other had escaped. Next morning communication between the lagers was opened, and the full extent of their loss became known. Their first care now was to concentrate and strengthen an encampment, in case the Zulus should renew the attack, and then a general assembly was held to decide what was to be done. One or two men proposed that they should leave Natal, but they were put to shame by the women, who declared they would never abandon the country till the Zulus were punished for shedding so much innocent blood. This feeling was general, for it was regarded as a duty to bring the murderers to account. Then they put up an earnest prayer to the God of heaven that He would not forsake His people, nor allow the heathen to triumph over them. From the bible—the only book with which they were thoroughly conversant—they drew consolation and hope, which enabled them to bear up against their trouble, and to take courage for the prosecution of the task before them.

When these events took place, Pieter Uys was at the top of the Drakensberg in readiness to go down, and Hendrik Potgieter was at Winburg, as his party preferred to remain on the interior highland. Both of them now collected as many fighting men as possible, and hastened to the assistance of the distressed people in Natal. The Englishmen at the port also, having lost two of their companions in the massacres, offered to help with all their followers, many of whom were trained soldiers who had deserted from the Zulu army.

When it came to a question of who was to be the leader, however, jealousy of each other—the bane of the emigrants—showed itself at once. Even Pieter Retief could not preserve perfect concord among the various heads of parties, and after his death there was no one whom all the others would admit as a superior. At length it was arranged that the English chiefs with their people should attack Dingan on one side while Potgieter and Uys attacked him on another, and Maritz should remain at the camp to protect it.

The two commandants, with three hundred and forty-seven men, rode directly towards the Zulu capital. After five days' march through an uninhabited country, they came in sight of a division of the Zulu army, which they attacked impetuously, and were drawn into a skilfully planned ambuscade. Before them were two parallel ranges of hills, with a long defile between them, and into this the farmers were led by the Zulus apparently retreating before them. Uys's division was in advance. When in the narrowest part of the gorge they found themselves surrounded by an immense force which had been lying in ambush, and by which they were so hemmed in that they could not fall back rapidly after firing and again load and charge, as was their mode of fighting with Moselekatse. They therefore directed all their fire upon the mass of the enemy behind them, when, having cleared a path by shooting down hundreds, they rushed through and escaped. Ten of them were killed, and they were obliged to leave their led horses, baggage, and spare ammunition behind. Among the slain was Commandant Uys, who was assisting a wounded comrade when he received a stab from an assagai. His son, Dirk Cornelis Uys, a boy of fifteen years of age, was some distance off, but, looking about, he saw his father on the ground, and a Zulu in the act of stabbing him. The gallant youth turned his horse and rode to help his parent, but could only die at his side.

A few days later seventeen Englishmen left Port Natal with about fifteen hundred blacks, of whom between three and four hundred were armed with muskets. A few miles south of the Tugela they came upon a Zulu regiment, which pretended to take to flight, left food cooking on fires, and even threw away a number of shields and assagais. The

Natal army pursued with all haste, crossed the Tugela, took possession of a kraal on the northern bank, and then found it had been drawn between the horns of a Zulu army fully seven thousand strong.

The battle that was fought, on the 17th of April 1838, was one of the most desperate contests that ever took place on that bloodstained soil. Three times in succession the Natal army beat back the regiments that charged furiously upon it. Then a strong Zulu reinforcement came in sight, and renewed the enemy's courage. Another rush was made, which cut the Natal army in two, and all hope of successful resistance was over. One of the divisions tried to escape by the only open path, which was down a steep bank of the Tugela and across that river. A Zulu regiment hastened to cut off the retreat of the fugitives, and many were killed in the water; but four Englishmen and about five hundred blacks managed to get through. The other division was entirely surrounded. But no lion at bay ever created such havoc among hounds that worried him as this little band caused among the warriors of Dingan before it perished. The young regiments were selected to charge upon it, while the veterans watched their prowess from a neighbouring hill. Whole masses went down before the withering fire, the survivors recoiled, but again they were directed to charge. At last a rush of a regiment, with another in reserve close behind, carried everything before it, and the stubborn fight was over. Thirteen Englishmen lay dead on the field of battle, with a thousand Natal blacks and probably three times that number of Zulus.

After these disasters the emigrants were unable to take the offensive again for some time. Owing to the excessive jealousy between the leaders, Potgieter and his adherents left Natal and went to reside along the Mooi river, where they founded the village of Potchefstroom. Those who remained behind did not venture far from their fortified camp, and suffered much from sickness and insufficiency of food. While in this distress, however, they were strengthened by the arrival of many of their friends from the colony, and they never once gave up hope of ultimate success. During the winter Dingan sent an army to attack them, but they were careful not to be drawn out of the lager by stratagem, and all attempts to reach them behind their defences failed.

In November a man of great natural ability, named Andries Pretorius, arrived in Natal, and was elected commandant-general. He at once assembled a force of four hundred and sixty-four men, all that could be spared from guarding the camp, and marched towards Umkungunhlovu. He took with him a sufficient number of waggons to form a lager, and at every halting-place these were drawn up in a circle and lashed together. While on the march scouts were patrolling in all directions to guard against surprise.

The commando resembled an itinerant prayer meeting rather than a modern army, for the men were imbued with the same spirit as the Ironsides of Cromwell, and spoke and acted in pretty much the same manner. There was no song, no jest heard in that camp, but prayers were poured forth and psalms were sung at every halting-place. The army made a vow that if God would give them victory over the cruel heathen, they would build a church and set apart a thanksgiving day in every year to commemorate it. The church in Pietermaritzburg and the annual celebration of Dingan's day bear witness that they kept their pledge. They did not wish to fight merely for the sake of revenge. On three occasions the scouts brought in some captured Zulus, and Mr. Pretorius immediately sent these to Dingan to inform him that if he would restore the property taken from the emigrants they were prepared to enter into negotiations for peace.

Dingan's reply came in the form of an army ten or twelve thousand strong, which attacked the camp at early dawn on Sunday the 16th of December 1838. For two full hours the soldiers persevered in the attempt to force a way in, notwithstanding the terrible havoc created among them by the fire from the farmers' guns and several small pieces of artillery. When at length they broke and fled, over three thousand corpses were lying on the ground, and a stream that flowed past the field of carnage was discoloured with gore. It has ever since been called the Blood river.

Pretorius marched to Umkungunhlovu as rapidly as possible, but before he could reach the Zulu capital Dingan set it on fire, and fled. He was pursued, but escaped to a part of the country where cavalry could not act, so the commando returned to Natal with four or five thousand cattle, all that were seen. In the campaign six white men were killed and three were wounded.

Since the commencement of hostilities Dingan had lost about ten thousand warriors, but his army was still so large that he was by no means humbled. When the farmers retired he rebuilt his capital, and though he pretended to fall in with overtures which were made for peace, it soon became evident that he was only watching for an opportunity to destroy the emigrants. It was therefore not considered advisable to scatter upon farms, so a town, named Pietermaritzburg, was laid out in such a manner that each family could have a large garden, and the cattle could be kept under constant protection.

In September 1839 a very important event took place in the Zulu country. Panda, a half-brother of Dingan, conspired to seize the chieftainship. A great number of the incorporated Zulus — the remnants of tribes that had come under Tshaka as the only means of saving themselves — were ready to rally round any leader who could give them reasonable hope of deliverance from incessant bloodshed, and when the induna Nongalaza, who was in command of the district along the northern bank of the Tugela, declared for Panda, they joined him. The rebel chief with a large following then crossed the Tugela, and sent to ask assistance from the Europeans.

The emigrants at first regarded him with suspicion, as it was by no means certain that his flight was not merely a pretence to draw them to destruction. But he soon convinced them of his sincerity, and an arrangement was then entered into by which he became a vassal of the emigrants in consideration of receiving their support. He remained in Natal under their protection until January 1840, when a burgher force of four hundred men under Commandant-General Pretorius marched with him against Dingan. His own army was about five or six thousand strong, and was commanded by Nongalaza. It marched in a parallel line, but at a distance of twelve or fifteen miles from the burgher commando.

Dingan now realised the danger of his position, and attempted to come to terms with the emigrants. There were two officers immediately under him, whose advice he frequently sought, and through whom he carried on his government. Their names were Tambusa and Umthlela. The first named he sent to the European camp to negotiate for peace.

Upon Tambusa's arrival, he and his servant Kombazana were made prisoners, and contrary to all law and justice were brought to trial before a court-martial for having taken part in the massacre at Umkungunhlovu, were sentenced to death, and were executed.

A few hours after this great crime was committed a messenger from Nongalaza brought word to the burgher column that on the preceding day, 30th of January 1840, he had fought a great battle with Dingan's army led by Umthlela, and had won a complete victory.

This battle proved a decisive one. At its commencement Dingan's army was superior in number, but during the action a body of his troops went over to Panda's side, and turned the scale. Those who were faithful stood their ground, and fell as became Zulu warriors. The slaughter on each side was enormous. The two best regiments of Dingan perished, for the veterans who had won their plumes under Tshaka preferred to die rather than show their backs to the traitors who had deserted their cause. Umthlela placed himself at the head of the reserve, and went into the hottest part of the field, where he was pierced through the heart with an assagai. Still the issue of the day was doubtful, when the cry echoed along Nongalaza's ranks: "The farmers are coming!" It was not so, but the belief that it was answered Nongalaza's purpose. The remnant of Dingan's army, the men who could not flee from a foe armed with spear and shield, gave way in their fear of those dreaded horsemen who had power to deal out death without meeting it themselves. A bushy country spread out before them, and favoured their escape. The battle was over, and the terror which the Zulu name had inspired was a thing of the past.

Dingan fled northward to the border of the Swazi country, where he was soon afterwards assassinated by a man who stole upon him unawares. Those who had adhered to him in his misfortunes then tendered their submission to Panda, by whom they were received with every mark of favour.

After the decisive engagement an enormous booty

in cattle fell into the hands of the conquerors. About forty thousand head were delivered to Mr. Pretorius, and were subsequently distributed among the emigrants in proportion to their losses.

Mr. Pretorius then formally installed Panda as chief of the Zulus, but in vassalage to the volksraad, to which he promised fidelity. The republic of Natal was declared to extend from the Umzimvubu to the Tugela, and the land between the Tugela and Black Umvolosi was proclaimed an appanage of that republic, set apart for the use of the Zulu people.

XVIII.

SEIZURE OF NATAL BY BRITISH FORCES. CREATION OF TREATY STATES ALONG THE FRONTIER OF THE CAPE COLONY.

THE emigrant farmers had now freed South Africa of the destructive Zulu power, and had driven the ferocious Matabele into regions unknown to Europeans. Seldom have such great events been accomplished by means apparently so feeble. Yet they took no credit to themselves for what they had done, because in their view it was God who had wrought the great deliverance, and they were merely humble instruments in His hands. No Israelite of old ever held a belief of this kind more firmly than did these wanderers who had suffered so much and acted so bravely.

It was, however, soon evident that they were less qualified for self-rule than for war, as the government which they established was the weakest and most imprudent that ever existed. It could not be carried on efficiently without a suitable revenue, and they refused to pay any but the most trifling taxes. Every measure of importance after adoption by the volksraad had to be referred to the burghers in primary assembly, and nothing but confusion was the result. The public offices from the highest to the lowest—with a solitary exception—were held by uneducated men, who could barely write an ordinary letter, and who were of course ignorant of routine duties. Above all, the utmost prudence was needed to avoid irritating the British government, and they acted as if they could afford to be indifferent to English opinion.

The elevation of the coloured races was then a leading—and surely a praiseworthy—idea in England, but, unfortunately, the great philanthropic and missionary societies had made up their minds as to the precise manner in which this should be effected, and condemned as unchristian all views that differed from their own. Applying their principles to South Africa, the formation of large Bantu states under missionary guidance and British protection was what they desired, and the reverend Dr. Philip, the exponent of their views, was urging this scheme upon the Cape government. Time has shown how faulty it was, but no one even in this country could foresee the full extent of the harm it would cause to the black people as well as to the white. The devastations which the Zulus and Matabele had wrought were unknown in Europe, and therefore when intelligence reached England that many thousands of the men of those tribes had fallen before the farmers' guns, public opinion was shocked. No one suspected that the destruction of those fierce warriors meant life to all other black people in the country. The great societies brought their influence to bear upon the government, in order—as they believed—to stop further bloodshed by compelling the emigrants to return to the Cape Colony. Hardly any one considered it advisable that the British dominions in South Africa should be enlarged by the annexation of the territory which they occupied.

While this was the feeling in England, the republican government resolved not to allow Bantu from beyond the borders to settle in Natal, and to confine those who were already there to certain locations. A commando was also sent against a marauding chief who lived between Natal and the Cape Colony, and he was severely dealt with. If the emigrants had sought to provoke the British government, they could hardly have devised a surer plan. As soon as the intelligence reached Sir George Napier, who was then governor of the Cape Colony, a body of troops was sent to protect the Bantu, and a military camp was formed within a short distance of the southern boundary of the republic.

For some time after the arrival of the emigrants in Natal, every possible effort had been made by the authorities in Capetown to cut off their supply of ammunition, but all attempts to do so had failed. They had now a port of their own, and foreign vessels were beginning to find their way to it. This naturally caused English merchants engaged in the South African trade to feel irritated, for it was supposed that the harbour of Natal might become the principal gateway to the interior.

A resolution of the volksraad to compel some recent Bantu immigrants to retire to a location on the southern side of the republic brought matters to a crisis. The troops on the border were reinforced, and were ordered by Sir George Napier to move on and take possession of Port Natal.

Accordingly two hundred and sixty-three soldiers of all ranks and of different arms, under Captain Thomas Smith, marched forward, meeting with no molestation on the way, and formed a camp at Durban. The volksraad sent a protest, but no notice was taken of it. Commandant-General Pretorius then assembled a number of farmers, and formed a camp at the head of the inlet, from which he sent a demand that the English troops should leave without delay. He claimed for the emigrant farmers perfect independence, but Captain Smith maintained the English view, that they had not ceased to be British subjects and could not by any act of their own throw off their allegiance to the crown of England.

A contest was now inevitable. Captain Smith, who altogether underrated the vigilance and courage of his opponent, thought to crush out opposition by a single blow, and left his camp one evening at the head of a hundred and thirty-seven soldiers with the intention of falling by surprise upon Pretorius, who had then with him two hundred and sixty-four men. No military operation could have been worse planned. It was clear moonlight, yet it was thought that the troops would not be noticed. The distance was a march of three miles, and the road was along the shore of the inlet, which was bordered at one place by dense scrub.

The troops were marching fully exposed past the thicket, with two field-pieces drawn by bullocks, when a sharp fire was opened upon them. They returned the volley, but without doing the slightest damage to the farmers, who were well protected and thoroughly concealed. Another discharge from the thicket wounded some of the oxen, which broke loose from the yokes and rushed furiously about, adding to the confusion. There was no remedy but retreat. Sixteen killed and thirty-one wounded were found by the farmers next day, and three others were drowned. The two guns, the oxen, and indeed everything that could be left behind, fell into the hands of the farmers.

Mr. Pretorius now again demanded that the troops should leave Natal, and to gain time to strengthen his camp, Captain Smith agreed to a truce of a few days, under pretence of considering the matter. A messenger, provided with two good horses, was directed to ride with all speed through Kaffirland to Grahamstown with a request for help, and he managed to get safely away.

When the truce expired the English camp was invested, and fire was opened upon it from the farmers' batteries, on which three small cannons were mounted. Captain Smith caused deep trenches to be dug, in which the soldiers could remain in security, and he increased his stock of provisions by slaughtering his horses and drying their flesh. The men were put upon short allowance, which, as the siege advanced, became less and less, until they had nothing more than a few ounces of biscuit dust and dried horseflesh daily. Fortunately for them there was no want of water, which was obtained from wells sunk within the camp.

The force under Pretorius increased by fresh arrivals until it amounted to six hundred men. They fortified the entrance to the inner harbour, and pressed the siege with vigour. Their cannon balls having become exhausted, they manufactured others by casting leaden ones over links cut from a chain cable. But so well were the soldiers protected that the fire against them was almost harmless, only eight men being killed and eight wounded on the British side during the twenty-six days that the siege lasted, though six hundred and fifty-one cannon shot were fired at the camp. On the other side four men were killed, and eight or ten—the exact number cannot be given—were wounded.

The messenger sent by Captain Smith overland, who was familiar with the language and customs of the Bantu tribes on his way, reached Grahamstown in safety, and informed the military authorities of what had happened. A hundred soldiers were thereupon embarked in a schooner at Algoa Bay, and sailed for Port Natal. A wing of a regiment was also taken on board a frigate at Simon's Bay, and proceeded to the same destination.

On Sunday, the 25th of June 1842, the schooner sailed into the inner harbour with a fair wind, having as many soldiers on board as could find room, and towing a number of boats containing others. The frigate at the same time opened fire with her heavy guns upon the high land commanding the entrance.

Three men were killed and five were wounded when passing under the farmers' batteries, but no further resistance was offered, for as soon as the fresh troops landed and Captain Smith was relieved, the burgher force under Pretorius dispersed.

Natal thus became a British possession. Some of the farmers remained in it, but most of them packed their effects in their waggons, and moved over the Drakensberg into the interior. More than three years elapsed, however, before a government under English officials was established, and during that time great numbers of Bantu—chiefly refugees from Zululand—moved into the nearly vacant territory. An arrangement was made with Panda, by which he ceded to the British government the ground between the Buffalo and the upper Tugela river, so that the boundary was extended on the north beyond the passes through the mountain range. Thereafter the Zulu chief was treated as an independent sovereign, and immediately the process commenced of building up again that great military power which cost so much English blood in later years to overthrow. On the south all the land beyond the Umzimkulu river was given to the Pondo chief Faku, and thus Natal was much reduced in size in that direction.

The farmers who went back over the Drakensberg settled in the territory between the Magalisberg and the Vaal river, that had previously been occupied by Commandant Potgieter's adherents. These now moved away to the north-east, in hope of being able to open communication with the outer world through Delagoa Bay, which, as it belonged to the Portuguese,

SCENE IN PONDOLAND.
(*Sketch by Captain Gardiner.*)

they thought would be safe against attack by Great Britain. They halted on the head waters of some streams flowing into that bay, and built a village which they named Ohrigstad. There, however, they suffered very severely from fever, so that they were obliged to move again. They then divided into two parties, one of which founded the village of Lydenburg, and the other, under Potgieter himself, went away north to the Zoutpansberg and settled there.

In England the conduct of the emigrants in thus persistently retiring from British authority was regarded as very objectionable. The opinion was general that something should be done not only to compel the wanderers in the interior of the continent to return to their old homes, but to prevent others from abandoning the colony and joining them. The project of forming a barrier along the colonial border, by means of the creation of a chain of large native states, had for some time been advocated by the great societies, and was now determined upon by the government. Such a barrier, it was imagined, would cut off commercial communication with the emigrants, and leave them no alternative but to retrace their steps.

In carrying this scheme into execution, Sir George Napier followed the method suggested by the reverend Dr. Philip, who made the preliminary arrangements. His plan was to select in a given area the most competent chief, that is the one supposed to be most amenable to missionary guidance, to enter into treaty with him as a sovereign, and to support him with all the influence of the British government.

At Thaba Bosigo one such chief was found in the person of the wise and able Moshesh, the friend and patron of missionaries. He had already built up a considerable power, which it was the great object of his life to increase and solidify. Nothing, therefore, could have been more in accordance with his desires than the scheme which was proposed: alliance with the British government, a subsidy in money, a vast extension of territory, and supremacy over all other chiefs within the area assigned to him. In 1843 a treaty was concluded, in which he was acknowledged to be the sovereign of a large vacant tract of land north of the Orange river, of the basin of the lower Caledon, where European farmers were settled, of the territory along the western bank of the Caledon higher up, which was occupied by various clans brought there by Wesleyan missionaries, and of all the land on which his own people lived. He was to have a subsidy of £75 a year, payable either in money or in arms and ammunition, as he might choose. It will be seen in future chapters that no other document ever signed in South Africa cost so much blood and treasure as this, or was so productive of evil in various ways.

West of the territory assigned to Moshesh there were no Bantu, but at and around a mission station of the London society, named Philippolis, there were some fifteen hundred or two thousand Griquas, under a captain named Adam Kok. These people were of mixed European, Hottentot, and negro blood, and most of them had recently migrated from the Cape Colony. They were supposed to be under missionary guidance and to be partly civilised, but the men lived chiefly by hunting, and their character was far from stable. It was not then known that they were a perishing race. For one or two generations the hybrid offspring of Europeans and coloured people

GRIQUA MAN AND WOMEN.
(*From a Sketch by Mr. Thos. Baines.*)

possess a fair amount of fertility, but they must then intermix with one of the pure original stocks, or die out. Within fifty years the Griquas, by attempting to live as a separate people, have decreased to little more than one-fourth of their original number.

There were more white people than Griquas living in the territory between the Modder river and the Orange, but at the same time that the treaty was made with Moshesh a similar one was made with Adam Kok, and thereafter this petty captain was officially regarded by the British government as the sovereign of all the land from the new Basuto boundary to the territory claimed by Andries Waterboer under the treaty of 1834. He was to receive a subsidy of £100 a year in money and the use of a hundred stand of arms with a reasonable quantity of ammunition. The London society was to receive £50 a year for the maintenance of a mission school.

Thus, as far as paper treaties could make states, there was now a barrier along the whole northern border of the Cape Colony from the Kalahari desert upward. A little later, by another treaty, the Pondo chief Faku became the nominal ruler of all the territory between the Umtata and Umzimkulu rivers, the Drakensberg and the sea, and thus the girdle was made complete.

But it was soon found that for the purpose intended the treaty states were useless. The emigrant farmers ridiculed the idea either of their removal or of their subjection to the puppet sovereigns thus set up, and matters went on pretty much as before, so far as they were concerned. In the territory assigned to Moshesh trouble of an unexpected kind immediately arose. The chiefs of the clans along the Caledon indignantly refused to acknowledge him as a superior, and the Wesleyan missionaries took part with them in doing so. The French missionaries, on the other hand, did their utmost to support and build up the Basuto power. Thus jealousies and quarrels were fomented, and the clans were kept in perpetual disturbance.

In the territory assigned to Adam Kok many of the white people had come to fear that such anarchy as had prevailed in Natal was inseparable from a republican form of government, and they were not only willing but anxious to see the country annexed to the British dominions. There were circumstances in their condition and in the manner of their removal from the colony that made them the least disaffected of all the Dutch-speaking people of South Africa. But they, too, repudiated the sovereignty of Adam Kok, and refused to acknowledge him as anything but a Griqua captain. Besides these people there were two large parties of emigrants in the country bitterly hostile to England, and they at once declared that if Kok attempted to interfere with them in any way whatever they would resist with arms.

The treaty states were thus no barrier to commercial intercourse with the emigrants in the interior, they did not prevent further emigration, nor did they cause a single individual to retrace his steps. They provoked disputes and quarrels among people who were before friendly, and they enabled Moshesh to build up a power antagonistic to the interests and welfare of South Africa.

XIX.

EVENTS TO THE CLOSE OF THE SEVENTH KAFFIR WAR.

SIR PEREGRINE MAITLAND, who succeeded Sir George Napier as governor of the Cape Colony, determined to support Adam Kok with a military force if he should be attacked, and a promise to that effect was made to him. Thereupon he assumed a very haughty tone towards the white people, and shortly afterwards sent a band of his followers to arrest a farmer who ignored his government. The farmer was not at home when the Griquas arrived at his house, so they poured a storm of abuse upon his wife, and took possession of his guns and ammunition.

Upon this the burghers formed a lager about thirty miles from Philippolis, and having placed their families in safety within it, they left a guard for its defence and took the field. There was at the time a body of British troops stationed at Colesberg, on the colonial side of the Orange river, two hundred of whom now marched to Philippolis to aid the Griquas. Adam Kok was also supplied with muskets and ammunition from the military stores. He was thus able to defend himself until a regiment of dragoons, with some artillery and a company of light cavalry, could march to his support from Grahamstown. As soon as the force reached Philippolis, Colonel Richardson, who was in command, issued a proclamation calling upon the farmers to surrender unconditionally; but they took no notice of it. He then marched towards their lager, and by a stratagem drew two hundred and fifty men out of it, who were nearly surrounded before they were aware that British troops were acting against them. Taken by surprise, they did not attempt to make a stand, but in their efforts to escape three were killed. A little later in the same day possession was taken of the lager without resistance, when all the arms found there were confiscated.

Colonel Richardson next called upon the emigrants to take an oath of allegiance to the queen, when all those—three hundred and sixteen in number—who have been mentioned as not ill-affected towards the British government did so. The others were not arrested, as there were no means of supporting them in detention, so they moved away to Winburg, beyond the territory claimed by Adam Kok.

By this time Sir Peregrine Maitland had become convinced that the Griqua treaty state, as originally planned, could not be maintained without the constant presence of a considerable military force, and in that case to regard Kok as a sovereign would be an absurdity. But he did not know what change to make, and so he visited the country in order to learn its condition by personal intercourse with the different people there, and to devise some plan of action. At Touwfontein, where the emigrant lager had been, he met a great number of farmers, all the chiefs between the Orange and Vaal rivers, and most of the missionaries. During several days matters were discussed, and the views of the different parties were laid before the governor.

Adam Kok contended that he was a sovereign in alliance with Great Britain, that every one within his dominions who did not implicitly obey his orders was a rebel, and he requested that all the white people should be removed.

The farmers contended that as there was no one living in the territory claimed by Kok whose parents had been born there, all being recent immigrants, their right was equal to that of the Griquas. Much of the land they occupied was vacant when they took possession of it, and the remainder had been purchased or leased from individual Griquas who by an earlier selection had prior claims. They could not return to the colony, where they had no ground, nor could they submit to such a government as that of Adam Kok and his missionary.

Moshesh contended that as he was acknowledged to be the sovereign of the territory assigned to him by treaty, no one within it should be communicated with except through him.

The chiefs along the Caledon contended that their independence of Moshesh ought to be recognised, and declared that they would rather die with arms in their hands than submit to him.

Each of the missionaries supported the claims of the particular chief with whom he was living, so that their opinions differed greatly.

Out of this confusion Sir Peregrine Maitland saw but one way of establishing order. He gave up all idea of the return of the emigrants to the Cape Colony, and endeavoured to arrange for the proper government of those who were living in the treaty states. He proposed to Adam Kok that the land between the Modder and Riet rivers should be allotted to Europeans, and that between the Riet and Orange rivers to Griquas. The Europeans were to be governed by an English officer whom he would nominate, and to whom Kok was to give a commission. Quitrent was to be levied on their farms, one half of which was to be devoted to the payment of the English officer and his assistants, and the other half was to be handed over to Kok, whose sovereignty over the whole territory was in this manner still to be recognised. The Griqua captain at once closed with the offer, for it relieved him of a great difficulty and gave him an addition to his income. The Europeans also accepted the proposal, though some of them grumbled at having to pay tribute to a man whose right to the ground was no better than their own.

Major Warden was selected by the governor to rule the European community between the Riet and the Modder, and fixed his residence at a place named Bloemfontein. A few soldiers of the Hottentot regiment were stationed there to support his authority, and he received all his instructions from Capetown, so that practically the territory was a British dependency, though writs and other public documents ran in the name of Adam Kok. This arrangement worked fairly well, and a short period of peace and prosperity followed in that part of South Africa.

A similar proposal was made by Sir Peregrine Maitland to Moshesh, but that chief was in a very different position from the Griqua captain, and was loth to exchange power for money. He wanted to keep on good terms with the governor, however, and so he made an appearance of consenting to the plan while really thwarting it. He offered for the use of Europeans a tract of land in the angle of the Orange and Caledon rivers, so far away from the possessions of his own people that there was no likelihood of its ever being of value to him, and so small that no revenue derived from it could cover the salary of a British official. This offer he could not be induced to enlarge, and though negotiations were carried on with him after Sir Peregrine Maitland's return to Capetown, nothing came of them. Thus within the Basuto treaty state matters remained in a most unsatisfactory condition.

At this time the eastern frontier of the Cape Colony was exposed to depredations as it had never—even in the worst times—been exposed before. Earl Glenelg, through his agent Lieutenant-Governor Stockenstrom, had given up to the Kosas the whole country east of the Kat and Fish rivers, and had entered into treaties with the chiefs as sovereign rulers. This action they considered a proof of weakness, and in consequence they laid aside all respect for the British authorities. Within the next ten years over a hundred murders were committed by their people on colonial ground, and the country as far west as the Sunday river was harried and wasted almost as in a time of war. The unfortunate British settlers of 1820 were the principal sufferers, but their prayers for relief were altogether disregarded in England. Modifications of the treaties were made by Sir George Napier and Sir Peregrine Maitland, but the position was not improved, for it was the system itself that was the cause of the evil.

In other respects this period was marked by many beneficial changes. The cost of government was greatly reduced, so that every year a surplus could be applied to the reduction of the public debt. By the sale of the old drostdies, the conversion of a number of quitrent farms into freehold, and licenses for the removal of a quantity of guano from some small islands off the western coast, by 1847 the debt was entirely paid off. Magistrates were increased, and churches of various denominations were multiplied throughout the colony. Municipal government of the towns and villages was introduced. An excellent system of schools was brought into operation. Good waggon roads were made—principally by convict labour—through many mountain passes, where previously produce could only be transported with the greatest difficulty. The value of the exports was rapidly rising by increase in the production of wool.

More than all, four or five thousand English, Scotch, and Irish agriculturists and mechanics were brought into the colony by a system of aided immigration, and partly filled the places of those who had moved into the interior. No people in any country

SCENE IN MONTAGU PASS.

have thriven better than these. About seven hundred destitute children sent out from London by a benevolent society were apprenticed to carefully selected persons, and though a few turned out badly, most of them became useful and prosperous members of the community. Unfortunately, however, these were not the only immigrants. The Cape was made the station where all slave ships captured by British cruisers south of the equator were brought, and the negroes were apprenticed here for short periods, after which they became merged in the general coloured population. The farmers and townspeople, who were without a sufficient supply of labour, were very glad to get them, and the missionary societies welcomed them as material to work with; but they were not a class to add permanently to the prosperity of the country.

After the frontier colonists had been exposed for ten years to the depredations of the Kosas, an event took place which brought on open war. A Kosa, who was detected in an act of theft at Fort Beaufort, was arrested, and was being conveyed to the nearest magistrate's office for trial, when a party of his clansmen crossed the border, and after overpowering the constables and murdering a Hottentot, released their friend. Sandile, the legal heir of Gaika, was then the principal chief of Western Kaffirland. The governor applied to him to surrender the raiders for trial, as their crime had been committed on colonial ground, and he had bound himself by treaty to give up offenders of this kind. But he made light of the matter, and refused to carry out his engagement.

A military force was then directed to enter Kaffirland and occupy Sandile's kraal, so as to bring him to terms. A very long waggon train accompanied it, conveying provisions, tents, baggage, and ammunition; and, as if to invite attack, this tempting prize was almost unguarded. The movements of the expedition were, of course, closely watched by the keen eyes of Kosa scouts, and when in a spot convenient for the purpose, while the main body of the English troops was some miles distant, a strong band of warriors rushed upon the train, and without any difficulty made themselves masters of a great portion of it.

By this disaster the British force was compelled to retreat precipitately. After considerable loss it reached the Lovedale mission station, just within the colonial border, and hastily fortified a large stone building used as a boarding school, which enabled it to stay there in safety.

At once a great body of Kosa warriors poured into the colony, swept off all the cattle east of Uitenhage, burned many dwelling-houses, and murdered several individuals who had not time to escape to villages or lagers. Their success encouraged a large portion of the Tembu tribe to join them, and these people laid waste the country north of the Winterberg just as the Kosas had done south of that range. Thus the European settlement in the eastern districts was reduced to the towns and villages, which were crowded with helpless and destitute people. The farms—except a few where there were lagers—were abandoned.

Another disaster followed. The garrison of the most advanced fort on the frontier was in urgent need of supplies of food and ammunition, and a train of waggons, under military escort, left Grahamstown for its relief. In a thicket the train was attacked, the guard was obliged to retire, and the supplies fell into the hands of the Kosas.

The whole burgher force of the colony was called out, and every soldier that could be spared from duty in Capetown was sent to the front. Hottentots and other coloured people were enrolled, waggons and oxen were everywhere impressed, and in a short time a mass of combatants sufficiently large for offensive operations was assembled on the frontier. A greater difficulty than that of collecting men, however, was that of collecting provisions. It was not only the army that the government had to feed, but the unfortunate European women and children whose property had been destroyed, and the families of all the Hottentots of the frontier.

Some successes were gained, but operations were stayed by the collapse of the transport service, and the army was obliged at one time to encamp on the coast, where supplies could be obtained by sea, in order to escape starvation. After a while several regiments of soldiers arrived from abroad, the transport service was organised on a better plan, and provisions were sent from the western districts. Then a kind of lull took place, in consequence of a professal of submission by most of the hostile clans, whose object was to get a crop of maize and then renew the war.

During this lull Sir Peregrine Maitland was recalled, as every governor since Lord Charles Somerset has been in whose term of office war has broken out. He was succeeded by Sir Henry Pottinger, who was also appointed high commissioner for the purpose of dealing with matters beyond the colonial border. All succeeding governors of the Cape Colony have been high commissioners also.

The crops of maize were gathered, and the war was resumed. But soon afterwards Sandile found himself hardly pressed, and surrendered, upon which there was another general profession of submission. In later years the Kosas laughed at the ease with which the white people were deceived, and ridiculed the idea of their being beaten in this war. But the governor, judging them by a European or an Indian standard, believed that they were subdued, and was about to proclaim peace when he received news of his transfer to Madras.

The enormous expense of the war had brought home to the imperial government the folly of the treaty system, of which it was the result, in a manner that the prayers of the colonists had never done. The ruined eastern farmers were clamouring for compensation from the British treasury for their losses, on the ground that they had protested against the measures which led to the war, and earl Glenelg had accepted the responsibility of carrying them out. They did not get what they asked for, but the whole military and commissariat charges were of necessity borne by England. Both Sir Peregrine Maitland and Sir Henry Pottinger had come to the conclusion that

Sir Benjamin D'Urban's system of dealing with the Kosas should be reverted to, and even Sir George Napier was of the same opinion.

The imperial authorities then resolved upon another complete change, and to carry it out they selected as governor and high commissioner Sir Harry Smith, who, as Colonel Smith, had been Sir Benjamin D'Urban's most able lieutenant in South Africa, and who had recently won high military renown in India. But while making this resolution they were beginning to comprehend that it was impossible at a distance of six thousand miles to direct the affairs of a country either safely or satisfactorily, especially under such pressure as could be brought by the great societies to bear upon a government in England; and they were already impressed with a belief that the best course they could adopt would be to let the affairs of the Cape Colony be settled by its own people. To the Kaffir war of 1846-7 more than to any other event is due the liberal constitution that was granted a few years later.

XX.

EVENTS DURING THE ADMINISTRATION OF SIR HARRY SMITH.

No governor has ever been more heartily welcomed in South Africa than Sir Harry Smith. Every section of the inhabitants of the colony hailed him as an old and tried friend, and there was a general hope that better days had now set in. He was not long in making known the details of the changes which he came to effect. Hurrying to the eastern frontier, he issued a proclamation, extending the Cape Colony on the north to the Orange river from its mouth to the junction of the Kraai, and on the east to the Keiskama and the Tyumie.

The territory between the Keiskama and Tyumie on one side, and the Kei on the other, he then proclaimed a British possession, but to be kept entirely for the use of the western clans of the Kosa tribe, just as Sir Benjamin D'Urban intended when he annexed it under the name of the province of Queen Adelaide. Colonel Mackinnon was appointed a commissioner to exercise general authority over the clans, an office which the governor himself had once

PORTRAIT OF SIR HARRY SMITH.

held. The chiefs remained the rulers of their people in many matters, but vicious customs were no longer to be tolerated, and punishment of persons accused of dealing in witchcraft was to be suppressed. A strong body of troops was to garrison various forts in the territory, and to support the authority of the commissioner and his assistants. The new province was named British Kaffraria.

The whole of the chiefs who had been in arms agreed to this arrangement, and those who resided within the province took an oath to maintain it. The others, who lived east of the Kei, were left perfectly independent. The governor, the colonists, and the missionaries—whose views were greatly modified by the late war—alike considered this settlement satisfactory, and to all outward appearance the Kosas were pleased with it; but within three years the chiefs declared that they had only agreed to it as a truce, in order to get material together for another trial of strength with the Europeans.

As soon as these arrangements were made, Sir Harry Smith proceeded to the territory north of the Orange river. Treaties between the British government and Bantu chiefs he regarded as agreements between a full-grown man and little children, and he repeatedly and emphatically declared that there should be no more of them. As for the treaty states on the northern border, he looked upon them as the creations of supreme folly, and he therefore intended to destroy them. But as neither Adam Kok nor Moshesh had violated any of the conditions of the treaties, he could not declare the documents annulled, and it was thus his object by some means to induce those persons to consent to their own effacement as sovereign rulers.

The emigrant farmers between the Riet and Modder rivers gave him an enthusiastic reception, for many of them had fought under his command thirteen years before, and they had always liked him as he had liked them. They had no complaint to make against Major Warden, but they had a grievance, in that half of the land tax which they paid went into the pocket of Adam Kok, and they had no return for it. Was it not scandalous, too, they asked, that they should be officially termed subjects of that petty captain of a mongrel band?

By the governor's desire, Kok went from Philippolis to Bloemfontein to meet him. At the conference Sir Harry stated that he was about to place the white people in the territory under the direct rule of the queen of England, but he would not interfere with Kok's government of his Griquas. The whole of the land between the Riet and Orange rivers—which was ten times as much as the Griquas could make use of—would be regarded as their reserve, the captain should have a perpetual pension of £200 a year, and as some of his people had leased farms north of the Riet river, which would now be lost to them, they should have among them £100 a year in perpetuity as compensation. The captain demurred to these terms, and spoke of his dignity in such a way that the governor lost all patience and threatened him with speedy punishment. He then submitted, and affixed his name to a document which put an end to the Griqua treaty state, but left him far more than he had any reasonable claim to.

A little later the governor had an interview with Moshesh, to whom he made some valuable presents, at the same time professing his friendship in the warmest language. He then announced his intention as regarded the white people, and asked for the co-operation of the chief. Probably Moshesh felt somewhat overawed in the presence of the impetuous governor, and it is improbable that he fully comprehended what the proposals laid before him would lead to, but he attached his mark to a document which destroyed the Basuto treaty state.

These preliminaries having been settled, on the 3rd of February 1848 Sir Harry Smith issued a proclamation, adding to the British dominions the whole territory between the Vaal river, the Orange river, and the Kathlamba mountains, under the name of the Orange River Sovereignty. The Europeans in it were placed under the immediate rule of the queen, and a staff of officials was appointed to administer justice and collect taxes in her Majesty's name. Major Warden was appointed head of the new administration. The coloured people were left under the government of their chiefs, and the land then actually in their occupation was to be reserved for their use and secured against encroachment. What might be termed their foreign relations, that is everything affecting the dealings of one head chief with another, or of any chief with Europeans, were to be under the control of the British authorities.

Here, at last, was a policy such as nearly every

man in the Cape Colony approved of. Unfortunately, however, it came too late. The vast majority of the white people living between the Modder and Vaal rivers were indisposed to submit to British rule in any form, and prepared to fight for the independent government they had lived under for twelve years. Moshesh, who had by this time built up a power far greater than Sir Harry Smith was aware of, began to devise schemes for the destruction of the Sovereignty government as soon as he found that he was to be confined to a reserve covering only the actual ground on which his people lived, that his practice of incorporating members of other tribes with his own was likely to be severely checked, and that the clans along the Caledon were treated as independent of him.

Sir Harry Smith had not long returned to Capetown when he received intelligence that the farmers in the north of the Sovereignty had elected Mr. Andries Pretorius to be their commandant and had risen in arms, that Major Warden with the little garrison of Bloemfontein had been obliged to capitulate, and that the whole of the English officials had been driven over the Orange river and were then in a camp near Colesberg. The energetic governor at once directed a strong body of troops to march to the Orange, and followed himself to take command in person. Commandant Pretorius did not attempt to defend the passage of the river, but made a stand at a strong position called Boomplaats, where on the 29th of August 1848 a severe engagement took place, which ended in the defeat of the farmers.

All who were inveterately opposed to British rule

now made their way in haste across the Vaal river, and there was no attempt to follow them. The Sovereignty government was re-established, and a much larger garrison than before was left in Bloemfontein. The places of those white people who had moved away were filled by fresh emigrants from the Cape Colony, many of whom were Englishmen, so that from this time forward the European population of the territory consisted of people either well affected to the British government or not very bitterly opposed to it.

Leaving now the region beyond the Cape Colony for a short time, an event must be related which caused intense excitement throughout South Africa. This was a project of the imperial ministry of the day to make of the Cape a convict settlement. The tidings caused a feeling somewhat akin to what a proposal would have done to introduce a dreadful disease. Men and women of respectability everywhere raised their voices against it, for if a class of people that had either by choice or of necessity become criminal, and whose self-respect was destroyed by conviction, were once allowed to mix with the coloured races, the country would no longer be fit to live in. Petitions and protests against the measure were sent to England in great number, and when the ship *Neptune* with convicts on board arrived in Simon's Bay, the people of the Cape peninsula—with few exceptions—bound themselves together under a pledge not to supply anything whatever to persons who had dealings with her, nor to have any intercourse with them.

This pledge was so strictly carried out that not a particle of food could be obtained for the convicts, and it was with much difficulty that supplies for the troops in garrison were procured. Any one who opposed the popular will in the matter did so on peril of being assaulted and having his property destroyed. Sir Harry Smith was very much opposed to the scheme of making the country a convict settlement, but he was obliged to carry out the instructions which he received from England, and so he could not send the ship away, though the colonists were very anxious that he should.

Five months the *Neptune* lay at anchor in Simon's Bay. Her crew and the convicts on board could get nothing to eat but provisions out of ships of war. If the plague had been in her she could not have been more carefully avoided. All this time the greatest excitement prevailed in the colony, and great caution had to be used by the government to prevent a collision with the people. At length, to the joy of every one, instructions were received from England that the convicts should proceed to Tasmania, as the secretary of state had changed his mind, owing to the numerous petitions of the colonists.

The anti-convict agitation had hardly died out when the country became involved again in war with the Kosa and Tembu tribes. The principal chiefs of these people had never regarded the cessation of hostilities at the close of 1847 as anything but a truce, though they were crafty enough to conceal their views from even those Europeans who were most intimately acquainted with them, and it was only at a later date that this became known. The common people were ready to support their chiefs with their lives as well as their substance, and, from their point of view, they had at least one very serious grievance against the European authorities.

The Bantu believe most implicitly that diseases and disasters of all kinds are caused by wizards and witches, and in every clan there is a recognised witch-finder who, whenever any trouble occurs, goes through certain forms called "smelling out," and then points to an individual whom he pronounces guilty of having caused it. The individual thus accused is, without further investigation, subjected to torture of different kinds, often resulting in death, and may consider himself fortunate if he escapes with a few scars and the loss of all his property. The British authorities suppressed the practice of "smelling out," and punished the witchfinders. They believed that by so doing they were conferring a benefit upon the people, who would be grateful for relief from the danger of being despoiled and tortured without cause or guilt. But the people supposed to be relieved looked at the matter in a different light. The English, they said, are giving us over to the wizards and witches to do as they like with us. Their view was what ours would be if a government were to suppress punishment for murder and imprison the constables who arrested a man for committing it.

Only a slight pretext was therefore needed for a renewal of the war, and any accident might have precipitated it, but, as it happened, the frontier colonists received timely warning of what was coming. It became known that a man named Umlanjeni, who was credited by his people with great magical knowledge, was issuing charms which he asserted would turn bullets fired at their wearers into water, and the Kosa warriors were repairing to him in hundreds at a time to procure them.

On receiving a report to this effect, Sir Harry Smith proceeded to King-Williamstown, and convened a meeting of all the chiefs in British Kaffraria, in order to discuss matters with them. Sandile, the most powerful among them, did not appear. Still, as the others made no complaints of any kind, and seemed to be prosperous and happy, the governor thought they could not have war in their minds. He returned to Capetown, but reports followed him that there would surely be a speedy outbreak.

With all the soldiers that could be mustered, Sir Harry was soon back in King-Williamstown, and as Sandile was known to be in one of the forests at the sources of the Keiskama, a body of troops was sent to arrest him. On the way the troops were attacked in the Boomah pass by thousands of Kosas, and lost twenty-three men killed and as many wounded in fighting their way through. A few hours later in another part of the country a patrol of fifteen soldiers was met by some of Sandile's people, and all were put to death.

On the following morning—Christmas 1850, three villages named Auckland, Woburn, and Johannesburg, close to the colonial side of the border, were surprised by Kosas, when forty-six men were murdered in cold blood, and the houses were burned to the ground.

In this manner the eighth Kaffir war commenced, and it was the longest and most costly in blood and treasure that the Cape Colony has ever been engaged in. The frontier districts were ravaged once more, and the burghers of all parts of the country were obliged to leave their homes and take up arms. The Kosas were joined by a great part of the Tembu tribe and by several hundreds of Hottentots from the settlement at the Kat river and other places. Even some of the soldiers of the Hottentot regiment deserted and went over to them, as the colonists had always feared would some day happen.

A very sad event was the loss of the transport steamship *Birkenhead*, which was sent from England with troops to assist in the war. She was proceeding to Algoa Bay when in the middle of the night she struck on a reef running out from Danger Point. The women, children, and sick people were put into the boats, while the soldiers were drawn up on the deck as on a parade ground. The sea was swarming with sharks, the shore was so far distant that the strongest swimmer could not hope to reach it, and the wreck was breaking up fast. Yet those brave men stood calmly there till the boats with the helpless ones got away. Then, just as the ship fell to pieces and sank, they leaped into the sea, and a few, by clinging to floating wreckage, got to land. Four hundred perished.

There had never before been so strong a force in South Africa as there was in Kaffraria at this time. For more than two years the soldiers, burghers, and auxiliaries of various kinds were employed against an enemy that could not be brought to a decisive action, but that seemed to go from one forest to another with the facility of birds, and that carried on war by doubling upon pursuers, cutting off stragglers, and seizing everything that was not strongly guarded. At length, however, the food of the hostile clans was completely exhausted, and the chiefs then asked for peace, which was gladly granted.

It was not Sir Harry Smith's fault, but his misfortune, that the war had taken place. It would have been beyond the power of any man to have staved it off permanently, for even the settlement made at its close, as will hereafter be seen, was only regarded by the Kosas as a truce. But, following the invariable custom in such cases, the secretary of state recalled the governor. Sir George Cathcart, who was sent out as his successor, took over the duty on the 31st of March 1852, and thereafter directed operations in person until the conclusion of peace.

He located the Tembus—who were really subdued—in the district that is now called Glen Grey, and gave much of the remainder of the land they had occupied for the last quarter of a century to colonists to be held under military tenure. It was for a time called North Victoria, but subsequently became known as the district of Queenstown, from the neat and flourishing village that was built near its centre. The Fingos, who had fought well on the European side, received the best of the land along the foot of the Amatola mountains and some extensive tracts forfeited by the Tembus. The in-

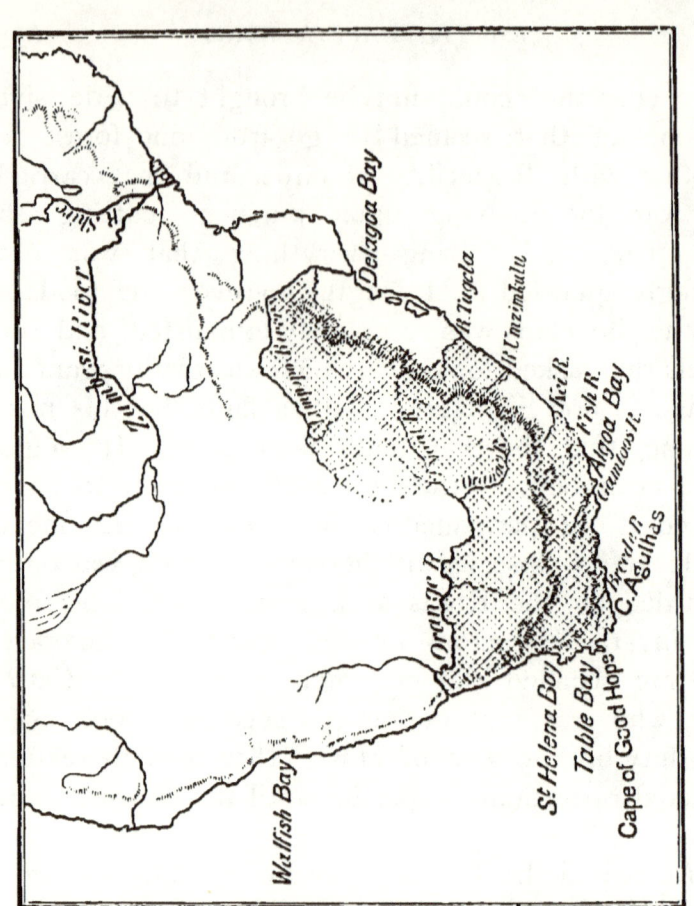

EXTENT OF TERRITORY UNDER EUROPEAN RULE IN 1850.

dependent section of the Kosa tribe, under the chief Kreli, was left in possession of the territory between the Bashee and the Kei; and the western clans of this tribe, who had been British subjects since 1847, had all the open ground from the Kei to the Keiskama assigned to them.

The government of British Kaffraria was re-established with a strong and reliable force to support it. Before the war there had been a large body of Kaffir police, but at the commencement of hostilities the men composing it had gone over to their own people. Their place was now taken by a corps composed chiefly of young colonists, with a few Fingos attached to it as detectives. The men, who were armed with the best weapons, were mounted, and proved a most useful body for either military or police purposes. Several regiments of British troops were also stationed in the province.

XXI.

ACKNOWLEDGMENT BY GREAT BRITAIN OF THE INDEPENDENCE OF THE SOUTH AFRICAN REPUBLIC, AND ABANDONMENT OF THE ORANGE RIVER SOVEREIGNTY.

For a short time after the restoration of British rule in the Orange River Sovereignty, everything went on smoothly, and the people appeared to be prosperous. But this satisfactory state of affairs did not continue long. Moshesh was unwilling that the growth of his power should be restricted, and as he did not wish openly to break with the British government, he endeavoured secretly to foment such disturbances as would destroy the arrangements then existing. He—a self-made Bantu ruler—cannot be blamed for doing this; but what can be said of the treaty system which enabled him to build up sufficient power to do it?

It was easy for him to bring about a collision between one of his vassal captains and the chief Sikonyela, while all the time he was professing to be an advocate of peace and apparently making sacrifices to secure it. Presently other clans became involved in the quarrel, and Major Warden, who had done all that was possible to restore order by advice and expostulation, then tried to quell the disturbance by force.

This course of action was regarded by the Europeans in the Sovereignty as a mistake. They maintained that the government ought not to meddle with matters affecting only Bantu clans, as it had no spare strength to squander, and should reserve its interference for occasions when Europeans were threatened with damage. But Sir Harry Smith thought differently. He had no idea that the Basuto power was as great as it afterwards proved to be, nor indeed had any other European in South Africa. He was of opinion that by adding the English soldiers at Bloemfontein and an equal number of farmers to any side in a quarrel in the Sovereignty, he could turn the scale against the other side. And so it was by his instructions that Major Warden attempted to punish the disturbers of the peace.

With one hundred and sixty-two soldiers, one hundred and twenty farmers, and from a thousand to fifteen hundred blacks, the major marched against Molitsane, the vassal of Moshesh who was held to be the cause of the disturbance, and at Viervoet was drawn into a trap and suffered a crushing defeat. No one was more surprised than Moshesh himself at the issue of the battle, for he had not believed that the troops and farmers under Major Warden's command could have been driven from the field so easily. He at once threw off the mask he had hitherto worn, and laid aside his assumed respect for British authority.

It has before been stated that the majority of the farmers in the Sovereignty were well affected towards England, but a strong minority were at heart opposed to English rule, though up to this time not inclined to offer open resistance. These last were hardly less surprised than Moshesh at the decisive success of the Basuto in the battle of Viervoet. They knew that no aid could be sent to Major Warden from the Cape Colony, which was then involved in a war of its own, and so, as a matter of self-protection, they set aside their duty to the Sovereignty government and entered into an engagement with Moshesh. They promised not to take part in hostilities against him, and he engaged not to allow his people to molest them. On both sides this agreement was faithfully kept.

The Europeans who were loyal to the British government, on the contrary, were sought out by bands of Basuto and plundered mercilessly. The clans along the Caledon were dispersed, and were reduced to great distress. Major Warden was perfectly helpless, for without a strong military force order could not be restored, and he had only men enough to guard the fort in Bloemfontein.

Some of the farmers now sent a request to Commandant Pretorius to come and devise some plan to put an end to the prevailing anarchy, and Moshesh joined in the invitation. Since the battle of Boomplaats Pretorius had been living north of the Vaal, with a reward of £2,000 for his apprehension hanging over his head all the time. When urged to interfere in matters in the Sovereignty, he wrote to Major Warden announcing his intention to do so, but intimating that he would prefer to make a treaty of peace with the British government, in which the independence of his adherents should be acknowledged. Major Warden hereupon reported to Sir Harry Smith that the fate of the Sovereignty depended upon the movements of a proscribed man. He had been instructed to act strictly on the defensive until troops could be spared from the Kaffir war to aid him, but if Pretorius and the emigrants north of the Vaal united with the Europeans who ignored his authority and with Moshesh, he would be entirely at their mercy.

Under these circumstances the governor decided to acknowledge the independence of the Transvaal emigrants, as the imperial ministers had announced their determination not to add another square inch of ground in South Africa to the queen's dominions, and advantages which could be obtained by a convention were not to be had in any other way. Two assistant commissioners—Major Hogg and Mr. Owen —were therefore sent to make the necessary arrangements with Commandant Pretorius and a number of delegates from the Transvaal people. The conference took place on a farm in the Sovereignty, and there, on the 17th of January 1852, a document— known ever since as the Sand River convention— was signed, in which the British government guaranteed to the emigrants north of the Vaal the right to manage their own affairs without interference. The convention was confirmed by the secretary of state for the colonies, and was ratified by the volksraad, so that thereafter the South African Republic—as the country was named—had a legal as well as an actual existence in the eyes of the British government.

The Sovereignty was thus preserved from interference by Mr. Pretorius, and its government became somewhat stronger than before, because a good many of those who had ignored Major Warden moved over the Vaal. But Moshesh's people still continued to plunder and harass the loyal farmers, and the clans that had opposed him remained in great distress.

This was the state of matters until Sir George Cathcart was able to spare a strong body of troops from British Kaffraria, with which he marched northward to restore order. He reached Platberg on the Caledon with a splendidly equipped force, consisting of nearly two thousand infantry, five hundred cavalry, and some artillerymen with two field-guns, hoping that the mere presence of such a body of troops would enable him to settle everything to his satisfaction, without having recourse to hostilities. From Platberg, after a minute investigation of affairs, he sent an ultimatum to Moshesh, demanding that chief's compliance with certain conditions and the delivery within three days of ten thousand head of horned cattle and one thousand horses, as compensation for the robberies committed by the Basuto people.

Moshesh personally was willing to accede to the high commissioner's terms, for he dreaded a struggle with the British power now that the Tembus had been subdued, the Kosas were ceasing to fight, and the Transvaal farmers were pacified. He knew that the army at Platberg was only a small portion of the force at Sir George Cathcart's disposal, and he was in that condition that any serious reverse might ruin him. The great tribe that called him master was composed of the fragments of many others that had not yet thoroughly blended, and disaster would cause its disintegration. There were numerous individuals in it of higher rank by birth than he, so that elements of discord were present, though they did not show themselves in times of prosperity. In short, to save his dynasty it was necessary for Moshesh to avoid defeat.

But the Basuto people preferred a trial of strength to the surrender of so many cattle and horses as the high commissioner demanded, and the great chief could not afford to act in opposition to their wishes, as a ruler by hereditary right could have done. The result was a kind of compromise. Moshesh sent in three thousand five hundred head of cattle, with a faint hope that they would be accepted as sufficient, and then assembled his warriors at Thaba Bosigo to resist the British army if it should advance.

The country of the Basuto is an exceedingly difficult one to penetrate. It is the Switzerland of South Africa. Resting on the interior plateau of the continent, five thousand feet above sea level, it rises like a gigantic billow in successive waves of mountains until the summit of the Drakensberg is reached, the highest peaks of which are over eleven thousand feet above the ocean. The lower valleys are remark-

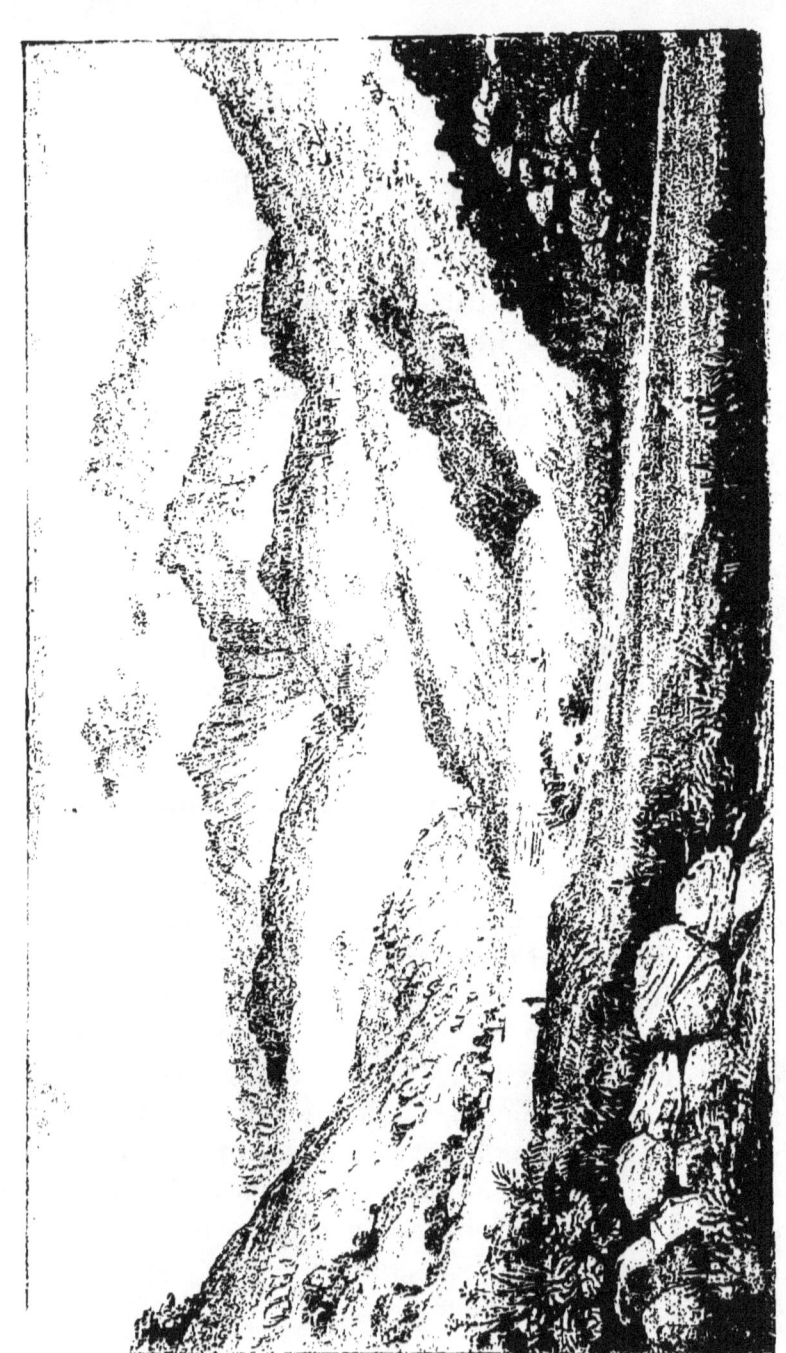

THE GIANT'S CUP, AS SEEN FROM THE SEAWARD SIDE OF THE DRAKENSBERG.
(From a Sketch by Captain Gardiner.)

ably fertile, so that the country can support a large population, though no other use is made of the higher lands than to pasture cattle in summer. There are many hills with flat tops and precipitous sides that can easily be defended against an enemy, and of all these Thaba Bosigo, the seat of Moshesh's government, is the strongest.

On the 20th of December 1852 Sir George Cathcart crossed the Caledon from Platberg, and entered Basutoland, with the intention of occupying Moshesh's mountain. He made the great mistake of underestimating the strength and courage of his opponent, and not giving him any credit for ability as a strategist. His officers took no thought about the matter, but looked upon their occupation of Thaba Bosigo as a certainty, and their march as a pleasant excursion. The army entered the Basuto territory in three divisions.

By a simple stratagem—that of exposing an immense herd of cattle in a position on the Berea mountain where their capture appeared easy—one of the British divisions was drawn into an ambush, and after suffering considerable loss was obliged to retreat to the camp at Platberg. It drove before it, however, some four thousand horned cattle, with a few horses and sheep, which the enemy was unable to recover.

Another of the divisions, under Sir George Cathcart in person, suddenly found itself face to face with about six thousand Basuto horsemen armed with European weapons, and though the discipline of the soldiers enabled them to keep the untrained mass from breaking their ranks, no further advance was now thought of. A little before dusk the third division managed to join the commander-in-chief, and a defensible position among rocks was then taken for the night. At daybreak next morning the army commenced its retreat to the camp at Platberg. It had lost thirty-seven men killed, fifteen wounded, and one prisoner, who was murdered by his captors.

Though he had gained such a success, the wise Basuto chief's first thought after the battle was to obtain peace. He sent for the reverend Mr. Casalis, one of his missionaries, and after consulting with him, the most politic document that has ever been penned in South Africa was written. It was as follows:—

"THABA BOSIGO,
"*Midnight, 20th December,* 1852.

"YOUR EXCELLENCY,—This day you have fought against my people, and taken much cattle. As the object for which you have come is to have a compensation for Boers, I beg you will be satisfied with what you have taken. I entreat peace from you— you have chastised—let it be enough, I pray you; and let me be no longer considered an enemy to the Queen. I will try all I can to keep my people in order in the future.

"Your humble servant,
"MOSHESH."

It was some time before a messenger could be found who would venture near the English sentries, and when at length one left Thaba Bosigo with a flag of truce, Sir George Cathcart was retiring to his camp at Platberg. The messenger followed and delivered the letter.

The English general, on his part, was not less anxious for peace. In his opinion there was everything to lose in a war with a tribe so strong as he had found the Basuto to be, and so he eagerly availed himself of the opening for escape from a grave difficulty which Moshesh's letter afforded. He announced that he was satisfied with the number of cattle captured, that he considered past obligations fulfilled, and that he would at once retire. There was much murmuring in the English camp when this announcement was made, but the general shut his ears to it all, and before the end of the month the army reached the Orange on its return march.

For some time the imperial government had been undecided whether to retain the Sovereignty as a British possession or not, but as soon as intelligence of the engagement with the Basuto reached England a decision was formed. The next mail brought a despatch from the secretary of state for the colonies that the territory was to be abandoned.

To carry this resolution into effect, Sir George Clerk was sent out as special commissioner. He called upon the European inhabitants to elect a body of representatives to take over the government; but when the representatives assembled, they objected in the strongest terms to be abandoned by Great Britain, for even while they were debating, Moshesh was crushing Sikonyela and another of his opponents, and adding their territory to his own. In effect, the representative assembly said to Sir George Clerk that they held England in honour bound to reduce the great barbaric power she had done so much to build up. When that was done, they would not need military assistance, and would be prepared to take over the government of the country, though they wished to remain permanently connected with the British empire. The special commissioner, however, was prevented by his instructions from paying any attention to language of this kind, and was obliged to term those who used it "obstructionists." The assembly then sent two delegates to England to implore the queen's government and the parliament not to abandon them, but those gentlemen met with no success in their mission.

Sir George Clerk now encouraged the remnant of the party that was at heart opposed to British rule to assert itself openly. With his concurrence, one of its ablest leaders returned from beyond the Vaal, and went about the country addressing the people and arguing that connection with England meant nothing but restraint, for no protection whatever was received. In the special commissioner's phraseology, Mr. Stander and those of his way of thinking, who used language to that effect, were "well-disposed."

This party elected a body of delegates, who met in Bloemfontein, and opened negotiations with Sir George Clerk. The "obstructionist" assembly protested, and was thereupon dissolved by the special commissioner, when most of its members and supporters, finding resistance to the will of the British government useless, went over to the "well-disposed" side, and tried to get as good terms as possible.

Gold was freely used to suppress complaints—it was termed part compensation for losses,—and nothing that was possible to be done was neglected to make the abandonment acceptable to the people generally. The result was that on the 23rd of February 1854 a convention was signed at Bloemfontein by Sir George Clerk and the members of the "well-disposed" assembly, by which the government of the territory previously termed the Orange River Sovereignty, thereafter the Orange Free State, was transferred, and its future independence was guaranteed.

There were now in South Africa five distinct European governments, namely of—

1. The Cape Colony,
2. Natal,
3. British Kaffraria,   } British Possessions.
4. The South African Republic,
5. The Orange Free State. } Independent Republics.

In 1854 the Cape Colony comprised all the land between the Orange river on the north, the Indian ocean on the south, the Atlantic ocean on the west, and British Kaffraria and the rivers Indwe and Tees on the east.

Natal comprised the territory between the Buffalo and Tugela rivers on the north-east, the Umzimkulu river on the south-east, the Kathlamba mountains or Drakensberg on the west, and the Indian ocean on the east.

British Kaffraria comprised the territory between the rivers Klipplaats, Tyumie, and Keiskama on the west, the river Kei from the junction of the Klipplaats to the sea on the north-east, and the Indian ocean on the south-east.

The boundaries of the South African Republic were undefined, but, roughly speaking, they were the Limpopo river on the north, the Vaal river and a line a little above Kuruman on the south, the Kalahari desert on the west, and the mountainous country corresponding with the Drakensberg on the east.

The Orange Free State comprised the territory between the Vaal river, the Orange river, and the Drakensberg, except Basutoland and the reserves set apart for coloured people.

XXII.

THE CONSTITUTION OF THE CAPE COLONY.

THE story of the Cape Colony from this time onward is very different from that of the preceding period. Arbitrary rule is henceforth a thing of the past, and a constitution of a liberal nature, granted by Great Britain, gradually removes the memory of old grievances, and creates a strong feeling of loyalty to the throne and the empire in all sections of the civilised inhabitants.

The imperial authorities having resolved to confer upon the Cape people the privilege of parliamentary institutions, the details were referred for arrangement to the legislative council, and when everything was settled, on the 11th of March 1853 the constitution was promulgated by an order in council. By it two chambers—termed the legislative council and the house of assembly—were created, both of which are elective. The upper chamber for some years consisted of fifteen members, but in course of time this number was increased to twenty-two, beside the chief justice as president. For the purpose of electing the members, the colony was divided into two provinces, more recently into eight circles. The members hold their seats for seven years. The house of assembly on its creation consisted of forty-six members, elected by twenty-two divisions, Cape-town having two more representatives than any of the others. It now consists of seventy-six members, elected by thirty-seven divisions, and holding their seats for five years. Parliament is summoned to meet by the governor, but a period of twelve months must not elapse between the sessions.

The right to vote for members of both chambers was conferred upon every male British subject over twenty-one years of age, who occupied a house or land worth £25, or was in receipt of a salary of £25 a year with board and lodging or £50 without. There was no distinction as regards race, or colour, or religion, or manner of living. In course of time, however, it was found expedient to alter these qualifications, as in the Cape Colony there is a large class of people unable to comprehend the nature of representative institutions, and yet in possession of sufficient property to bring them within one of the conditions specified above. In 1892 the right to vote was restricted to such adult male subjects as are able to sign their names and write down their addresses and employment, and who either occupy property worth £75, or receive £50 a year as salary or wages.

Parliament met for the first time in June 1854. Since that date no law can be made without the approval of both houses and the sanction of the governor. The right is reserved to the queen to disallow any law so made within two years of its reaching England, but in practice this right is very rarely used. The ordinary yearly sessions of the parliament usually last about three months, from early in June to the end of August.

Naturally the colonists were gratified with the change from arbitrary to representative government,

PARLIAMENT HOUSE, CAPETOWN.

but there was still much to wish for. The officials of highest rank, who formed the executive council and were therefore the governor's advisers, continued to be sent out from England, and held their appointments during the pleasure of the secretary of state for the colonies, no matter whether parliament liked them or not. They framed all government bills, and no measure involving the expenditure of money could be brought before the house of assembly unless introduced by them. They possessed the right of discussion, though not of voting, in both chambers.

This condition of things lasted eighteen years. In 1872 responsible government was introduced, and the ministers—as the high officials are termed—have since that time been the leaders of the party in parliament that can command the largest number of votes in support of their measures. They are the colonial secretary, the treasurer, the attorney-general, the commissioner of public works, and the secretary for agriculture. There is also the premier, or prime minister, who may hold any of these appointments, or none of them; but who, in any case, has all matters connected with the aboriginal races directly under his care. When any important measure, introduced by the government, fails to secure the support of a majority of the members of parliament, the ministers must resign, and the leader of the opposition is entrusted by the governor with the task of forming a new cabinet.

In practice this system gives to the men who are chosen by the people the power of making and altering laws, of levying taxes and controlling the manner of using the public money, and of creating and doing away with offices. But it is a system adapted only for races of high civilisation. The majority of the day possesses supreme power, and if it came to consist of men whose constituents were incapable of acting with moderation, the minority could be more grievously oppressed than under the purest autocratic rule. There are many thinking people in the colony who regard the franchise as still too low for perfect safety, with the existing form of government and the political equality of the various races that compose the population.

Until 1882 the English language only could be used in debate in parliament, just as in the proceedings of courts of justice or in transactions in the public offices. This was decidedly unfair, for Dutch is habitually spoken by fully three-fifths of the white people in the colony, and by a still larger proportion of the coloured inhabitants, exclusive of Bantu. It will be remembered that its suppression as the official language was one of the chief grievances that rankled in the breasts of the old colonists. The parliament could not be said in truth to represent the people as long as the language of the majority was proscribed, and in point of fact comparatively few of the old stock sought admission into it. It was some time before they realised the full significance of responsible government, but when they did, one of their first acts was to secure the same rights for their own tongue as for the English. Either can now be used in parliament, courts of law, and public offices, at the choice of the speaker, and no one is admitted into the ordinary branches of the civil service without a perfect knowledge of both.

It would be incorrect to say that this measure has raised the tone of debate in parliament or improved the administration of justice in the slightest degree, but it certainly has made the parliament more truly representative of the people, and it has removed a serious obstacle to the perfect blending of the colonists of Dutch and British blood, which is now happily in rapid progress.

XXIII.

THE PROVINCE OF BRITISH KAFFRARIA.

BEFORE 1857 there were hardly any Bantu in the Cape Colony except the Fingos who had been introduced by Sir Benjamin D'Urban and the Tembus of Glen Grey, while British Kaffraria—the territory between the Keiskama and the Kei—had very few white inhabitants except soldiers, as the land there was reserved for the section of the Kosa tribe that was under English rule. After that date many thousands of Kosas were scattered over the country as far west as Port Elizabeth, and a population of European blood occupied a considerable portion of the land eastward to the Kei. This change in the position of the two races was caused by an event more astounding than anything in the pages of the wildest romance.

The chiefs had accepted the terms imposed upon them at the close of the last war, but resolved to renew the struggle with the white people as soon as circumstances would permit it. Shortly after the conclusion of peace, Sir George Cathcart was succeeded as governor and high commissioner by Sir

THE GREY HOSPITAL, KING-WILLIAMSTOWN.

George Grey, one of the ablest administrators the country has ever had, and he immediately took steps to prevent, as he hoped, another outbreak of hostilities.

As high commissioner he exercised supreme control in British Kaffraria. Provided with a large amount of money from the imperial treasury, he attempted to pacify the chiefs by giving them pensions, payable monthly, as compensation for the power they had apparently lost, and he tried to break the belief in witchcraft by building a large and beautiful hospital in King-Williamstown, where any sick black person was attended by skilful medical men and provided for free of charge. Further, he commenced to make roads in the province, and to build a great sea wall at the mouth of the Buffalo river—called the port of East London—with the express object of teaching the Kosas the advantage of earning money by labour. In the same spirit he encouraged the Wesleyan and Free Church missionary societies to establish industrial institutions, where young Fingos and Kosas could be trained as gardeners, carpenters, blacksmiths, and waggon-makers, and where a number of the most intelligent boys could be educated as interpreters, schoolmasters, and evangelists. One of the institutions which he thus assisted with funds is still in existence. This is Lovedale, an establishment of the Free Church, where an exceedingly good training has ever since been given, and where at the present time some five or six hundred youths of both sexes are living as pupils.

These truly philanthropic measures, however, required many years to produce a good effect, and even then a very small proportion of the people would be benefited by them. They had not well been taken in hand when tidings reached the high commissioner in Capetown that cattle in unusual numbers were being slaughtered in and beyond British Kaffraria, and that the Kosas were assuming a defiant attitude. Colonel Maclean, who had succeeded Colonel Mackinnon as head of the local government, was not long in finding out and reporting the cause.

One morning in May 1856 a girl named Nongkause went to draw water from a little stream that flowed past her home. On her return, she stated that she had seen by the river some men who differed greatly in appearance from those she was accustomed to meet. Her uncle, whose name was Umhlakaza, went to see the strangers, and found them at the place indicated. They told him to return home and go through certain ceremonies, after which he was to offer an ox in sacrifice to the spirits of the dead, and to come back to them on the fourth day. There was that in their appearance which commanded obedience, and so the man did as they bade him. On the fourth day he went to the river again. The strange people were there as before, and to his astonishment he recognised among them his brother who had been many years dead. Then, for the first time, he learned who and what they were. The eternal enemies of the white man, they announced themselves as having come from battle-fields beyond the sea to aid the Kosas with their invincible power in driving the English from the land. Between them and the chiefs

Umhlakaza was to be the medium of communication, the channel through which instruction would be given. For strange things were to be done, stranger than any that had ever been done before, if the proffered assistance was welcomed. And first, he must tell the people to abandon dealing in witchcraft, to kill fat cattle and eat.

Such is the tale which the Kosas told each other of the manner in which Umhlakaza and Nongkause became acquainted with the secrets of the spirit world. Umhlakaza and Nongkause! What terrible visions of suffering and death are called forth in Kaffirland now at the mention of those two names!

Kreli, the paramount chief of the tribe, hailed the message with joy, and indeed it is generally believed — though it cannot be proved — that he was the instigator of the scheme. His word went forth that the command of the spirits was to be obeyed, that the best of all the cattle were to be killed and eaten. Messengers from him hastened to the chiefs in British Kaffraria to inform them of what had taken place, and to require their co-operation. Instantly the clans were in a state of commotion. Most of the chiefs commenced to kill, but one, Sandile, timid and hesitating, for a time held back. The high commissioner sent word to Kreli that though in his own territory he could do as he pleased, he must cease from instigating those who were British subjects to destroy their property, or it would become necessary to punish him. But he cared little for such a threat, as the time was at hand when it would be for him to talk of punishing.

The revelations communicated through Umhlakaza grew apace. The girl, standing in the river in presence of a multitude of deluded people, heard strange unearthly sounds beneath her feet, which Umhlakaza pronounced to be the voices of spirits holding council over the affairs of men. The first order was to slay cattle, but the greedy ghosts seemed insatiable in their demands. More and more were killed, but still never enough. And thus the delusion continued month after month, every day spreading wider and embracing fresh victims in its grasp. After a while Sandile gave way to the urgent applications of his brother Makoma, who asserted that he had himself seen and conversed with the spirits of two of his father's dead councillors, and that they commanded Sandile to kill his cattle if he would not perish with the white man.

Before this time the last order of Umhlakaza had been given, that order whose fulfilment was to be the final preparation of the Kosas, after which they would be worthy of the aid of a spirit host. Not an animal out of all their herds must be left living, every grain of corn in their granaries must be destroyed. But what a future of glory and wealth was predicted for the faithful and obedient! On a certain day myriads of cattle, more beautiful than those they were called upon to kill, were to issue from the earth and cover the pastures far and wide. Great fields of millet, ripe and ready for eating, were in an instant to spring into existence. The ancient heroes of the race, the great and the wise of days gone by, restored to life on that happy day, would appear and take part in the joys of the faithful. Trouble and sickness would be known no more, nor would the frailties of old age oppress them, for youth and beauty were to return alike to the risen dead and the feeble living. Such was the picture of Paradise painted by the Kosa prophet, and held before the eyes of the infatuated people. And dreadful was to be the fate of those who opposed the will of the spirits, or neglected to obey their commands. The day that was to bring so much joy to the loyal would bring nothing but destruction for them. The sky itself would fall and crush them together with the Fingos and the whites.

Missionaries and agents of the government tried in vain to stay the mad proceedings. A delirious frenzy possessed the minds of the Kosas, and they would listen to no argument, brook no opposition. White men who attempted to interfere with them in any way were scowled upon and warned to take care of themselves. Yet these fanatics, with their imaginations fixed on boundless wealth, were eagerly purchasing trifles from English traders, bartering away the hides of two hundred thousand slaughtered cattle. Most of them acted under the influence of superstition alone, though there is no doubt that some of the leaders viewed the proceeding as calculated solely for purposes of war. To throw the whole Kosa tribe, fully armed and in a famishing state, upon the colony, was the end kept steadily in view by these. The terrible odds against the success of such a venture they were too blind to see or too excited to calculate.

Some there were who neither believed the predictions of Umhlakaza nor looked for success in war, and who yet destroyed the last particle of their food. Bukhu, Kreli's uncle, was one of these. "It is the chief's command," said he, and then, when nothing more was left, the old man and his favourite wife sat down in their empty kraal and died. Kreli's principal councillor opposed the scheme till he saw that words were useless. Then, observing that all he had was his chief's, he gave the order to kill and waste, and fled from the place a raving lunatic. Thus it was with thousands. The chief commanded, and they obeyed.

In the early months of 1857 an unwonted activity reigned throughout the country from the Keiskama to the Bashee. Great kraals were being prepared for the reception of the cattle, so soon to appear like stars of the sky in multitude. Enormous skin bags were being made to contain the milk shortly to be like water in plenty. And even as they worked some were starving. East of the Kei the prophet's command had been obeyed to the letter, but the resurrection day was still postponed. It was in mercy to the Gaikas, said Umhlakaza, for Sandile had not finished killing yet. Nothing surely was ever more clumsily arranged, more blindly carried out than this mad act of the Kosas. One section of the tribe was literally starving, while another section was still engaged in destroying its resources.

The government did all that was possible to protect the frontier. Every post was strengthened, and every available soldier was sent forward. The colonists, too, were prepared to meet the expected shock, come when it would. And then, after defence was provided for, stores of food were accumulated for the purpose of saving life. For there could be no heart so cold as not to feel pity for those misguided beings who were rushing so frantically into certain destruction.

At length the morning dawned of the day so long and so ardently looked for. All night long the Kosas had watched with feelings stretched to the utmost tension of excitement, expecting to see two blood-red suns rise over the eastern hills, when the heavens would fall and crush the races they hated. Famished with hunger, half-dying as they were, that night was yet a time of fierce, delirious joy. The morn, that a few short hours, slowly becoming minutes, would usher in, was to see all their sorrows ended, all their misery past. And so they waited and watched. At length the sun approached the horizon, throwing first a silver sheen upon the mountain peaks, and then bathing hillside and valley in a flood of light. The hearts of the watchers sank within them. "What," said they, "will become of us if Umhlakaza's predictions turn out untrue?" But perhaps, after all, it might be midday that was meant, and when the shadows began to lengthen towards the east, perhaps, they thought, the setting of the sun is the time. The sun went down—as it often does in that fair land—behind clouds of crimson and gold, and the Kosas awoke to the reality of their dreadful position.

A blunder, such as a child would hardly have made, had been committed by the managers of this horrible tragedy. Under pretence of witnessing the resurrection, they should have assembled the warriors of the whole tribe at some point from which they could have burst in a body upon the colony. This had not been done, and now it was too late to collect them together. An attempt was made to rectify the blunder, and the day of resurrection was again postponed, but fierce excitement had given place to deepest despair. The only chance of life that remained was to reach the colony, but it was as suppliants, not as warriors, that the famished people must now go.

The horrors that succeeded can only be partly told. There are intelligent men living now, then wild naked fugitives, who cannot recount the events of those days. The whole scene comes home to them as a hideous nightmare, or as the remembrances of one in a state of delirium. In many instances all the ties were broken that bind human beings to each other in every condition of society. Brother fought with brother, father with son, for scraps and shreds of those great milk sacks so carefully made in the days when hope was high. The aged, the sick, the feeble, were abandoned by the young and vigorous. All kinds of wild plants, and even the roots of trees, were collected for food. Many of those who were near the sea coast endeavoured to support life upon the shellfish found there. Being unaccustomed to such diet, they were attacked by dysentery, which completed the work of famine. In other instances whole families sat down and died together. From fifteen to twenty skeletons were afterwards often found under a single tree, showing where parents and children met their fate when the last ray of hope had fled. A continuous stream of emaciated beings poured into the colony, young men and women mostly, but sometimes fathers and mothers bearing on their backs half-dying children. Before the farmhouses they would sit down, and ask in the most piteous tones for food, nor did they ask in vain.

Between the first and last days of 1857 the official returns of British Kaffraria showed a decrease in the population from one hundred and five thousand to thirty-eight thousand of both sexes and all ages. Sixty-seven thousand had perished or dispersed. In the centre of this territory was King-Williamstown where the government had provided a quantity of corn, by which the lives of thousands were saved. Between the Kei and the Bashee there was no such storehouse, and flight, except to rival and unfriendly tribes, was next to impossible. The death-rate there was consequently higher than in British Kaffraria. The lowest computation fixes the number of those who perished on both sides of the Kei at twenty-five thousand, ordinary calculations give double that number. The power of the Kosa tribe was for the time completely broken.

Large tracts of land in British Kaffraria having become waste by this mad act of the Kosas, Sir George Grey allotted farms of about fifteen hundred acres in size to a considerable number of selected individuals from the Cape Colony, to be held under tenure of military service and a small quitrent. A strong body of European settlers was thus stationed in advance of the most formidable Kaffir strongholds. Some regiments of the German legion, raised by Great Britain during the Crimean war, were sent out, and were disbanded in the province, where plots of land were assigned to the officers and soldiers on a military village system. Many of these men prospered, and they were undoubtedly of great service to the country, but on the whole the villages were failures. The proportion of women was too small to give reasonable hope of permanency to the settlements, and the men were better adapted for life in towns than as tillers of the soil. Most of them dispersed as soon as the issue of rations ceased.

A body of agricultural labourers selected from the hardy peasantry of Northern Germany was introduced shortly afterwards. The men were accompanied by their wives and children, and were inured to toil and accustomed to rough living. In 1858 and 1859 these people, in number rather over two thousand, landed at East London. They were sent out under a contract between Sir George Grey and a merchant in Hamburg, and were bound to refund within a certain period the cost of their transport and to pay twenty shillings an acre for the ground allotted to them. They were located in different parts of the province, but chiefly in the valley of the Buffalo river. No better settlers could have been introduced. By their industry, in the course of a few years they became possessed of a considerable amount of stock and brought their little farms to a high state of cultivation. As market gardeners they were unrivalled in South Africa. Frugal, temperate, industrious, and religious, they contributed very largely to the prosperity of the province.

King-Williamstown soon grew to be a place of no little importance. It was garrisoned by a strong body of British troops, and was the centre of a large trade, besides being the seat of the local government.

In theory the Cape parliament had no power to legislate for British Kaffraria, but in practice as soon as an act was passed in Capetown the high commissioner proclaimed it of force in the province, and thus secured uniformity in the laws. The revenue was small, and required to be supplemented by grants in aid from the imperial treasury. But now that the territory had ceased to be occupied exclusively by Bantu, it seemed to the queen's ministers that it might with advantage be incorporated with the Cape Colony, and this burden be removed from the British taxpayer. Proposals to that effect were therefore brought before the Cape parliament on several occasions, but were always rejected. At length the imperial parliament passed an act of union, which was, however, only to take effect after the lapse of a certain period, and provided the Cape parliament did not in the meantime annex the province. Armed with this document, Sir Philip Wodehouse, Sir George Grey's successor as governor and high commissioner, introduced a bill which provided for the incorporation of British Kaffraria as two electoral divisions—King-Williamstown and East London—and after much opposition it was passed by a majority of both houses of the Cape legislature, and in 1865 was carried into effect.

XXIV.

THE COLONY OF NATAL AND THE DEPENDENCY OF ZULULAND.

NATAL became a British possession at a very unfortunate time for the good of the country. Sentiment in England was then running so strong in favour of black people, that this beautiful and fertile country, which might have been made the home of many thousands of industrious European families, was given away to any Bantu who chose to enter it.

There are, of course, different ways of looking at this matter. The Bantu themselves, who regard their mode of life as vastly preferable to ours, inasmuch as it is comparatively free of care and toil, certainly think their possession of Natal proper and desirable. The missionary looking for raw material to work with is naturally of the same opinion. But the man who believes that the strengthening of the European element would be a blessing to Africa itself, who is convinced that the native tribes of the continent can never become civilised except under European government and under the guidance and control of a strong body of European settlers, must look upon the alienation of the soil of Natal to the Bantu as a very great mistake.

As soon as Great Britain was dominant there, all who were in fear of Panda made their way into the country, where they were sure of being protected and of being allowed to live as they chose. Their birthplace and that of their fathers might be far away, but they were all termed natives by the government, and as soon as arrangements could be made tracts of land were assigned to them to live upon. Missionaries settled among them, and in course of time a few became converts to Christianity and made some advance towards civilisation. But the great majority remain what their forefathers were, for it cannot be said that their use of a few articles of European manufacture is an indication of any real change.

There are no people in the world more prolific than the Bantu of South Africa, and though their death rate in towns partly occupied by Europeans is high, in their own kraals where they live after the custom of their ancestors it is low. The consequence is an amazingly rapid increase of population, wherever the old checks of war and punishment for dealing in witchcraft are removed. At the present day there are no fewer than half a million of these people within the borders of Natal. They are permitted to live according to their own laws and customs, but they pay a small hut-tax, and the government exercises general control over them.

Owing to their presence in such numbers the country has failed to attract European settlers, and only one large body of white immigrants has ever entered it since the British conquest. Between 1848 and 1851 some four or five thousand English people arrived, to whom small plots of ground were given; but many of them afterwards removed to Australia, and few remained as cultivators of the soil. White people from abroad settle in the country every year, but never in large numbers. At the present day they are not more than forty-three thousand all told, that is, for every twelve African blacks there is only one white person.

Although the disparity in number is so great, the Bantu have not often disturbed the peace of the country, and only on two or three occasions has it been necessary to use military force against defiant chiefs. They have as yet ample space for living comfortably in their own way, and taxation is so light that they do not feel it as a burden. But this condition of things cannot be permanent, for they are multiplying so rapidly that there must some day be a struggle for more room. What form it may take cannot, of course, be foreseen.

Only once since the British occupation of the country has there been a serious disturbance within its borders. In 1848 a section of the Hlubi tribe fled from Zululand, and had a location assigned to it at the sources of the Bushman's river, under the Drakensberg. The Hlubi had once been the largest tribe in South-Eastern Africa, but in Tshaka's wars most of its members were killed, and those who survived were dispersed far and wide. "There was a white mark from the Tugela to Thaba Ntshu, and that mark was our bones," said once an old Hlubi to the writer of this volume, in recounting his personal adventures. He might have added that there was a similar line from the Tugela to the Kei. Along both these routes a few fugitives were scattered, and these have multiplied so greatly that if their descendants could all be collected together to-day the Hlubi would again stand out as the largest tribe of the country.

The great chiefs had perished in Tshaka's wars, and the one of highest rank that was left was Langalibalélé—in English "The Sun is burning"—the head of the clan that sought refuge in Natal. A stranger visiting his location in 1873 would have regarded him as a man of little importance, with a following of not more than ten thousand souls, all told; but those acquainted with his history knew that he was held in strong attachment by clans as far away as the Caledon in one direction and the Fish river in another.

There was a law in Natal, required for public safety, that no Bantu should have guns in their possession without being registered. In other parts of South Africa guns were obtainable, and Langalibalélé, setting the law at defiance, sent his young men away to earn money and purchase these weapons, which were brought by hundreds into his location without the necessary formalities being observed. When this became known, the chief was called upon to account for his guns, but he declined to do so. Message after message was sent, requiring him to appear at Maritzburg, but he made excuses, and never went. It was subsequently proved that he was in treasonable correspondence with other chiefs, and he must have felt himself strong enough to maintain his independence against the Europeans.

Peaceable means having failed to secure his obedience, an armed party was sent to enforce the demands of the government. Upon its approach Langalibalele abandoned his women and children, and with his cattle and most of his warriors fell back upon the mountains. In the Bushman's pass Major Durnford and a small party of volunteers overtook the rearguard of the rebels. The chief was in advance, and as the volunteers had orders not to fire first, they attempted to communicate with him. The induna in command pretended to send for the chief, and while waiting for him to arrive, the volunteers were being surrounded. At the same time threatening gestures and language, coupled with taunts, were used towards them. They fell back in a panic, when too late, and as they did so five of them were shot down.

The colonists at once awoke to a sense of their danger. They did not know how far the inclination to rebel extended, but of one thing they were certain: that nothing but the prompt punishment of the Hlubis would prevent all who were disaffected from rising in arms. Volunteers at once came forward. Everywhere in South Africa the Europeans were ready to help. The government of the Cape Colony took immediate measures to render effectual assistance, and the two republics expressed a willingness to give aid if needed. It was recognised that not only the peace of Natal, but of the entire country, was imperilled, for if time was given for all the sections of the Hlubi tribe to unite with the clan in rebellion a general war of races might ensue.

Langalibalélé and his warriors crossed the Drakensberg to Basutoland, in expectation of being joined there by one of Moshesh's sons; but such prompt measures were taken by the governments of the Cape Colony and Natal that the rebels were surrounded before they reached their destination, and the chief, with some of his principal men, who were in advance, were obliged to surrender to the Cape frontier armed and mounted police. The main body made an attempt to resist, but were dispersed after a sharp action, and all the cattle were captured.

During this time the excitement of the Natal colonists was naturally very high, and what, under ordinary circumstances, would be regarded as undue severity was exercised towards the people Langalibalélé had left behind, as well as to another clan that sympathised with him. But as soon as the danger was over, violent measures of every kind ceased.

Langalibalélé was tried by a special court, which sentenced him to banishment for life; and as Natal had no outlying dependency to send him to, an act was passed by the Cape parliament authorising his detention on Robben Island. His clan was broken up, and the ground it had occupied was resumed by the government.

This event attracted a great deal of attention in England, chiefly through the action of the Aborigines Protection Society and of Bishop Colenso, who represented the conduct of the white people and of the government as in the highest degree cruel and unjust towards the Hlubis. The Natal clergy, some sixty ministers and missionaries of different denominations, did their utmost to show that it was not so; but their opinions were in general unheeded, as were also the statements of the South African press. The imperial ministry reflected the sentiments of the people. Sir Benjamin Pine, the governor of Natal, was recalled. Compensation was ordered to be given from the colonial treasury to the clan that had suffered loss owing to its sympathy with the rebels; various Hlubis who had been condemned to terms of imprisonment had their sentences commuted; and it was required that Langalibaléle should be removed from Robben Island to a farm on the mainland, where he could have the society of his wives and be treated as a prisoner of state. These orders were of course promptly carried out. Langalibaléle remained an exile for twelve years, during which time he was provided with every possible comfort. He was then permitted to return to Natal, and died there shortly afterwards.

The belt of land along the coast north of the Umzimkulu has a tropical vegetation, though it is perfectly healthy for Europeans. It seemed therefore to present a favourable field for the production of coffee, sugar, ginger, arrowroot, cotton, and tea, and no long time elapsed before experiments began to be made. Not a plant among them all but throve wonderfully well, so that it was hoped and expected that Natal would shortly become one of the most valuable dependencies of Great Britain. Here was a favourable soil and a favourable climate, and here, thought people at a distance, in the teeming Bantu locations was a great reservoir of labour that could be utilised for the good of both employers and employed. But the Bantu declined to be utilised in this way. Some of them were willing to work for a while when the whim seized them and they had a particular object in view, but they could never be depended upon, and were prone to leave service just when they were most needed.

The planters then turned to India for a supply of labour. Coolies were engaged there, and were brought over under contracts for a term of years. By their assistance the soil was made to bring forth tropical products in considerable quantities, but eventually some were destroyed by diseases and others were found not to pay. Sugar has succeeded best. After providing for home consumption, in 1892 sugar was exported to the value of £119,461, tea to the value of £2,374, coffee to the value of £444, and arrowroot to the value of £228.

It was supposed that the coolies would return to India when their contracts expired, as they were entitled to free passages back; but they had found a goodly land, and many of them had no mind to leave it. Some of their countrymen of the trading class were next attracted by the accounts spread by those who returned, and soon quite a little stream of Indian immigrants set in. As they can live upon the merest trifle, European competitors were rapidly driven out, and retail dealing, with all kinds of light labour, fell into their hands. They contribute nothing

PORT NATAL AND DURBAN IN 1860.
(*From a Sketch by Rev. L. Grout.*)

towards the military strength of the country and very little towards its revenue. They are now equal in number to the white people, so that Natal cannot be regarded as an English colony in the same sense as Canada or Australia. It is more like a miniature India, a country occupied chiefly by alien races, but with a government and upper caste of Europeans.

The circumstances under which they lived determined the mode of life of the white people of Natal. They became for the most part traders and forwarders of goods to the interior republics. There are planters and farmers among them, but more than half of the whole number reside in the two towns, Maritzburg and Durban, and a large proportion of the remainder occupy villages along the trade routes. Their spirit and sentiments are largely affected by this circumstance. It has been observed as something strange that an Englishman long resident on a farm in the Cape Colony feels himself perfectly at home if he visits the Orange Free State, yet is like an alien in Natal. But the cause is easily explained: in the one case he is among people of familiar instincts, in the other he is not.

Maritzburg and Durban have thriven greatly of late years. Durban is the gateway through which passes the commerce not only of the colony itself and of Zululand, but of part of the Orange Free State and the South African Republic. Extensive works have been constructed to improve the entrance to the inner harbour, and large ships can now cross the bar and lie beside a wharf as safely as in a dock. Numerous handsome buildings, chief among which is the grandest municipal hall in South Africa, embellish this town.

From Durban a railway has been constructed to Charlestown, on the border of the South African Republic. It passes through Maritzburg, and also through the villages of Estcourt, Ladysmith, and Newcastle farther inland. From Ladysmith a branch line runs by way of Van Reenen's pass in the Drakensberg to Harrismith in the Orange Free State, and taps the trade of the eastern part of the republic. It goes up the Drakensberg in a series of zigzag sections, but in places the gradients are very heavy, as they are likewise on the Charlestown line. It is in contemplation to continue the railway from Harrismith until it meets the great northeastern line through the Cape Colony and the Orange Free State, which will give unbroken communication between Capetown and Durban. The Charlestown line will probably be continued at no distant date to the gold fields in the South African Republic. Close to the coast there is a branch line northward to the village of Verulam, and one southward to Isipingo. These lines are in all 399 miles in length.

The main branch of this system of railways has the great advantage of passing through an extensive field of coal of fair quality, from which fuel can be obtained at a cheap rate. It is on the plateau at the foot of the Drakensberg, so that it is centrally situated, and the coal, which is easily worked, is conveyed to the coast along a descending gradient. It is not the least important of the natural riches of Natal. Besides furnishing fuel for the railways and the towns, in 1892 nearly sixty thousand pounds' worth was exported.

The legislature of the colony has undergone many changes. For some years there was a council entirely of nominees, but in 1856 a charter was granted by the queen, when it became chiefly elective. From that date until 1893 the proportion of elective to nominee members was frequently altered, and then responsible government was introduced. There are now two chambers: a legislative council of eleven nominee members, holding their seats for ten years, and a legislative assembly of thirty-seven elected members, holding their seats for four years.

The franchise differs in principle from that of the Cape Colony, or representative government of any kind would be an impossibility. Male British subjects, not being Bantu, who own land worth £50, or who pay £10 a year for rent, or who have lived three years in the country and are in receipt of salaries of £96 a year, are entitled to vote. Bantu are excluded, except those who possess the above qualifications, and in addition have been by their own desire for seven years exempted from tribal and subject to colonial law. This provision secures equal rights with Europeans for the few who have embraced Christianity and live in a civilised manner, while it withholds from the great barbarous mass a privilege of which they are incapable of making proper use.

The public debt of Natal is rather over seven million pounds sterling, apparently a very large sum for a colony of only forty-three thousand Europeans to owe, as it means an indebtedness of £163 for each individual. But the Indians should count for something in apportioning the public debt, though it would be difficult to say in what ratio they should be classified with Europeans. The great mass of Bantu, if reckoned at all, must appear on the other side of the ledger. The railways are public property, and a considerable portion of the debt was incurred for the purpose of constructing them.

The history of Zululand is so closely connected with that of Natal that it can conveniently be included in the same chapter. Panda, who became independent of foreign control in 1843, was much less intelligent than either of his predecessors, Tshaka or Dingan. Soon after his accession to power he grew so stout as to be unwieldy, and never afterwards displayed activity of any kind, bodily or mental. Two of his sons, however, Umbulazi and Cetywayo by name, grew up to be men of superior ability. Though the discipline of the army was greatly relaxed, the military system introduced by Tshaka was still kept up, and the regiments were divided in their attachment to the young chiefs. "Two young bulls cannot live together in the same kraal," said Panda; "one must drive the other out or be gored." The brothers were of the same opinion. In December 1856 a battle was fought between their adherents on the northern bank of the Tugela, which resulted in complete victory for Cetywayo. His brother must have been killed, though the body was not found, for he was never seen again. Then a dreadful massacre of the defeated chief's adherents took place, when not only the men, but the women and children related to them, were put to death. About one-fourth of the Zulus perished.

From that day Cetywayo was the real ruler of the tribe, though his father lived until 1872. The young chief was a man of prepossessing appearance, dignified in manner, and gifted with mental power in a high degree. But he was as pitiless as a piece of steel, and human life under his government was sacrificed with as little compunction as the life of oxen and cows. Much as one could wish it otherwise, observation shows that this is the kind of rule which brings out what is best in the Bantu character as well as what is worst, and under Cetywayo the Zulus were recognised by every one as the most intelligent, the most active, and the most fearless of all the blacks in South Africa. They were the most handsome too, for constant exercise in arms and in military drill greatly improved their appearance. Discipline had become relaxed during the fifteen years following Panda's accession, but by Cetywayo it was restored to the same condition as under Tshaka.

As time went on the Zulus became more and more a menace to their neighbours. Hemmed in between the South African Republic, Natal, and the sea, if they used their arms at all, it could only be against a civilised power.

In 1877 Sir Bartle Frere became governor of the Cape Colony and high commissioner for South Africa. No man had a kinder heart or a more earnest desire to promote the welfare of the people of the country, white and black, the Zulus as well as British subjects.

But war with Cetywayo had become a necessity, and he could not avoid it without betraying his trust. It was his duty to protect the queen's subjects, and there was no question that many of them were in imminent peril, and must so remain until the Zulu military system came to an end. Unfortunately he did not know how strong the Zulu army really was, and none of those upon whom he depended for information were able to tell him. Cetywayo gave him more than one provocation. A powerful Zulu force paraded along the British border, and the chief spoke of it as a mere hunting party. English officials who were sent into Zululand as envoys were treated by the indunas in a contemptuous manner. Zulu subjects crossed the boundary, seized two women on Natal soil and carried them away to death, and Cetywayo, when called upon for redress, treated the matter as of trifling importance. In several serious disturbances by Bantu tribes in distant parts of South Africa the agency of the Zulu chief was clearly traced, and in many other respects he showed himself an enemy to the civilised governments of the country.

In December 1878 Sir Bartle Frere, having collected a military force in Natal which every one believed to be strong enough for the purpose, sent an ultimatum to Cetywayo, in which he demanded redress for the injuries sustained, and called upon the chief to disband his army. As no notice was taken of the message, on the 10th of January, 1879, an English army entered Zululand in three divisions, consisting partly of British soldiers, partly of colonists, and partly of blacks.

Ten days after crossing the Buffalo the central column formed a camp at the foot of the hill Isandlwana—that is The Little Hand—within sight of the Natal border. The country was so rough that it needed all that time to construct a road along which provisions could be conveyed. On the following morning part of the column, with Lord Chelmsford, the commander-in-chief, left the camp and moved away to attack a kraal several miles distant. Some Dutch farmers had advised the English officers to take precautions against surprise, and had told them of the encounters with Dingan, but their warnings were disregarded. Nothing was done for protection at Isandlwana, though there were waggons enough to form a lager. Not a trench was dug nor a spadeful of earth thrown up in a bank. No one there even dreamed of danger until a little before noon on the 22nd of January 1879, when the horns of a Zulu army about twenty thousand strong were closing around the camp.

The fight for life was stubborn, but the odds on the enemy's side were too great, and all was soon over. A few, principally mounted irregulars, managed to make their way out of the circle of Zulu spears before it was quite closed, but the ground was full of boulders and dry beds of occasional torrents, so that many of these even were overtaken and killed. With them were Lieutenants Melvill and Coghill, who were trying to save the colours of the first battalion of the 24th regiment, and who reached the Natal bank of the Buffalo before they were struck down. The colours were found in the river some days afterwards.

At Isandlwana nearly seven hundred British soldiers and over one hundred and thirty colonists perished, for the Zulus gave no quarter. The victors lost about three thousand men.

Information of the terrible disaster reached Lord Chelmsford in the afternoon. An officer had ridden towards the camp, and had seen it in possession of the Zulus. The party with the general, though weary from marching in the hot sun, at once commenced to retreat, for all its stores of every kind were lost. Isandlwana was reached shortly after nightfall, and there, among the corpses of their slain comrades, officers and men, alike worn out with anxiety and fatigue, lay down and tried to rest. The Zulus, after plundering the camp, had retired. At early dawn the retreating band resumed its march, and reached Natal without being molested.

At Rorke's Drift, where the column had crossed the Buffalo, there was a small depôt of provisions and a hospital, and there a hundred and thirty soldiers, under Lieutenants Bromhead and Chard, had been left to keep open communication with Natal. About five o'clock in the afternoon of the day of Isandlwana this post was attacked by between three and four thousand of the very best of the Zulu soldiers, commanded by Dabulamanzi, a brother of Cetywayo. Fortunately the garrison had received warning in time to enable them to make a lager of sacks of maize and boxes of biscuits, behind which they maintained such a gallant defence until four o'clock in the morning of the 23rd that Dabulamanzi then thought it prudent to retire. Over three hundred of his men were lying dead around the lager. Of the garrison seventeen were dead and ten were wounded. This splendid defence saved Natal from invasion, for if the post had fallen the colony would have been open to the Zulus.

The other columns fared better than the one whose fate has been told. Colonel Pearson, with about two thousand European combatants and the same number of blacks, crossed the Tugela near the sea, and marched towards Ulundi, the Zulu capital, where the whole of the invading forces intended to unite. At Inyesane he was attacked by a Zulu army between four and five thousand strong, but beat it back with heavy loss, and on the 23rd of January reached the Norwegian mission station Etshowe. Here he learned of the disaster at Isandlwana, so he sent his cavalry and blacks back to Natal, and fortified the station, where he remained until reinforcements arrived from England.

The third column consisted of about seventeen hundred British soldiers, fifty farmers under Commandant Pieter Uys, and three or four hundred blacks. It was commanded by Colonel Evelyn Wood. This column was not attacked on its march, and after Isandlwana fortified a post at Kambula, where it remained. Colonel Wood managed to inflict much damage upon the Zulus in his neighbourhood by frequent sallies, but on one occasion, at a mountain named Hlobane, his patrol was nearly surrounded, and ninety-six of the party were killed. Among them were Commandant Uys, Colonel Weatherley, and the son of the latter, a mere youth, who died at his father's side just as Uys's brother had died by his father's side forty-one years before. On the day after this event the lager at Kambula was attacked by a great Zulu army, which suffered tremendous loss before it retired discomfited.

In the beginning of April Lord Chelmsford, with a strong force of soldiers and sailors, marched from Natal to the relief of Colonel Pearson at Etshowe. On the way he was attacked at Ginginhlovu, but beat back his assailants, and succeeded in reaching the station.

As soon as intelligence of the disaster at Isandlwana reached England strong reinforcements were sent out, and before June some nine thousand soldiers, cavalry and infantry, with a vast quantity of munitions of war and provisions, reached Natal. With them came the young prince imperial of France, who was fated to lose his life a few weeks later in a lonely dell in Zululand. He went out from a camp with a small reconnoitring party, which was surprised by a band of Zulus while it was resting, and the prince, being unable to mount his horse, was stabbed to death, his companions having abandoned him and ridden away.

Despatches now reached South Africa announcing that Sir Garnet Wolseley had been appointed commander-in-chief of the forces, high commissioner for South-Eastern Africa, and administrator of the territories bordering on the seat of war. Lord Chelmsford was at the time just completing his arrangements for an advance upon Ulundi. It seemed as if he was to be deprived of the satisfaction of bringing the war to an end, and, as actually happened, Sir Garnet Wolseley arrived before the 4th of July, when Ulundi was reached and the final battle was fought; but Lord Chelmsford was still in command of the column.

It is estimated that about ten thousand Zulu soldiers had been killed before the end of June. Some twenty thousand more had lost heart, as they had not succeeded in taking a single lager during the war, and they had consequently deserted and dispersed. With from fifteen to twenty thousand who were true to him still, Cetywayo awaited the British army at Ulundi. Lord Chelmsford formed his troops in a hollow square, upon which the Zulus dashed themselves in vain. Beaten back by a terrible storm of bullets, and having no hope of breaking the British square by even the heaviest sacrifice, they turned to retire, when the cavalry was let loose upon them. They dispersed, never again to rally, and Cetywayo was a fugitive seeking only concealment. After Ulundi and the military kraals near it were burned, the army fell back upon its base of supplies, and Lord Chelmsford resigned his command.

The war was over, the colonial volunteers were allowed to return home, and part of the large regular force in the field was sent to England, though until Cetywayo's person could be secured it was not considered advisable to remove the whole of the troops from the country. The people—all honour to them for it—were so loyal to their chief that for many weeks not one could be found to betray him, though thousands must have been acquainted with his hiding places. At length, however, a man, who was threatened with death if he did not divulge the secret, pointed out a secluded kraal on the border of a forest, and Cetywayo became a prisoner.

No captive ever conducted himself more decorously than the fallen chief of the Zulus. He was sent a prisoner to Capetown, and, after a short confinement in the castle, had a small farm close to the one occupied by Langalibalélé assigned to him as a residence. There he was attended by servants of his own choice, and was well cared for in every respect.

Zululand was divided by Sir Garnet Wolseley into thirteen districts, each of which was placed under the government of a chief independent of all the others, and nominally guided by the advice of a single British resident. But this plan of settlement did not answer at all, and in 1883 Cetywayo was allowed to return. In the meantime he had visited England, where he was very well received, and by his sensible observations and dignified deportment had acquired the favourable opinion of every one with whom he came in contact. It was thought that after the experience he had gone through he might without imprudence be allowed to return to his own country, upon making a promise to observe conditions that would prevent his power from becoming dangerous again.

Some of the people welcomed him back, but others adhered to a rival chief named Sibepu, who had found means to secure a large following. War at once broke out between them, and when Cetywayo died in the following year, it continued between his son Dinizulu and Sibepu. Dinizulu secured the aid of a body of farmers, in return for which he ceded to them

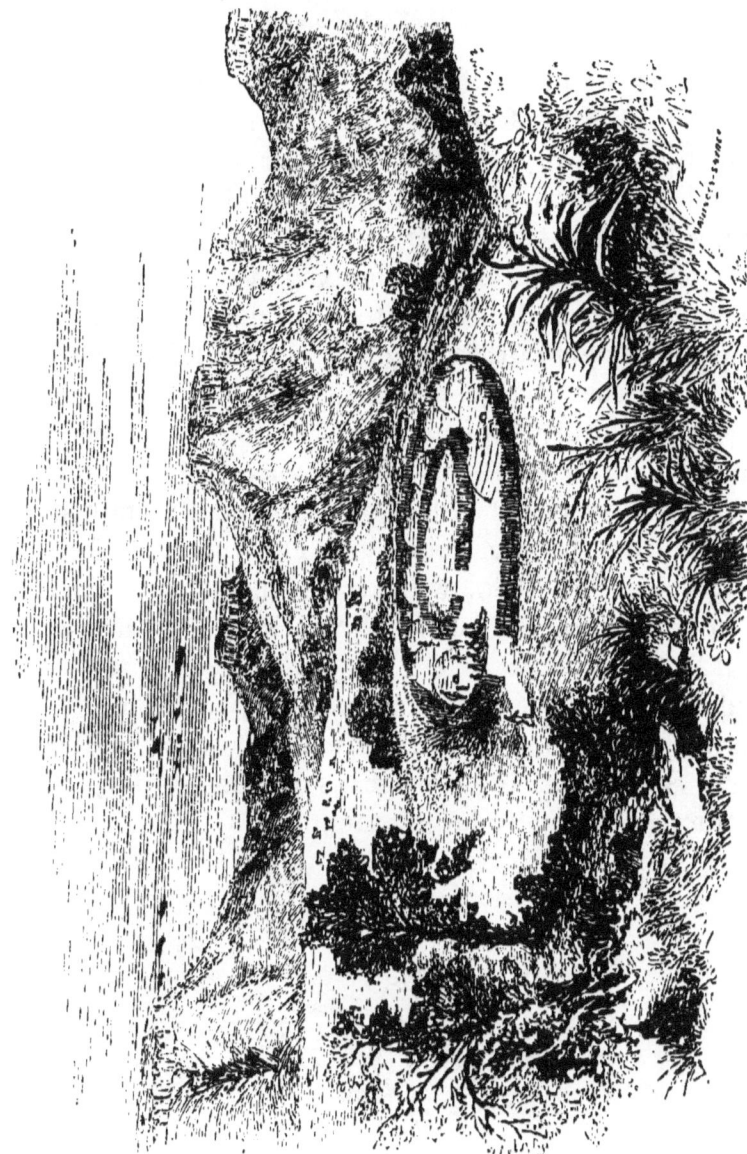

SCENE IN ZULULAND.
(From a Sketch by Rev. L. Grout.)

a large tract of land, which was afterwards united to the South African Republic, and is now known as the district of Vryheid. With their assistance he subdued his rival, but confusion and strife still continued, so that in 1887 what remained of the country was of necessity annexed to the British Empire. It was divided into six districts, and a European magistrate, supported by soldiers and police, now has charge of each.

Not unnaturally Dinizulu objected to this arrangement, and he caused such disturbances against the English authority that order could not be maintained while he was in the country. He was therefore arrested, and in 1889, with two other chiefs, was sent to reside on the island of St. Helena, where he is still living.

Zululand has not been annexed to Natal, but the governor of the one country is also governor of the other. Settlement by Europeans in the territory is not practicable to any large extent.

XXV.

THE ORANGE FREE STATE AND BASUTOLAND.

THE history of the world may be searched in vain for an instance of a community in a more unenviable position than the burghers of the territory between the Orange and Vaal rivers when they were abandoned by Great Britain. They were scattered thinly over a great plain, and beside them in a mountain land like a strong fortress was a hostile tribe armed to the teeth, under the ablest chief in South Africa, exulting in its recent victory over a British army, and vastly exceeding them in number of combatants. To the policy of forming a powerful Basuto state they had been resolutely opposed, yet now they were made to bear the consequences of its creation. Their country was without roads or bridges, almost without churches and schools, so that these were to be provided as well as the ordinary machinery of government, while they received no share of the customs duties on their trade levied in the ports of Natal and the Cape Colony. That they surmounted these difficulties and made their state one of the most flourishing in South Africa is something that they are justly proud of.'

The form of government that they adopted was republican. There is a president, who is the principal executive officer, and who is elected by the burghers for a term of five years. He must carry out the resolutions of the volksraad, and has no veto upon its proceedings. He is assisted by an executive council. The volksraad is the supreme authority, and consists at present of fifty-six members, one for each fieldcornetcy and one for each seat of magistracy. They are elected for four years. The president and the state secretary have the right of debate, but not of voting, in the volksraad. All European males of full age born in the State are electors, and also all European immigrant males of full age who have become burghers and are in possession of unmortgaged landed property to the value of £150, or are lessees of landed property at a yearly rental of £36, or are in receipt of a fixed yearly income of £200, or have been resident in the State for three years and possess movable property worth £300. Men of coloured blood who live in all respects as Europeans may have the privilege to vote accorded to them by special resolution of the volksraad, and some of very dark tint living in the same way go to the polls unquestioned. But the principle is kept clearly in view that the government is to represent the civilised inhabitants of the country, and that those who are uncivilised can have no voice in its formation, though they are to be protected equally with electors and have the same right in courts of justice.

The fundamental law of the State, like that of all other European communities in South Africa, is the

Roman as modified by the legislature of Holland before 1652. The official language is Dutch, and the courts of law are after the Dutch pattern, though considerably modified. In each district there is a landdrost, with a body of heemraden to assist in settling important cases, and over all is a supreme court of judges, who must previously have been qualified barristers.

When the British flag was withdrawn the community was split into factions, but the common danger forced them to unite in choosing a president acceptable to Moshesh. Mr. Josias Hoffman, a farmer who was intimately acquainted with the great chief and on excellent terms with him, was therefore elected. During his short tenure of office, however, the burghers felt that concession to the Basuto power was carried further than was consistent with the dignity of an independent state, and early in 1855 the volksraad took advantage of his having made a present of a keg of gunpowder to Moshesh without reporting the circumstance and clamoured so loudly against him that he was compelled to resign.

Mr. Jacobus Nicolaas Boshof, a man of education, of high moral character, and of considerable ability, was then elected president. Having had a training in official work in the civil service of the Cape Colony, he was able to put the different departments of the government in good order. But from the day of his assuming duty he was so incessantly harassed by the all-important question with Moshesh that he could do little or nothing else for the general welfare of the country.

Moshesh's object, from a Bantu point of view, was so praiseworthy that his followers were ready to do everything in their power to promote it. He wished to recover for his tribe the whole of the territory south of the Vaal and west of the Drakensberg that had been in occupation of black people before the wars of Tshaka. The remnants of the tribes that in olden times had occupied the ground were now his followers, and he wanted the soil that once was theirs. Sir George Napier had given him by treaty a large portion of it, and that much, at any rate, he was determined to have.

The object of the Free State government and burghers was to retain the boundary fixed by Sir Harry Smith, which, in their opinion, was a fair one. When white people moved into the territory it was a vast waste, and if they had not come Moshesh could never have had a quarter of the land that was now in his possession. Certainly Bantu had at some former period occupied ground nearly as far west as Bloemfontein, but they had irrecoverably lost it during the Zulu wars. To admit Moshesh's claim would be to consent to the annihilation of the State, and the burghers had no mind for that. Here, in brief, was the cause of the long and desperate struggle between the Orange Free State and the Basuto tribe.

For several years Moshesh directed his efforts towards the south, leaving the farmers on his other borders undisturbed. In that direction the herds of the white people were plundered mercilessly by his followers, and as a rule he would give no redress. Sir George Grey once tried to arrange matters amicably between the two parties, and through his agency an agreement of peace and friendship was signed; but Moshesh did not long observe it. At length actual possession of occupied farms was taken by parties of armed Basuto, and hostilities could be staved off no longer.

In March 1858 the burghers of all parts of the State were called out, and entered Basutoland in two divisions, the object being to try to confine the war to the enemy's country. But Moshesh was much too skilful a strategist for their commanders to cope with. He kept them closely occupied until after some severe fighting they arrived in front of Thaba Bosigo, where they learned that swarms of his light horsemen were ravaging their farms. Before them was a mountain stronghold which could not be taken by storm, and they had not the means of laying siege to it. Under these circumstances the burghers dispersed, and made the best of their way to the localities where they had left their families.

President Boshof had already applied to the South African Republic for aid, but as the burghers of the northern state were holding out for special terms of union, and there was no time to be lost, he requested the mediation of Sir George Grey. Moshesh consented to an armistice, and promised to abide by the decision of the governor. He was wise enough to recognise that if he pushed his advantage too far he would have to deal with the northern republic as well as the southern, and he felt certain that the governor would give him, as the conqueror, a good strip of territory.

Sir George Grey accepted the office of mediator. He took from Moshesh a far outlying mission station which was a kind of semi-independent fief of the Basuto chieftainship, but gave him a large extent of territory south of Sir Harry Smith's line. Thus the first struggle with the Basuto ended in very serious loss to the Orange Free State.

Shortly after this Mr. Boshof resigned, and was succeeded as president by Mr. Marthinus Wessel Pretorius, son of the famous commandant-general. He represented a strong party that desired the union of the two republics, but as there were many conflicting interests in the way, besides the declaration of the high commissioner that union would dissolve the conventions with Great Britain, every attempt at amalgamation failed.

During these years the Free State was continually growing stronger. The Griqua captain Adam Kok sold his territorial rights to the republic, his people sold their ground to farmers from the Cape Colony, and then the whole clan moved away to a new country below the Drakensberg and south of Natal, given to them by Sir George Grey. With the exception of a little tract of almost unoccupied land belong to the Griqua captain Nicholas Waterboer between the Modder and Orange rivers and a location belonging to the Barolong chief Moroko, the whole territory between the Vaal and the Orange up to the Basuto border was now in possession of white people, and sheep farming and cattle rearing could be carried on in a large portion of it with greater profit than in any other part of South Africa.

Along the Basuto border, however, there was a continual state of unrest. Moshesh had conquered the clans on the northern bank of the Caledon, and had annexed their ground. The white people maintained that the boundary should remain as before, but the chief said contemptuously that he had never

PORTRAIT OF PRESIDENT BRAND.

agreed to it, and he showed clearly that he would not respect it. President Pretorius did all that was possible to induce him to act fairly in the matter, but in vain. His people pressed across the line, settled on farms, and plundered the country for miles in front of them.

In 1865 Advocate Jan Hendrik Brand was elected

president. Of him it may be said that South Africa knows no worthier name, for no one has ever contributed more to the welfare of the people than he. Sir Philip Wodehouse had succeeded Sir George Grey as governor of the Cape Colony and her Majesty's high commissioner for the regions beyond. President Brand requested him to mark off the northern boundary between the Free State and Basutoland, and the volksraad empowered him to alter Sir Harry Smith's line if he saw fit to do so, as they were willing to lose some ground if only they could secure peace. Sir Philip was no lover of republics, and he never concealed his dislike of the South African farmers; but in a matter of this kind he could be depended upon to act with the strictest justice. Moshesh very reluctantly agreed to abide by his decision. He visited the country, carefully inspected it, heard the arguments on both sides, and after much consideration confirmed Sir Harry Smith's line. The president then called upon Moshesh to withdraw his followers from the farms they had taken possession of, and upon the chief's failure to do so, the burghers were called out to drive them back by force, when open war began.

The laying waste of a large extent of territory in the Free State by Basuto horsemen could not be prevented, and a number of people were massacred in a shocking manner; but, on the other hand, the burgher forces were victorious in several engagements and took some mountain strongholds by storm. Thaba Bosigo, however, resisted every attack upon it. After ten months' fighting Moshesh asked for peace, and offered to cede a considerable part of his country, but a year later he declared that he had only done so in order to secure a harvest. The president and the burghers were deceived, and in April 1866 terms were agreed to and a treaty of peace was signed.

His gardens were planted, and when his harvests were gathered Moshesh threw off the mask. He declined to fulfil the terms of the treaty, and in July 1867, President Brand was obliged to call the burghers again to arms to compel him to observe his engagements. Both sides recognised that the struggle must now be a final one, and each put forth its utmost strength. But Moshesh no longer possessed the mental vigour of his earlier years, and in his tribe there was no one who could take his place as a strategist. His sons were mere ordinary barbarians. Soon fragments of the tribe began to drop off and move over the Drakensberg. Then one after another all the Basuto strongholds fell, except Thaba Bosigo, Moshesh's own mountain, which defied attack. The granaries were destroyed, and the bulk of the tribe, driven into the mountains, was suffering severely from hunger and disease.

The Free State was in a fair way of being able very shortly to dictate its own terms when Sir Philip Wodehouse interfered. At Moshesh's request he proclaimed the Basuto tribe British subjects, and sent an armed force to protect them. British interests, he declared, would not permit of their being dispersed over the country as fugitives. Naturally the people of the Free State regarded this action as unfriendly and unfair, and the volksraad sent deputies to England to protest against it; but the imperial authorities left the matter entirely in the governor's hands. The president then tried to secure as good terms as possible, and in February 1869 an agreement was concluded by which the Free State obtained all the land north and west of the Caledon and south of a line almost identical with that of Sir Harry Smith between the Caledon and the Orange.

The republic sorely needed rest when the struggle with the Basuto was over, though it was less exhausted than its opponent. Paper money had been issued to a large amount, and the notes were greatly depreciated in value. Farming operations had been neglected, and individuals as well as the state had been compelled to incur heavy debts. There was hardly a homestead in the land which did not bear evidence that a crisis of no ordinary nature had been experienced. The loss of life too had been heavy in proportion to the population. But the hearts of the people beat high, and government and burghers alike set to work resolutely to repair their losses.

A little before this date a discovery was made that created a perfect revolution in South African life. One day in 1867 a child on a farm in the north of the Cape Colony was observed to be playing with a remarkably brilliant pebble, which a trader, to whom it was shown as a curiosity, suspected to be a gem of value. It was sent for examination to a qualified person in Grahamstown, who reported that it was a diamond of twenty-one carats weight, and that its value was £500. Search was immediately commenced in the neighbourhood by several persons in odd hours, and soon another, though much smaller, was found. Then a third was picked up on the bank of the Vaal river, and attention was directed to that locality.

During 1868 several were found, though as yet no one was applying himself solely to looking for them. In March 1869 the Star of South Africa was obtained from a Korana Hottentot, who had been in possession of it for a long time without the least idea of its value except as a powerful charm. It was a magnificent brilliant of eighty-three carats weight when uncut, and was readily sold for £11,000. From all parts of South Africa men now began to make their way to the banks of the lower Vaal to search for diamonds, and trains of waggons conveying provisions and goods were to be seen on every highway to the interior. Some of the diggers were fortunate in amassing wealth, but this was by no means the case with all. Diamond digging, in fact, was like a great lottery, with a few prizes and many blanks. But it had a powerful attraction, and shortly many hundreds of adventurers from Europe and America were also engaged in it.

The quiet, simple, homely life of the South African farm and village in olden times—rarely disturbed except by wars with Bantu tribes—had passed away for ever, and a bustling, struggling, restless mode of existence was rapidly taking its place. The wealth of the country was enormously increased, for diamonds soon attained a high place in the exports; but it may be questioned if the people are on the whole as happy as they were before.

The southern bank of the lower Vaal was Free State territory, but the ownership of the northern bank was disputed. Before the discovery of diamonds it was regarded as of so little value that no actual government existed there, though the South African Republic, the Orange Free State, the Batlapin tribe, and the Griqua captain, Nicholas Waterboer, all claimed the ground. The consequence was that each mining camp on that side of the stream formed a kind of government for itself, and a great deal of confusion and lawlessness was the result.

After a while much richer diamond mines than those along the Vaal were discovered on some farms to the southward, and most of the diggers removed to them. The public offices of the district in which they were situated were at a considerable distance, but as soon as arrangements could be made by the government, a resident landdrost was appointed, a post-office was established, and some policemen were engaged.

In the minds of people at a distance the various camps were confused with each other, and all were supposed to be in the lawless condition of those north of the Vaal. Most of the diggers were British subjects, so that her Majesty's high commissioner considered it his duty to interfere in the interests of order. At that time one of the shrewdest men in South Africa was agent for the Griqua captain, Nicholas Waterboer, and on behalf of his client had laid claim to a large part of the Orange Free State, including the locality in which the diamond mines were situated. No pretension could be more shadowy, but when Mr. Arnot, on behalf of Waterboer, offered the territory to the British government, it came to be regarded, on one side at least, as having some real foundation.

The high commissioner proposed arbitration, which President Brand declined. The territory which Mr. Arnot claimed south of the Vaal, he said, had been part of the Free State ever since the convention of 1854. Before that date it had been part of the Orange River Sovereignty, and some of the farms in it were held under British titles issued at that time. Nicholas Waterboer and his people lived far away, and, as well as could be ascertained, had never occupied ground there. Under these circumstances he would not admit that there could be any question of ownership. The right of the state to land beyond the Vaal, however, he was willing to submit to arbitration, as it had been acquired by purchase, and the seller's title might be open to doubt.

While the high commissioner and the president were corresponding on this subject, Mr. Marthinus Wessel Pretorius, who was then president of the South African Republic, agreed to submit some disputes between that country and the Barolong, Batlapin, and Griquas, to arbitration, in consequence of which a court was appointed, with Mr. Keate, governor of Natal, as final umpire, and proceedings were opened at the little village of Bloemhof, on the northern bank of the Vaal. The Free State government was not represented in the court.

The interests involved were greater than were recognised at the time. It was supposed that the sovereignty of some of the diamond mines was the great question at issue; now it is seen that access by Great Britain to the distant interior was also involved. On one side the proceedings were a perfect farce. President Pretorius and his attorney did nothing whatever to work up their case; they did not attempt to meet evidence that might have been disproved with the greatest ease; they even put in a spurious document given to them by one of their opponents purposely to befool them. On the other side was Mr. Arnot, who knew exactly what to withhold as well as what to bring forward. The result was that Mr. Keate, acting solely on the evidence before him, gave judgment against the South African Republic, and in defining the territories of the disputants included within Nicholas Waterboer's boundary the part of the Free State which that captain claimed.

As soon as the Keate award was issued—October, 1871—Sir Henry Barkly, who was then high commissioner, proclaimed Waterboer's country a British dependency, with boundaries enclosing the mines along the Vaal, and at Dutoitspan, De Beer's, and Kimberley. An armed force was sent to take possession of it, and the Free State officials withdrew under protest. The territory, which was named Griqualand West, then became a crown colony. It remained in that condition until 1880, when it was annexed to the Cape Colony, of which it now forms part.

Some time after Griqualand West came under the

British flag, a special court was created to decide upon conflicting claims to ground. For many weeks evidence was taken, and the most minute research was made into the history of the land and its people. When at length judgment was given, all claims within the diamond mining area that rested on grants by Waterboer were thrown out, because that captain never had any rights there.

President Brand then went to England and laid his case before the Imperial authorities. In brief it was this—that Great Britain had taken the land from the Free State under pretence that it belonged to Waterboer, and that a British court, after careful examination, had since decided that Waterboer had no right to it. The reply which he received was to the effect that it was a necessity for the paramount power in South Africa to be in possession of the diamond mines, but he would receive £90,000 from Griqualand West as a solatium.

The president wisely accepted the offer, and with the money reduced the public debt of the state. The sore feeling entertained by the burghers passed away, and they began to reflect that perhaps after all it was better for them to be relieved of the responsibility of maintaining order among the diggers. A diamond mine at Jagersfontein had been left to them, and it was turning out much richer than had once been anticipated. Then they had all the advantages which the other mines offered as markets for farm produce, so that they might have a good deal of gain with no risk.

Since this settlement the Free State has enjoyed

constant peace, and no part of South Africa has made greater progress. Roads, bridges, and good public buildings have been constructed, and an excellent system of public schools is maintained by the government. The railway from Capetown to Pretoria, in the South African Republic, passes through the state, and there are lines to Port Elizabeth and East London, all of which were constructed by the government of the Cape Colony under a very liberal convention. From Harrismith there is a line to Durban, constructed by the government of Natal. The Free State is without a public debt. Its boundaries on every side are undisputed, and it has no semi-independent clans within its borders. The Barolong of Moroko, the last who were in that condition, came completely under the government after a feud in which the chief was killed by one of his brothers. The Cape Colony, the Orange Free State, and the smaller British dependencies in South Africa, except Natal, form a customs union.

President Brand was elected again and again until 1888, when he died in office. Mr. F. W. Reitz, previously chief justice, was then chosen to fill the vacant place. According to the census of 1890 the population consists of seventy-eight thousand Europeans and one hundred and thirty thousand coloured people. The industries of the state are almost entirely pastoral and agricultural, but there are valuable coal fields which are beginning to be worked, and there are diamond mines at Jagersfontein and Koffyfontein: the last-named, however, not being of great importance.

COMMON STYLE OF SOUTH AFRICAN FARMHOUSE.

When Basutoland was taken over as a British possession, an agent was appointed by the high commissioner, who, with a few magistrates and some police, guided rather than governed the tribe. Moshesh died soon afterwards, and his principal heir, Letsie by name, had none of the old chief's ability. Molapo and Masupha, two other sons, were at the head of considerable sections of the tribe. All were unwilling to part with any real authority over the people, and gave just sufficient obedience to the British officials to ensure protection, but carefully avoided conceding more.

In 1871 the territory was attached to the Cape Colony, which thus became responsible for the preservation of order within it. The system of administration continued as before. Bantu law was recognised, except in a few of its worst features, but it was intended gradually to assimilate it to the law of the colony. Sufficient hut-tax was easily collected to cover the cost of administration and to leave a small amount for public works, besides providing for liberal allowances to the chiefs.

In a short time the tribe recovered from its losses in property, and increased in number as only Bantu can in a period of peace. Europeans believed that the British officials were gaining control over the people, and that the power of the chiefs was waning; but it was soon to be proved how little foundation there was for such a belief. In 1877 a wave of disturbance began to pass along the Bantu tribes connected with the Cape Colony, and when it subsided the government resolved upon a general disarmament. As soon as the measure was applied to Basutoland, the people rose in rebellion. Some clans, indeed, professed to be loyal, but only because others with whom they were at feud were on the opposite side. The colony spent a vast amount of treasure in trying to reduce the rebels to submission, but failed in the attempt, and the end was that in 1884 Basutoland was transferred back to the imperial government.

The country since that date has been nominally under the direction of a British administrator, with magistrates to assist him; and these officers appear to have some moral influence, though the people obey only when it pleases them. Letsie died recently, and was succeeded by his son Lerothodi, who is now the actual ruler of the tribe.

Basutoland contains at present about two hundred and twenty-five thousand Bantu, and six hundred Europeans. The white people are officials, missionaries, or traders. No others are permitted to settle in the country.

XXVI.

THE SOUTH AFRICAN REPUBLIC.

THE vast tract of land north of the Vaal, that became the property of the emigrant farmers after the expulsion of Moselekatse, contained ground suitable for almost every variety of agricultural and pastoral industry, and, though the circumstances was then unknown, in mineral wealth it is not surpassed by any country in the world. It's eastern and northern valleys, well watered and of great fertility, had for a time a strong attraction for settlers, but experience proved them to be less healthy than the open highlands, and they were therefore partly abandoned. In some places the tsetse fly abounded, and this scourge of domestic cattle prevented settlement in its neighbourhood until the large game was exterminated, when it disappeared. The fever too, that was once so prevalent on the borders of forests and streams in the lowlands, in course of time became almost unknown in the same localities if the ground was cultivated and the rank grass burnt off before it began to decay.

The farmers were only fifteen or sixteen thousand

in number, all told, so they naturally selected what appeared to them the choicest spots, and no one considered it worth his while to settle on the great plains of the west. There was no such thing as union among them. An attempt was made to form a kind of common government, by the election of a single volksraad for legislative purposes, but with four executive heads, one for each of the principal factions. This system, as may be imagined, was accompanied by much disorder, and was soon succeeded by four republics, independent of each other: Potchefstroom, Zoutpansberg, Lydenburg, and Utrecht. Matters were not mended by this arrangement, and it may almost be said that the white people beyond the Vaal were without government at all.

A notable evil that resulted from this condition of things was that the outskirts of the occupied area offered a refuge to vagabonds of every stamp, who resorted to them from other parts of South Africa. Men capable of the most abominable cruelty and meanness, but possessing the quality of brute courage, roamed along the frontier nominally as hunters and traders, and their lawless deeds were attributed by people at a distance to the whole community.

When Europeans first entered the country, it was in a similar condition to Mashonaland in 1890. North and west, as far as it was known, the native tribes had been destroyed by the Matabele, and only a few wretched remnants were living either along the margin of the Kalahari desert or among almost inaccessible mountains. The greater portion of the territory south of the twenty-second parallel of latitude was literally without inhabitants, for Moselekatse's bands were in the habit of traversing it yearly in one direction or other, and no clan could live in their way. The arrival of the white people and the flight of the Matabele gave new life to the dwellers in the mountains and deserts. They could come out into the open country once more, and make gardens and sleep in safety. The Europeans were masters and owners of the land, but in accordance with the ancient Dutch custom, they permitted each little Bantu community to be governed by its own chief in all matters that did not affect the ruling race.

The kraals were made subject to a labour tax, and under a strong government no better tax could be imposed upon a barbarous people. But under the weak rule of the emigrant farmers the system was liable to great abuses, though the Bantu thought lightly of it until the dread of the Matabele was forgotten. Life was now safe, and the occupants of the kraals were multiplying at a prodigious rate, besides which fugitives were coming in from the regions beyond the Limpopo, where Moselekatse was lord.

Ten years passed away, and the clans had become so strong that they began to chafe under the restraints imposed upon them by the white men and to aspire to independence. The anarchy and strife among the Europeans appeared to give them the opportunity they wanted. But among themselves also there was the remembrance of ancient feuds, which caused so much jealousy that combination was impossible, and instead of rising altogether, it was in succession that the most disaffected among them took up arms. Then, too, as will be seen on a much more memorable occasion at a later date, in presence of an opponent the farmers stood shoulder to shoulder, and were therefore able to suppress the various risings against their authority.

These disturbances were brought prominently to the notice of the English people by the reverend Dr. Livingstone, the greatest explorer of modern times, who was then a missionary with the Bakwena, under the chief, Setyeli, and whose house and furniture were destroyed during the war. Dr. Livingstone was a strong partisan of the Bantu, and did his utmost to oppose the claim of the emigrant farmers to dominion over the clan with which he was living, so that his statements are those of an advocate rather than those of a judge. He represented Setyeli as wholly in the right, and the farmers as wholly in the wrong: but any impartial writer who examines Setyeli's own account of the matter, as given by himself personally to the governor in Capetown, must come to a different conclusion.

War cannot be carried on without cruelty, but in these contests acts were sometimes performed by the Europeans which exceeded the limit regarded as permissable by civilised nations. It should be remembered, however, that the provocation on such occasions was very great, as, for instance, when white women and children were murdered in cold blood, or when corpses were mutilated, or captives put to death by torture. Men belonging to the most refined circles in Europe would probably retaliate under such circumstances as cruelly as the emigrant farmers did.

Early in 1857 the Potchefstroom faction adopted a new constitution, under which Mr. Marthinus Wessel Pretorius became president, though with no other power than to carry out the resolutions of the volksraad. In the following year Zoutpansberg gave in its adhesion to this constitution, and, in 1860, Lydenburg and Utrecht, previously united, were also incorporated, so that the whole country north of the Vaal became a single republic. The different factions now began to strive for the supreme power in the state, and a civil war broke out, in which some blood was shed. Peace was restored in May, 1864, when Mr. Pretorius was accepted by all parties as the legally elected president, and Mr. S. J. Paul Kruger as commandant-general or military head.

Meantime the Baramapulana tribe, which was living in a mountainous tract of land in the north of the republic, had become very strong in number, owing to an influx of broken clans from beyond the Limpopo. It was in possession of a good many guns, procured from the vagabond whites in the neighbourhood, and was disposed to resent any interference with its actions. In a feud a brother of the chief was obliged to flee, and was protected by the Government, a circumstance which greatly annoyed his opponents. In April 1865, when searching for a fugitive offender, some of the lawless Europeans and a party of blacks who were assisting them committed acts of great violence upon the outposts of the tribe, and a general war was brought on.

For more than three years the republic strove in vain to subdue the Baramapulana. There was no money in the treasury, and the government was actually at one time unable to raise funds sufficient to pay for the carriage of ammunition from Durban. The burghers of the southern part of the state refused to take part in the war. Commandant-General Kruger did all that man could do with the slender means at his disposal, but he was at length obliged to withdraw discomfited. The village of Schoemansdal, the centre of the ivory trade and the residence of a landdrost and a clergyman, was abandoned by its inhabitants when the feeble commando retired, and was afterwards burnt by the enemy. The Europeans were obliged for their safety to withdraw from a large part of the district of Zoutpansberg, to which they were never able to return. The Baramapulana, however, felt the want of commercial intercourse, and in July 1868 expressed a desire for a renewal of friendship, at the same time offering to pay tribute, when peace was gladly made on conditions which by no means secured the absolute supremacy of the republican government.

The white people had thus lost ground, and the fact of their having done so made it more difficult than before to preserve order among the Bantu farther south. In one respect only the country showed signs of progress: in the number of churches built and clergymen engaged. Yet even in religious matters there was constant strife among the sections of what outsiders can only regard as one church, so trifling are the differences that break it into distinct communions. A generation had grown up without a knowledge of books or of events beyond their own little circle. The rivers were unbridged, there were no public offices worthy of the name, the treasury was always empty, and the salaries of the officials, trifling as they were, could seldom or never be paid when they fell due. Commerce was carried on chiefly by means of barter, as gold and silver were exceeding scarce. Still on the farms anything like want was unknown, for the flocks and herds throve and increased in the rich pastures, and the fertile soil produced grain and vegetables and fruit in abundance.

The war with the Baramapulana was hardly concluded when fresh difficulties arose through the Barolong of Montsiwa and other clans on the west setting up a claim to independence and to the possession of a territory of immense extent. The republic was not in a position to assert its authority by force of arms, and indeed the matter was hardly considered worth much notice until the discovery of diamonds along the lower Vaal gave importance to the claim. Then President Pretorius and her Majesty's high commissioner for South Africa arranged that it should be settled by arbitration, and each party appointed a representative to form a court, with Governor Keate, of Natal, as final umpire. The manner in which the case for the republic was conducted has been related in the preceding chapter. Governor Keate's award gave to the tribes the independence and the territory that they claimed, and even took from the government at Pretoria a large district that had been occupied by white people ever since the great emigration.

As soon as the award was known President Pretorius was obliged to resign, for the volksraad maintained that he had exceeded his authority in making the agreement with the high commissioner, and declared that they were not bound by his action. The high commissioner, however, announced that he would enforce the award, though he did not take possession of the territory cut off from the republic by it. And now there was a general cry that a clever man, capable of conducting business on equal terms with the queen's representative in Capetown, must be found to fill the office of president. The reverend Thomas François Burgers, a clergyman who had abandoned the orthodox church and whose name was then prominently before the public on account of the skilful manner in which he had conducted some difficult cases in the law courts of the Cape Colony, seemed to possess the requisite ability, and he was elected by a nearly unanimous vote.

Mr. Burgers was an able and an active man, with large persuasive powers, but he was a dreamer. He dreamed of a powerful and prosperous republic, with colleges and telegraphs and railways, with a high name among the nations of the earth; and he imagined that it could be formed off-hand out of a few thousand uneducated men with seventeenth-century ideas and such immigrants as he could induce to join him from Holland. Two years after his election he induced the volksraad to send him to Europe to negotiate a loan for the purpose of constructing a railway from Pretoria to Delagoa Bay and to engage teachers for a number of state schools.

In Holland £90,000 was subscribed towards the loan, and with the money railway material was purchased and sent out to rust and rot away at Lourenço Marques, for no more could be borrowed. A superintendent-general of education and a few other officials were engaged, with whom the president returned to Pretoria, to find that during his absence the Bapedi tribe, under the chief Sekukuni, that occupied a wild and rugged tract of land in the valley of the Olifants river, had acted in a manner that no government could tolerate.

A large commando was called out to punish the insurgents, but the burghers assembled in fear and trembling. The president was to lead it in person, and as he was in religion an agnostic, they—with their thorough orthodox creed—feared much that the blessing of God could not rest upon the enterprise. So strong had this feeling become throughout the country that a large number of families, rather than remain under his government, were moving away to seek a new home beyond the Kalahari desert, and were even then marking the road to Mossamedes in the Portuguese province of Benguela, where they ultimately settled, with a line of graves showing the terrible sufferings of their march. The passionate feeling at the time of his election had passed away, and hardly anything was now remembered except the failure of many of his plans.

One strong place was taken, which the president in overdrawn language wrote of as the Gibraltar of the south, but this success did not give heart to the farmers. An attempt to take another stronghold failed, chiefly owing to the conduct of the burghers themselves, and then there was a perfect stampede homeward, which all the efforts of Mr. Burgers could not prevent. Some days later the fugitives reached Pretoria, and no hope of suppressing the rebellion speedily was left.

The volksraad was hastily convened, when it was resolved to engage men wherever they could be obtained, at £5 a month, rations, and a farm of four thousand acres when the disturbance was quelled. To meet the expense heavy war taxes were imposed.

But the country was quite unable to bear this strain. The ordinary charges of government and the interest on the public debt could not be met, much less an additional burden. And so the whole administrative machinery broke down. The republic was really in a pitiable state, without money or an army, with rebellion triumphant, and a general election approaching that was feared might be attended with civil war.

While things were in this condition Sir Theophilus Shepstone, previously secretary for native affairs in Natal, was sent by the British government as a commissioner to Pretoria with very large powers. It is admitted by every one that a country is entitled to interfere with a neighbour whose weakness is a cause of common peril; but whether Great Britain was justified in this instance in taking possession of the South African Republic is a question upon which opinions differ. One of the reasons assigned by Sir Theophilus Shepstone for the action which he took was that the territory was in danger of being overrun by the Zulus, and if that was really so, the circumstance would go a long way to support his proceedings. But the farmers never expressed a fear of such a danger, and always alleged that they could repel Cetywayo's armies much more easily than besiege a fortified mountain stronghold. The Zulu chief at the time was trying to play off the republic against Natal, and his declarations to one party concerning the other cannot be regarded as evidence, though the British commissioner seems to have attached much value to them. Further than this, the residents of the villages, who were principally English and Germans, requested the commissioner to declare the country a British dependency, as the only remedy against anarchy, and the farmers did nothing to oppose him and his slender escort. The government managed to patch up a kind of peace with Sekukuni, but otherwise matters remained in the condition described until the 12th of April 1877, when Sir Theophilus Shepstone issued a proclamation declaring the country a British possession, and thereupon assumed supreme control, the president retiring under protest.

A considerable military force now entered the

Transvaal territory, as the country was re-named, and apparently the new government was firmly established. Trade revived, money flowed in, and property of every kind increased in value. But the farmers were dissatisfied with the loss of their independence, and sent Mr. Paul Kruger and Dr. Jorissen to England to endeavour to get the annexation withdrawn. The deputation failed in its purpose, and at that time the British ministry appear to have believed that a large proportion of the people of the territory—if not the majority—were in favour of English rule. As a proof that this was not the case, memorials were sent round against the annexation, and received the signatures of over six thousand five hundred individuals, representing practically the whole rural population. Another deputation, consisting of Messrs. Paul Kruger and Pieter Joubert, with Mr. Eduard Bok as secretary, was now sent to England, in hope that with so strong an argument in its favour it would meet with success. But it returned disappointed, and thereafter repeated declarations were made by the highest officials in South Africa that under no circumstances would the British flag be withdrawn from the Transvaal.

Sir Theophilus Shepstone was personally not disliked, and if any one could have made the farmers contented under English rule he would have done it. But in March 1879 he was succeeded as administrator by Sir Owen Lanyon, a man of haughty disposition, who was incapable of even attempting to conciliate the people of the country. The feeling now rapidly gained ground that if peaceable means to obtain the restoration of independence did not soon succeed, an appeal to arms ought to be made. The women of South Africa have always had great influence in public affairs, and on this occasion their voice was decidedly in favour of war. Mothers encouraged their sons, wives their husbands, to act as men, and if they were beaten they could die the death of patriots or move away to the unknown north as their fathers had done before them.

At this time Sekukuni again gave trouble, but Sir Garnet Wolseley with a strong body of troops and a band of Swazis marched against him, inflicted great damage upon his tribe, and brought the chief himself a prisoner to Pretoria. Shortly after this event intelligence reached the country that Mr. Gladstone had succeeded the earl of Beaconsfield as prime minister of England, and as the new premier when in opposition had denounced the annexation as unjust, the farmers not unnaturally thought that he would give them back their independence. For a while therefore the agitation almost ceased. Some of the troops were withdrawn from the territory, and Sir Garnet Wolseley, having been relieved as commander-in-chief by Sir George Colley, returned to Europe.

As soon as it was known, however, that Mr. Gladstone declined to withdraw the British flag, the general discontent came to a head. An attempt to seize the waggon of a farmer who refused to pay a tax brought a number of his friends to the rescue, and the officials at Potchefstroom, though supported by a strong military force, were openly set at defiance. A great meeting took place at Paardekraal, where

Krugersdorp now stands, and after several days' discussion it was resolved to commit their cause to the Almighty God and live or die together in a struggle for independence. Messrs. S. J. Paul Kruger, M. W. Pretorius, and Pieter J. Joubert were elected a triumvirate to conduct the government, and the volksraad resumed its functions as the supreme legislative power. It was decided that Heidelberg should be the capital until Pretoria could be recovered, and there, on Dingan's day, the 16th of December 1880, the flag of the republic was hoisted again.

The act certainly proved that the European blood has not degenerated in courage by removal to South Africa, as many persons had previously assumed. And here it may be asked how it was that the same men who dared not face danger in the commando under President Burgers went through this war for independence with the bravery and devotion of ancient Spartans, yet afterwards claimed no glory for what they had done. The reply is short: religion caused the change. In one instance they believed that the Almighty was against them because their leader was not of the true faith, in the other they believed most thoroughly that the Almighty was with them, guiding and strengthening them in the unequal fight. It was this, and this alone, that turned the fugitives from Steelpoort into the men of Majuba hill.

On the same day that the flag was hoisted the first blood was shed. A party of burghers, under Commandant Cronjé, went to Potchefstroom to have a proclamation printed, and was fired upon by the soldiers there, when one of them was badly wounded. Colonel Winsloe, who was in command of the soldiers, had a camp outside the village, and had also fortified the landdrost's office and some adjoining buildings, in which a garrison was stationed under Major Clarke. Commandant Cronjé returned the fire, and then laid siege to the buildings occupied by Major Clarke, who after holding out two days was obliged to surrender. Colonel Winsloe held the camp throughout the war, and only surrendered it after an armistice was entered into.

Disaster after disaster now attended the British arms.

Colonel Anstruther was directed to march from Lydenburg with two hundred and sixty-four men to reinforce the garrison of Pretoria, and was warned that he might meet with resistance on the way, but having a very poor opinion of the fighting powers of the farmers he took no precautions whatever. On the 20th of December he was marching carelessly with a long waggon train, when at Bronkhorst Spruit, thirty-eight miles from Pretoria, he suddenly found himself in front of a force of about the same number of farmers under Commandant Frans Joubert. The commandant demanded that he should proceed no farther, and upon his replying that he would go on, a volley was poured in by the farmers. The soldiers made a very feeble resistance, and in a few minutes so many were disabled that the colonel—who was himself mortally wounded—was obliged to surrender.

From the garrisons in Natal Sir George Colley now

collected a body of rather over a thousand men, and set out to assist the troops in the Transvaal, who with the loyalists were beleaguered in the various villages. On learning of this movement, Commandant-General Pieter Joubert, who was one of the triumvirate, entered Natal with a force superior in number, and occupied a strong position at Lang's Nek, on the road along which the British general must march. On the 28th of January 1881 Sir George Colley attempted to force the passage of the Nek, but was beaten back with heavy loss. He then fortified a camp at Mount Prospect, four miles' distant, and awaited reinforcements which were on the way from England.

On the 8th of February with nearly three hundred men General Colley left his camp to patrol the road towards Newcastle, and near the Ingogo river was drawn into an engagement with a body of farmers under Commandant Nicolaas Smit. Up to dusk neither side could claim victory, but when night fell the remnant of the English patrol returned to camp in a heavy fall of rain, leaving two-thirds of those who went out in the morning dead and wounded on the field.

In the three engagements here mentioned the British loss was about six hundred men, nearly half of whom were killed. The farmers had seventeen men killed and twenty-eight wounded. Military critics attribute the difference largely to steady aim and skill in shooting on one side, the farmers attribute it entirely to the working of Providence in their favour.

The crowning disaster was yet to come. During

the night of the 26th of February General Colley left his camp with six hundred men, and climbed to the top of Majuba hill, posting two pickets on the way. From this position he hoped to command the farmers' camp at the Nek two thousand feet below, and when at dawn on the next morning Commandant-General Joubert observed the soldiers on the crest above him, he at once realised the danger. Some hundred and fifty volunteers now offered to try to take the hill, and actually made their way up in face of the superior force above, the bullets passing over them as if they were charmed. A little before noon Commandant Nicolaas Smit with seventy or eighty men reached the crest, and then the soldiers were seized with a panic and fled. Ninety-two killed, one hundred and thirty-four wounded, and fifty-nine prisoners represented the British loss that day, against one man killed and five wounded on the farmers' side. General Colley himself was among the slain.

In the meantime the soldiers and British adherents in the Transvaal villages were closely besieged, and a good many lives were lost in sorties and skirmishes, but none were reduced to surrender.

After Sir George Colley's death, Sir Evelyn Wood took command of the English forces, and as troops were fast arriving in Natal, he soon found himself at the head of twelve thousand men. But now came instructions from the imperial government not to advance, and on the 5th of March an armistice was concluded between the general and the triumvirate. This led to the arrangement of terms of peace and the restoration of independence to the republic. The territory occupied by the Swazis was cut out, however, and on the other side the Keate award line was made the boundary until by some modifications of a later date that border was extended nearly to the great western trade route to the interior of the continent.

Four years after the re-establishment of the republic very extensive and rich goldfields were discovered in the district of Lydenburg, and a little later in the highland that forms the watershed between the Vaal and Limpopo rivers. Long before that time gold mines were worked in different parts of the territory, but the metal produced was not sufficient to attract the attention of the outside world. People now began to migrate to the fields from all parts of South Africa, and shortly from Europe as well. A town, named Barberton, was built in the centre of the eastern mines, and for some months it was the busiest place in the country, but most of its inhabitants then removed to the more important fields of Witwatersrand. Here the city of Johannesburg arose, almost as by magic, with streets of handsome and substantial buildings and all the appliances of modern times.

The production of gold has gone on increasing year after year, until in the twelvemonth that ended in June 1893 the quantity exported was worth nearly four and a half million pounds sterling. New fields are continually being opened, and though most of them prove too poor to cover the expense of working, it is very unlikely that all that are payable have already been found.

The republic possesses also iron in the greatest

abundance, coal of good quality and practically limitless in quantity, silver, copper, lead, and several other minerals which will certainly be turned to account at no distant date.

The great majority of the people engaged in the mining industry are English speakers, while the farming population speak Dutch. The intercourse between them is upon the whole friendly, and each section certainly exercises considerable influence upon the other. In the legislature, however, the English-speaking section is almost powerless, and taxation is arranged so as to fall lightly upon agriculture. In other respects no one has anything to complain of. The farmers, who acted as one man in the war of independence, are now divided as before into opposing church factions, which keep the country in a state of unrest.

After the discovery of gold the revenue of the republic rose by leaps and bounds, and public works could be undertaken that were undreamed of before. Many new villages have been laid out, and some of the buildings in them are among the best in South Africa. Telegraphs have been constructed, rivers have been bridged, and waggon roads have been made, though, of course, a great deal still remains to be done in regard to all these matters. A system of state-aided schools has been established, but as instruction through the medium of the Dutch language is greatly favoured, private schools in which English is used are much more largely attended in the towns and villages. The farmers, who control the government, are afraid to encourage the use of the English language, or to modify the franchise so that Englishmen after a short residence might have electoral rights, lest their independence should be imperilled. The theory upon which they act is that while the country is the home of themselves and their children, English people only visit it to make money, and when they have accumulated sufficient wealth return to Europe.

A railway will shortly be completed from Pretoria to Delagoa Bay, with a branch line to Barberton. It is being constructed by a company called the Netherlands South African, which is aided by the Portuguese and republican governments. A line from Pretoria to Vereeniging on the Vaal river, passing Johannesburg, is now open, having been constructed by the Netherlands South African Company with assistance from the Cape government. At Vereeniging it is connected with the great trunk line through the Orange Free State, which branches off to the three chief ports of the Cape Colony. From Krugersdorp there is a railway through Johannesburg to the Springs, passing over a great coal mine which supplies fuel to the city and to the quartz-crushing machinery along a route of fifty-four miles.

The republic is not within the customs union of South Africa. The public debt is about six million pounds sterling.

The country is governed by a president, who is elected for five years. Since the restoration of independence Mr. Paul Kruger has uninterruptedly filled the office. He is aided by an executive council, which consists of three heads of departments and two non-official members appointed by the first volksraad. For military purposes a commandant-general is elected by the burghers every ten years.

The legislative power is vested in two chambers, each consisting of twenty-four members, elected for four years. The first volksraad is by far the more important of the two. Its members are elected by burghers of European blood, born in the republic or naturalised after a residence of five years. The second volksraad has very little power, being intended chiefly as an advising body in matters connected with the mining industry. Its constituency is somewhat larger than that of the first volksraad, as foreigners can make themselves eligible to vote after a residence of two years.

According to the census of 1890, which was very incomplete, the white population of the South African Republic consisted of one hundred and nineteen thousand souls. It is now probably not below one hundred and thirty thousand. The Bantu are supposed to number fully six hundred and fifty thousand.

XXVII.

DEPENDENCIES OF THE CAPE COLONY.

During recent years the greater portion of the territory between the Indwe and Kei rivers on one side and Natal on the other has been annexed to the Cape Colony, but in some respects it is regarded as a dependency rather than as an integral part.

It is a very beautiful and fertile tract of land, resembling Natal in appearance, though the temperature along the coast is not quite so high. On the elevated belt just below the Drakensberg the winter nights are too cold to be pleasant to Bantu, and consequently no one except Bushmen resided there permanently until quite recently. There are some fine forests on the lower terraces. The rainfall is abundant, and the drainage perfect, the rivers on account of their great fall speedily carrying off all superfluous moisture. The climate is therefore exceedingly healthy, though the grass is so rich and other vegetation so luxuriant that had the country been nearly level fever would certainly be endemic.

South Africa abounds in waterfalls. The most celebrated of these are the great falls of the Orange,

SOUTH AFRICAN BOULDER.

the Tugela's leap of sixteen hundred feet over the face of the Drakensberg, and the fall of the Umgeni a few miles from Maritzburg, but perhaps the most imposing is in the Tsitsa, in the territory now being treated of. Ordinarily the stream tumbles over the precipice in three or four rills, but in times of flood a volume of water from four to five hundred feet wide drops nearly four hundred feet into a narrow chasm.

When white men first visited this territory, more than two centuries ago, four tribes were found occupying it: the Pondos, the Pondomisis, the Tembus, and the Kosas. All are there at the present day, and the fragments of many others as well. The Pondos are still independent, but during recent years the whole of the people outside the boundary line assigned to that tribe have come under British authority.

In 1858, after the destruction of their cattle and grain by the Kosas, Kreli and his people were driven over the Bashee by a body of the colonial armed and mounted police. A few hundred Fingos and some Kosas who professed to be attached to the British government were then located in the district of Idutywa, part of the vacant territory, and an English official was stationed there to preserve order among them. The rest of the old Kosa country continued to be without inhabitants until 1864, when Sir Philip Wodehouse believed it necessary to strengthen the European element of the population west of the Kei, as the military force on the border was being reduced. He therefore resolved to make room for farmers by inducing some of the Bantu to move eastward.

The first step taken was an attempt to turn Kreli from an enemy into a friend, and with this view he was offered the districts of Kentani and Willowvale, with a pension of £100 a year as long as he should behave himself to the satisfaction of the governor. The chief joyfully accepted the offer, and immediately moved in with his people. The first clan in the colony to whom an exchange of ground was proposed declined to move; but some of the Tembus of Glen Grey and of the Fingos west of the Keiskama consented. The former received the districts of Kalanga and St. Mark's, the latter the districts of Tsomo, Nkamakwe, and Butterworth.

Thus the whole of the land east of the Indwe and the Kei was again occupied by a Bantu population. British officials were stationed with all these people, but as the imperial government would not permit the territory to be formally annexed, they were really only diplomatic agents. Sir Philip Wodehouse's object in removing these Bantu was entirely frustrated, for not a rood of ground was obtained by the measure for Europeans. The Tembus and the Fingos in the colony simply threw off swarms, but took care not to abandon any part of their locations.

The main branch of the Tembu tribe lived between the Bashee and Umtata rivers. After 1863 its chief was a man named Gangelizwe, ordinarily a gentle-looking and soft-speaking individual, but subject to outbursts of violent passion. His great wife was a daughter of the Kosa chief Kreli, and his treatment of her was at times so inhuman that her father was exasperated to the last degree. There was an old feud between the Tembus and the Pondos, so that Gangelizwe had an enemy on the other side also. In 1875, in a mad fit of rage, he murdered one of his concubines, who was an illegitimate niece of Kreli and an attendant upon the great wife. His enemies on all sides were now ready to fall upon him, and as his tribe contained many fragments of others whose fidelity could not be depended upon in such a quarrel, the chief himself and his councillors requested British protection and offered to become subjects of the queen. To prevent a disturbance on the border the high commissioner consented, and in 1875 the districts of Slang River, Engcobo, Umtata, and Mkanduli were added to the empire in the same loose way as those previously mentioned.

Living on the eastern bank of the Bashee river, close to the coast, was a clan called the Bomvana, the fugitive remnant of a tribe destroyed in the early Zulu wars. This clan was nominally attached to the Kosa tribe, but it did not destroy its substance in 1857, and was consequently able to give shelter to Kreli when he was driven over the Bashee in the following year. From that time it was really independent, and remained so until 1878. Then the country around was involved in a war yet to be referred to, and Moni, the chief of the Bomvanas, who was too weak to maintain neutrality, applied to be received as a British subject. The high commissioner accepted his offer, and took possession of the district of Elliotdale, thus bringing the whole country between the colonial border and the Umtata river more or less authoritatively under the British flag.

It was regarded as being under the protection and control of the high commissioner as representing the empire, and no part of it was made subject to the Cape Colony until 1879, when the districts of Idutywa, Tsomo, Nkamakwe, and Butterworth were formally annexed. The districts of Kentani, Willowvale, Kalanga, St. Mark's, Slang River, Engcobo, Umtata, Mkanduli, and Elliotdale were annexed in 1885. It is now under the control of an officer styled the chief magistrate of Transkei and Tembuland, who has thirteen subordinate magistrates—that is one in each district—to assist him.

The whole of the territory between the Umtata and Umzimkulu rivers was allotted to the chief Faku, when in 1844 an attempt was made to form a powerful Pondo state. But that attempt was a failure, for the upper portion of the territory was nearly uninhabited, and the lower portion was filled with refugee clans from the north, some of whom were almost as strong as the Pondos themselves. The country therefore continued to be convulsed with feuds and wars, and Faku at length became only too glad to part with his nominal right to a portion of it that he might have a chance of conquering and holding the rest.

He first ceded the land along the coast between the Umtamvuna and Umzimkulu rivers to Natal, thereby getting rid of a number of his opponents, and then in 1861 he offered to the Cape government nearly two-thirds of the remainder. The line which he proposed cut off the Pondomisis, the Bacas, the Hlangwenis, and some others of less note, whom he desired to place under such control that they could not molest him while he subjugated the enemies that would be left on his side. His offer was not at once accepted, but thereafter the country north of the proposed line was not regarded as part of Pondoland. Shortly afterwards Sir George Grey gave a large portion of the unoccupied ground in it to Adam Kok's Griquas, who thereupon migrated from the Orange Free State. From them the country became known as Griqualand East. Later, some Basuto, Batlokua, and Fingo clans moved into it during the last war between the Free State and Moshesh.

Constant inter-tribal quarrels at length induced the high commissioner to interfere, as nearly all the chiefs declared their readiness to place themselves under British authority. In 1873 an officer with the title of resident was sent into the country, and the districts of Maclear, Mount Fletcher, Tsolo, and Kumbu—the last two occupied by the Pondomisi tribe—were taken over. In the following year the districts of Matatiele, Kokstad, and Umzimkulu, with Adam Kok's consent, were also taken over, as was in 1876 the district of Mount Frere, with the consent of the Baca chief. These eight districts comprise the whole of the territory north of the line proposed by Faku. In 1879 they were formally annexed to the Cape Colony. In 1886 the district of Mount Ayliff, occupied by the Kesibe clan, was also annexed. It is south of Faku's line, but it became a necessity either to take over the Kesibes, or to stand by and see a brave little clan massacred by the Pondos. The nine districts are under the charge of an officer styled the chief magistrate of Griqualand East, and under his supervision each district has its own resident magistrate.

The Bantu in these dependencies have given very little trouble during recent years, but there were some serious disturbances before they became accustomed to European guidance.

On the 3rd of August 1877 there was a marriage at a Fingo kraal just within the Butterworth border, and two petty Kosa captains, with a small party of attendants, crossed over to partake in the festivities. On such occasions custom demands that all who attend are to be made welcome. In the evening, when the guests were excited with dancing and drinking millet beer, a quarrel arose, no one afterwards was able to tell exactly how or why. At any rate the Kosas were ranged on one side and the Fingos on the other, and they used their sticks so freely that the two captains were badly bruised and one of their attendants was killed. The visitors were then driven over the border.

Strong bands of Kosas immediately mustered to avenge the insult offered to their friends, and began to sweep off the Fingos' cattle. The excitement on both sides soon became so great that the efforts of the officials to restore order were unavailing. The police were sent to the front, the colonial volunteers were called out, and an imperial regiment of the line marched to the border. Several sharp actions were fought with Kreli's people, who lost some seven hundred men, and then suddenly fled into Pondoland.

In the belief that the disturbance was over, the volunteers were now permitted to go to their homes; but they were hardly disbanded when the Kosas returned and attacked the police. In December Kiva, a relation of Kreli, crossed the Kei, and appealed to the Kosas in the colony to support the head of their tribe. Most of them, with the chief Sandile, responded to the appeal, and the country was involved in the ninth Kaffir war.

In February 1878 the colonial camp at Kentani was attacked by about five thousand Kosas, who charged in dense masses, but were mown down by a fire from heavy guns. Both Kreli and Sandile were present in the engagement. The principal column was led by the tribal priest, who had performed certain ceremonies which caused the warriors to believe that they were invulnerable; but this feeling of confidence being destroyed, they gave way to despair. When they broke and fled, the volunteer cavalry and the Fingos pursued and prevented them from rallying.

As far as Kreli was concerned the battle of Kentani was a decisive one. He did not attempt any further resistance, but with his adherents at once crossed the Bashee. After the conclusion of peace a small location was assigned to him in Elliotdale, and there he spent the remainder of his life.

West of the Kei the Kosas held out for many months, but at length Sandile was killed in action, and they then submitted.

In October 1880, just after the Basuto tribe rose in rebellion, the Pondomisis, the Basuto clans in Griqualand East, and several clans attached to the Tembu tribe rose also against the Europeans. They committed some atrocious murders and destroyed much property, but within four months they were completely subdued by a combined force of burghers and rival Bantu.

The two chief magistracies contain at present about half a million Bantu and barely ten thousand Europeans. The latter are government officials, missionaries, traders, and farmers on the highlands under the Drakensberg and on ground purchased from Griquas. The chiefs retain considerable judicial power, are regarded as officials, and are in receipt of salaries, for it would be useless to attempt to govern the people if they were ignored. Regulations for the conduct of affairs are made by the governor in council, and when published become law. No statutes of the Cape parliament have force in the chief magistracies unless they are specially applied by proclamation of the governor in council. Bantu law is administered by the magistrates except when Europeans are concerned, but persons charged with the commission of serious crimes are tried before a judge on circuit according to the colonial laws. The only direct tax paid is one of ten shillings a year on each hut, which brings in sufficient to defray the ordinary cost of government, including a considerable sum expended on mission schools. A strong police force is needed, but against that expenditure may be set trading licenses and the customs duties on goods sold.

The rate of increase of the population is amazing now that all the checks that kept it in bounds in ancient times have been removed. As far as can be ascertained, there is nothing like it out of South Africa. The food of the people consists of maize or millet, with pumpkins, sweet cane, curdled milk, and occasionally flesh plainly cooked. This simple diet, with living mostly in the open air, tends to keep them in robust health, and every girl becomes a wife and with rare exceptions a mother.

The port of St. John's, nearly in the centre of the coast of Pondoland, is another dependency of the Cape Colony. It consists of the mouth and tidal estuary of the Umzimvubu river, with a strip of land about sixteen square miles in extent on the western side above the sea, and was purchased in 1878 from a Pondo chief. There are other places along the coast where boats can effect a landing in fine weather, but Port St. John's is the only one worthy of the name of harbour between East London and Durban. It is at present little used, but may some day become of value. A magistrate is stationed here, and there is a population of nearly three hundred souls.

Pondoland—which completes the territory south of Natal—remains under the government of its own chiefs, but the coast is under British protection. The country is constantly convulsed with quarrels between the clans, many of which are alien in blood to the Pondo tribe.

Along the coast of Great Namaqualand there are several rocky islets upon which seabirds congregate in vast flocks, and as there is hardly any rainfall in that region the guano is of considerable value. These islets became dependencies of the Cape Colony many years ago. Their only inhabitants are the men employed to gather the guano.

Farther north on the same coast is Walfish Bay, the only port through which access can be had to Great Namaqualand and Damaraland. The country around is a dreary waste of sand, and a more uninviting spot can hardly be imagined. But on account of its strategical importance it was taken in possession by Great Britain, and in 1884 became a dependency of the Cape Colony. On the little strip of land which was declared British territory there are living some six or seven hundred Hottentots of a very low type. The only other inhabitants are the colonial magistrate with his staff of police, a missionary family, and a few traders and forwarders of goods to the interior.

XXVIII.

VARIOUS TERRITORIES NOT ALREADY DESCRIBED.

BRITISH BECHUANALAND.

THE Keate award was hardly delivered when the clans cut off by it from the South African Republic began to quarrel with each other, and their feuds continued with hardly any intermission until the British flag was hoisted at Pretoria. Then for a time there was comparative order, because the Transvaal authorities favoured the strongest chiefs and the military force in the country commanded respect.

When the republic was restored the old quarrels began afresh, and soon became more bitter than ever. Some of the chiefs now professed strong attachment to Great Britain, and as a matter of course their rivals professed equally strong attachment to the government of the farmers. Until we get to know these people thoroughly our national vanity leads us to believe that they all have a high regard for English justice and English benevolence, and it is with something like a shock that the truth bursts upon us that it is only English power for which they have any respect. Why should they like us better than other people? We do as much—even more—to destroy their national customs and everything else that they hold dear. How is it possible, then, that they can love us? They certainly respect strength, and they are always ready to profess attachment to that party which can give most. But in cases like that of the Bechuana tribes, if one chief declares himself a friend of the republic, his rival will most certainly announce himself as the devoted adherent of the queen.

At this stage a European renegade suggested to the chief with whom he was living that white men should be enlisted to fight for him, and as a result volunteers were called for, each to receive a farm in payment when the war was over. The other side adopted the same course, so that bodies of Europeans —decidedly of the vagabond type, however—were apparently pitted against each other in a cause that did not concern them in the least. In reality there was no fear of such combatants shedding each other's blood, except when an individual made himself particularly obnoxious; but it soon became a certainty that unless some power intervened the volunteers would divide the best part of the country among them and leave little worth having for their employers.

The western border of the South African Republic was the base of operations on one side, and President Kruger's government made little or no effort to prevent its being so used. The burghers of that state would not put themselves to trouble to protect clans that had thrown off their authority, and they had also an excuse that volunteers for the other side were enlisted at the diamond fields—on British soil—with hardly a show of secrecy. This implication in the disturbances caused people in England to regard the republic as being at the bottom of the whole matter, and public opinion supported the government in sending out a strong military force under Sir Charles Warren to protect the clans from being despoiled.

Meanwhile the volunteers—or freebooters—had taken possession of two considerable tracts of ground, and set up an independent government on each. One was termed the republic of Stellaland, the other the land of Goshen. When Sir Charles Warren approached, the people of Goshen, instead of preparing to resist, dispersed to other parts of South Africa, and the people of Stellaland submitted, so that there was no necessity to fire a shot in anger.

The expedition, though it had not to fight, was of the utmost service to British interests in the country. It restored the imperial prestige, which had suffered so greatly a few years before, and it secured an open highway to the interior of the continent. In September 1885 the territory which had been the scene of the disturbances was taken under British sovereignty. The original boundaries have since been enlarged, and are now the South African Republic on the east, the twentieth meridian from Greenwich on the west, the Molopo river and Ramathlabama Spruit on the north, and the Cape Colony on the south. It forms a crown colony, governed by a local administrator under her Majesty's high commissioner, and is divided into five magisterial districts: Mafeking, Vryburg, Taung, Kuruman, and Gordonia.

The best of the land was set apart as reserves for the Bechuana clans, but there are large tracts occupied by European farmers, and a great extent of ground is still open. It is well adapted for cattle runs, though agriculture only succeeds in limited localities, and in general there is a scarcity of surface water. No minerals of any importance except salt have yet been discovered. The climate is exceedingly healthy, and though the days in midsummer are unpleasantly warm, the nights are invariably cool and enjoyable.

Since the establishment of British authority order has been observed as well as in any part of the world. At present there are over five thousand Europeans in the province, and that number is likely to be largely increased in the immediate future, when some extensive blocks of farms are sold. Vryburg, the seat of government, is connected by rail with the ports of the Cape Colony, and the line is now being continued to Mafeking, on the northern border. This is along the great trade route to the interior of the continent, which is thus entirely under the British flag.

THE BRITISH PROTECTORATE.

The territory for a considerable distance north of British Bechuanaland is under British protection, which means that all white people living in it are under the jurisdiction of magistrates appointed by the high commissioner, and that the relationship of the native tribes to each other is controlled by the same authority, though the government of the chiefs over their own people is not interfered with. Much the greater portion of this territory is without surface water, and is very thinly inhabited by Bushmen and wandering Bechuana who were formerly held by the clans at the fountains in a condition of the most abject slavery. Their circumstances have improved of late years, but they still lead lives of want and misery, and are largely subject to the caprice of their masters. The protectorate is divided into two districts, over each of which there is an officer entitled an assistant commissioner. Order is preserved by a strong police force of mounted Europeans. This territory and the crown colony of British Bechuanaland are both within the South African customs union.

THE CHARTERED COMPANY'S TERRITORY.

Beyond the protectorate a vast territory, probably half a million square miles in extent, is being opened up by the British South Africa Company under a royal charter granted in 1889. It is often called Rhodesia, after Mr. Cecil J. Rhodes, the present premier of the Cape Colony, who was the originator of the Company, and is still its chief manager. Concessions have been obtained from native chiefs which give the Company proprietary rights over immense tracts of fertile land and extensive areas of gold-bearing quartz reefs. In some places shafts and tunnels indicate that at an unknown period in the past the mines were worked, and ruins of buildings far beyond the skill of Bantu to construct give evidence that the land was not always occupied solely by barbarians.

The Chartered Company was formed with a capital of a million pounds sterling. A strong body of police was sent into the territory to construct and occupy forts in commanding positions, and then immigration of Europeans was invited. An elevated plateau of great extent offers fruitful soil, a climate in which white people can enjoy life, and vacant ground waiting for settlement.

It came to be in its present thinly inhabited condition in exactly the same manner as the Transvaal country before 1836. When Moselekatse was driven to the north by the emigrant farmers he commenced to destroy the Makalaka tribes just as he had destroyed the Bechuana, and Lobengule, his son and successor, continued the murderous practice. Large areas were utterly wasted, and the remnants of the tribes retreated to the hills, where they made their kraals among rocks in places difficult of access. These situations, if they could not be defended, offered facilities for escape when the Matabele bands approached in their yearly raids. By those terrible invaders the lives of the Makalaka were held in no more esteem than the lives of so many antelopes. This was the condition of the country when the first expeditionary force of the Chartered Company entered it and built forts under a concession from Lobengule himself.

Naturally all the broken and impoverished clans

welcomed the white men, and there will be no difficulty in managing them while the Matabele power exists. That power, however, has within itself the elements of disintegration. It consists of three distinct castes. There are, first, the descendants of the pure Zulus who came up from the coast with Moselekatse, and who form a kind of nobility. Secondly, there are the descendants of the Bechuana boys who rose from bearers of burdens to be soldiers before the flight from the south. And, thirdly, there are the Makalaka who have been incorporated in the same way. These sections are not thoroughly fused, and the result of pressure, either peaceful or warlike, may be to cause the army to crumble away. It is at present about twenty thousand strong.

Already a great deal of the preliminary work in opening up the country has been done. There is telegraphic communication and a postal service between all the forts and the Cape Colony, and a railway is being constructed inland from Port Beira, which will give easy access to the north-eastern portion, while the south-western portion can be reached without much difficulty from the terminus of the Capetown-Mafeking line. Farming has been tested with good results. The limits of the districts which are healthy for Europeans have been fairly well ascertained. And many appliances of modern times, including even a printing press, may be found to-day in a region that half-a-dozen years ago was unknown except to a few explorers and hunters.

The Chartered Company's territory appears to have a brilliant future before it. There is every probability that its mineral wealth is enormous. It is perhaps the last great open place in the world for fresh European settlement. But it cannot remain long in that condition. The highlands southward from the Zambesi must either be occupied within a few years by civilised Europeans, to the gain of the whole human race, or they must revert to barbarians. The Chartered Company and the Matabele army cannot long exist side by side.[1] The last is doomed to destruction. Then, if Europeans are not in possession, every little remnant of a clan will lay claim to vast areas as having been the property of its ancestors, the now docile Mashona and Makalaka will become discontented plotters, and from outside hordes of refugees will pour in. That is the lesson which the history of Natal and the South African Republic teaches.

THE GERMAN PROTECTORATE.

In 1884 Germany commenced to secure a footing on the south-western coast of Africa, and her protectorate now extends from Cape Frio on the north to the Orange river on the south, and from the Atlantic ocean on the west to an irregular line running from the head waters of the Zambesi to the twentieth meridian from Greenwich on the east. From this vast territory must be excluded, however, the only port on the coast, Walfish Bay, which with

---

[1] As this is being printed, intelligence has reached England that war has been forced upon the Chartered Company by the Matabele.

a little tract of land around it belongs to the Cape Colony.

The southern part of this region is almost rainless, and fountains are few in number, but as one goes northward the moisture increases, though nowhere can the land be correctly described as capable of supporting an agricultural population. It is nevertheless well adapted for cattle-rearing. Copper is known to exist in large quantities, and it is generally believed that other minerals will be found. The population is Hottentot as far north as Walfish Bay, and Bantu beyond. The Europeans are chiefly missionaries and traders, with a small force of German soldiers and a few prospectors.

While this is being written, a war is being waged with a Hottentot clan that declines to acknowledge the German authorities, but with this exception the natives have as yet given no trouble.

THE PORTUGUESE POSSESSIONS.

During the early years of the sixteenth century the Portuguese took possession of the principal harbours on the south-eastern coast of Africa, but they did not attempt to plant colonies behind them. Portugal was too small and too thinly populated to spare men for such a purpose while the Indian commerce was in her hands. The magnificent harbour of Delagoa Bay did not escape their observation, and at times they occupied a small fort there, though as very little trade could be done on that part of the coast they were in the habit of abandoning it occasionally for many years together.

Mozambique was used as a resting-place for the royal fleets to and from the East, and on that account became a place of importance, but the other Portuguese stations were mere outlying trading posts.

Under these circumstances there never was a well-defined inland boundary of the territory which the Portuguese held, nor was one needed, for no European power was behind them as a rival. But though they planted no colonies, in the days of their glory and their prosperity they certainly exerted themselves greatly to open up the country. Their missionaries—chiefly of the Society of Jesus—penetrated the far interior, and sought to convert the natives even in the most deadly localities along the coast. Their traders crossed the continent from Angola to Mozambique, and brought gold and ivory and slaves to the ports to be shipped to Brazil and Europe.

Then came Portugal's decay, but the Dutch, who wrested India from her, cared nothing for the East African coast. They indeed occupied Delagoa Bay for some years in the eighteenth century, but nothing was to be made there, so they did not remain long. Thus the Portuguese retained their old stations along the shore, though in a condition of ruin or decay, and preserved a kind of shadowy claim to the interior lands where their missionaries had once lived and their traders had flourished.

Some years after the South African Republic was established it was mutually agreed that the Lebombo mountains should be the boundary between that state and the Portuguese territory. More recently the British Chartered Company took possession of the interior plateau farther north, and a dispute quickly arose as to the limit of the Portuguese rights. A boundary has been agreed upon, however, though it is not yet marked off. It gives to the Chartered Company nearly the whole of the land adapted for European colonisation, though the Portuguese area looks large on a map.

An attempt is now being made to turn the territory to some account, and charters have been granted by the government at Lisbon to several companies for the purpose. But it is difficult to see what can be done in a country where fever is so deadly to Europeans as it is on the East African coast belt. The contrast with the opposite side of the continent is very great. The Atlantic shore is parched with drought, and is consequently arid and treeless, but is extremely favourable to health. The eastern shore has a superabundant rainfall, so that vegetation is luxuriant and swamps abound, and where this is the case under a burning sun white men cannot thrive.

From Delagoa Bay a railway is being constructed to Pretoria, and undoubtedly there will be a great deal of traffic on it when it is completed. In the hot months, however, Lourenço Marques, the town at the bay, is so unhealthy that the death rate of the inhabitants is about two hundred in the thousand yearly. Few will care to make a home in such a place.

From Port Beira, at the mouth of the Pungwe river, a railway is being constructed inland, which will tap a large portion of the English Chartered Company's possessions. But the same cause which is disastrous to the welfare of Lourenço Marques affects this place also, and it is improbable that it will ever be more than a station for the transport of goods and passengers.

SWAZILAND.

This is a tract of land enclosed on three sides by the South African Republic, and on the fourth by the Lebombo mountain range. It contains valuable gold-fields, and is also fertile, well-watered, and healthy. The Swazis have always been regarded as one of the bravest of the Bantu tribes. They were friends of the early emigrant farmers, and have ever since continued to show good will to all Europeans. They are supposed at present to number from sixty to seventy thousand souls.

Their chief, Umbandine by name, who died four years ago, granted to different white men concessions of all kinds, to extract metals, to till ground, to graze cattle, and a great deal else, until there was very little left for his own followers. This led to a kind of government of the Europeans by a committee acting with the chief's approval. In 1890 the committee was replaced by a joint commission appointed by Great Britain, the South African Republic, and the Swazi chief, which is now the government of the Europeans in the territory. Bunu, successor of Umbandine, rules his own people without any interference.

XXIX.

THE PRESENT CONDITION OF THE CAPE COLONY.

SINCE the management of its affairs has been in the hands of its own people the Cape Colony has made an enormous stride in prosperity. Its principal industries are still pastoral and agricultural, but these are carried on now in a much better manner than formerly.

The great Karoo plains, thinly speckled with succulent plants, and the long grassy slope beyond to the north are covered with flocks of merino sheep and Angora goats, which are kept up to a high standard by the importation of the best foreign blood. In these parts of the colony agriculture is only possible where there is running water, but a great deal of labour has been expended in making reservoirs from which gardens and orchards can be irrigated, and recently much success has attended the sinking of artesian wells.

On the first and second terraces from the southern coast and in the districts adjoining the eastern border the rainfall is ample, and agriculture is carried on conjointly with cattle-breeding. Wheat and maize are the principal crops, but oats are extensively grown for horses, and almost every kind of vegetable and fruit is abundant.

In the south-western angle of the colony—the part settled in the seventeenth century—the cultivation of wheat and the vine is carried on. Sufficient wheat, indeed is not at present grown for home consumption and the supply of shipping, because the farmers have not been able to keep pace with the sudden and rapidly increasing demand caused by the mining industry in the north; but there is good reason to believe that the large importations of recent years will not continue much longer. The quality of the wines and spirits made has been much improved of late, though it does not yet satisfy the English palate.

Ostriches have been tamed, and their feathers form an important item in our trade returns. On the other hand, skins of wild animals have quite disappeared, for the large game with which the country once teemed has been exterminated. Ivory also has greatly fallen off, and the little that is now exported is brought from the distant interior of the continent.

In 1852 rich copper mines were opened in the district of Namaqualand and the part of the colony previously regarded as the least valuable has ever since been contributing its mineral wealth to the general prosperity.

It is impossible to give the value of the purely colonial products, but the quantity from the whole of South Africa exported in the year that ended on the 30th of June 1893 was valued at a little over thirteen and a half million pounds sterling, of which twelve millions and a quarter passed through the ports of the Cape Colony, and one million and a quarter through Durban, Natal. Of the items that made up this amount gold was first, being valued at four millions and a half, and diamonds came next, being valued at nearly four millions. The copper ore exported was worth over a quarter of a million, and the coal over £50,000. These figures—representing nearly two-thirds of the total exports—show the importance of the mining industry of South Africa, and it must be remembered that this industry is only in its infancy.

Taking the remaining exports alone into consideration, they are now about ten times as great as in 1850. Pastoral pursuits are represented by wool, to the value of £2,648,000; Angora hair, to the value of £597,000; hides, skins, and horns, to the value of £545,000; and ostrich feathers, to the value of £491,000.

Agriculture contributes but little to the exports, because nearly everything that is grown is required for home consumption. Still a little fruit and grain is sent abroad. Wine to the value of £18,000 finds its way out of the country. Aloes and argol contribute about £2,000 each, Natal sends away bark for tanning to the value of £9,000, and the Cape Colony dried flowers worth £21,000. The fisheries supply large quantities of food for use in the country, and an export to Mauritius to the value of £13,000. Natal disposes of sugar to the value of nearly £100,000. Small items of various kinds, which do not need special mention, make up the balance.

Altogether this means that South Africa has a

purchasing power at the present time of over thirteen millions sterling yearly, less the interest on the different public debts and on foreign capital invested in the country. The bulk of the trade is with Great Britain, and a large proportion of it originates in the Cape Colony.

Excluding the dependencies named in the twenty-seventh chapter, the colony has now a population of three hundred and sixty-six thousand Europeans and seven hundred and fifty-five thousand coloured people. Of these last, rather more than half are Bantu—Kosas, Tembus, and Fingos,—the others are mixed breeds, Asiatics, descendants of freed slaves, and Hottentots. All are subject to the same laws, except in a few particulars where it has been found necessary to make special provision for Bantu communities, such as the recognition of communal tenure of land in locations, the prohibition of the sale of spirituous liquors in certain defined areas, and the supervision of these people when they live in undue number on farms owned by Europeans.

Among the Bantu missionaries of nearly every Christian society have been labouring for many years, and two or three generations have grown up under their care. The result upon the whole is discouraging to those who look for high improvement, although a considerable advance has been made by a section of these people. Where youths have been separated from the surroundings of the kraals, and have been trained in habits of order, cleanliness, and—as far as practicable — industry, the most good has been effected. In this direction the Free Church of Scotland led the way, and its noble institution at Lovedale is now a model which other Christian bodies are copying. It has become generally recognised that the system of education carried out by most of the missionary societies was faulty. Their idea was to teach the children of barbarians to read and write, to give them a knowledge of grammar and geography, of arithmetic and history, and especially to instruct them in Christian doctrine and cause them to read

THE BOYS' SCHOOL, LOVEDALE MISSIONARY INSTITUTION.

the Holy Scriptures. The government subsidised the schools, and the rivalry among the different denominations was so keen that no location of any importance was lost sight of. And now, after a vast expenditure of energy and money, it is seen that education of this kind is by itself of little value, and industrial training is coming to be regarded as a necessity.

The mixed breeds, descendants of slaves, and Hottentots have also been the objects of missionary solicitude, and as they have long been in close contact with white people their mode of living is based upon the European model. Most of them profess Christianity. They do the rough work of the farms and the towns, but are in general averse to steady labour, and are thriftless to the last degree. The instances are rare of people of this class accumulating property, though they often have excellent opportunities for doing so.

The Asiatics in the colony are chiefly descendants of people from the Spice islands, who were sent here in the seventeenth and eighteenth centuries, and are commonly termed Malays. Those of pure blood are almost—if not wholly—without exception Mohammedans. But many Africans and people of mixed blood have adopted that creed, and as they have intermarried, the Malays present every variety of appearance between the pure Asiatic, the pure European, and the pure African, while some fluctuate between Christianity and Islam. They are decidedly of a higher type than the class previously mentioned. Many of the men are good mechanics, and the amount of property that they hold is considerable. They are confined entirely to towns. Some Indians from Hindostan have recently migrated to this colony, among whom are a few who profess the Roman Catholic faith.

Owing to the zeal of the missionaries, for many years greater efforts were made to give a good school education to coloured children than to white, and it is a lamentable fact that there is at present a large section of the European rural population without any knowledge of books. This condition of things, however, has attracted serious attention of late, and it will not be permitted to continue.

There is an excellent system of public schools, each under the joint control of a local board of management and the educational department of the government, half the cost being defrayed by the treasury. Those of the first and second class are attended almost exclusively by white children. Then there are several colleges in which higher education is imparted, and numerous excellent schools connected with religious societies. The Cape Colony has further a university, which is, however, only an examining body empowered to confer degrees.

No expense is spared to bring justice within reach of every one. There are seventy-eight stipendiary magistrates, holding courts in as many districts into which the colony is divided. All petty civil and criminal cases are tried by them. The supreme court consists of the chief justice and eight puisne judges, but as two form a quorum, in practice three of the judges sit in Grahamstown, three in Kimberley, and the others in Capetown. Twice a year a judge of the supreme court visits each district town, and tries cases which are beyond the jurisdiction of the magistrates.

The towns and villages are supplied with public libraries aided by government, hardly any are without two or three churches of different denominations, and banks, insurance offices, newspapers, and benevolent institutions are found in nearly all. Municipal government—in very rare instances abused—is in force in every community of the slightest note. Each

INNER DOCK, CAPETOWN.

district has a divisional council, with powers over a large area somewhat similar to those of municipal councils in the villages.

Good roads have been made even in the wildest parts of the colony, and the rivers on the principal routes have been bridged. There is scarcely a hamlet that is not now connected with all parts of South Africa by the post and the telegraph wire. The railway system has been referred to in other chapters, and a glance at the map at the beginning of this volume will show how extensive are the open lines.

Very great improvements have been made in the harbours, especially in Table Bay. Here in olden times the beach, after winter storms, was frequently strewn with the wrecks of costly fleets, now ships lie in a dock in perfect safety, and a magnificent breakwater protects the outer anchorage. The cost of these works, including a dry dock capable of containing a steamer of the first class, was nearly a million and a half pounds sterling.

On the coast numerous lighthouses stand as sentinels to warn seamen of danger by night, and the ancient terror of stormy seas off the Cape of Good Hope has long since been forgotten. It arose more from distance from home in the early days of circumnavigating Africa than from the real violence of the sea, for that is commonly trifling compared with the fury of the North Atlantic.

The colony is connected with Europe by two submarine cables, so that anything of importance that occurs there one day is known here through the newspapers on the next. Splendid steamships carrying mails and passengers arrive from and leave for England weekly, often making the run of six thousand miles in less than fifteen days, and the passage is certainly one of the pleasantest in the world.

Against the material prosperity which the colony has attained within the last forty years must be placed a public debt of rather over twenty-six million pounds sterling, or about £71 per individual colonist, if the coloured inhabitants are excluded. That rate per head, however, must be reduced by taking into account that the coloured people perform the rough labour of the country, and that their presence—except on the eastern frontier—does not constitute a danger; but in what proportion they should be classified with the whites it would be hard to say. They certainly stand in a very different position from the blacks of Natal, in that their relative number to the Europeans is only two to one, and nearly half of them imitate the European mode of living.

Never before was this country a land of good hope as much as at present. No one can tell what its mineral exports may be ten years hence, but they are advancing now at a very rapid rate. The mines furnish excellent markets for agricultural produce of every kind, and the farmer and grazier do not need to look for customers abroad. A vast open territory in the interior is inviting inhabitants, and the Company that owns it is offering land on most liberal terms. There is an opportunity for introducing civilisation far into the heart of Africa in the only way in which it can be successfully done, that is by means of European settlements sufficiently strong to rule without danger of revolt, and to be able at the same time to act with justice and kindness towards the native race.

The continuation of the Story of South Africa, when written at no very distant period, will be an account of either brilliant successes or disastrous failures, there will be little of mediocrity in it. The prospect certainly seems bright at present, but a stream of European immigrants of the right stamp is needed to make it continue so. In the movement northward the sons and the daughters of the Cape Colony are taking an active part, and there are no people on earth more fitted than they to be the pioneer settlers of a new land. The nationalities from which they spring are not those that recede, and the fusion that is taking place—notwithstanding there is still a small section of both Dutch and English who regard each other with hostility—is not diminishing the vigour derived from the parent stocks. But they are too few in number to occupy and hold the great interior plateau. As they go forward, men and women from Europe—of the class that wins success by industry, perseverance, and prudence—must come in and fill the places they leave, if South Africa is to have a really brilliant future.

CHRONOLOGICAL TABLE OF EVENTS.

A.D.
- 1486. Discovery of the Cape of Good Hope by Dias.
- 1497. Doubling of the African continent by Vasco da Gama.
- 1503. Discovery of Table Bay by Antonio de Saldanha.
- 1510. Defeat of Portuguese by Hottentots in Table Valley.
- 1591. First visit of English ships to Table Bay.
- 1595. First voyage of the Dutch to India.
- 1602. Formation of the Dutch East India Company.
- 1652. Commencement of the European settlement in South Africa.
- 1655. Introduction of the vine.
- 1657. Discovery of the Berg river.
- 1658. Introduction of slaves.
- 1659. First Hottentot war.
- 1660. Discovery of the Elephant river.
- 1672. Purchase of territory from Hottentot chiefs.
- 1673. Commencement of second Hottentot war.
- 1679. Foundation of Stellenbosch.
- 1685. Discovery of the copper mines of Namaqualand.
- 1688. Arrival of the first Huguenot settlers.
- 1700. First occupation of land on the second plateau.
- 1713. First outbreak of small-pox.
- 1722. Great loss of life by gale in Table Bay.
- 1737. Wreck of another fleet in Table Bay.
- 1742. First use of Simon's Bay in winter months.
- 1746. Foundation of Swellendam.
- 1752. Exploration of the country eastward to the Kei.
- 1755. Second outbreak of small-pox.
- 1761. Exploration of southern part of Great Namaqualand.
- 1767. Third outbreak of small-pox.

CHRONOLOGICAL TABLE OF EVENTS. 389

A.D.
- 1779. Commencement of first Kaffir war.
- 1781. Arrival of French troops to defend the Cape Colony against the English.
- 1786. Foundation of Graaff-Reinet.
- 1789. Commencement of second Kaffir war.
- 1792. Commencement of the Moravian mission.
- 1795. Surrender of the Cape Colony to the English.
- 1799. Commencement of the London Society's mission.
- —— Commencement of third Kaffir war.
- 1801. Exploration of the southern part of Bechuanaland.
- 1803. Restoration of the Cape Colony to the Dutch.
- 1806. Second surrender of the Cape Colony to the English.
- 1809 Subjection of all Hottentot inhabitants to colonial laws.
- 1812. Fourth Kaffir war.
- 1815. Slachter's Nek insurrection.
- 1818. Commencement of fifth Kaffir war.
- 1820. Arrival of large body of British settlers.
- 1822. Commencement of Zulu wars of extermination.
- 1824. Erection of first lighthouse on South African coast.
- 1830. Settlement of the Matabele in the valley of the Marikwa.
- 1834. Emancipation of the slaves in the Cape Colony.
- 1835. Sixth Kaffir war.
- 1836. Beginning of great emigration from the Cape Colony.
- 1837. Flight of the Matabele to the country north of the Limpopo.
- 1838. Dreadful massacres of Europeans by Zulus.
- 1840. Subjection of the Zulu tribe to the emigrant farmers.
- 1842. Occupation of Natal by a British military force.
- 1843. Creation by the British government of Griqua and Basuto treaty states.
- 1844. Creation of Pondo treaty state.
- 1846. Commencement of seventh Kaffir war.
- 1847. Creation of the province of British Kaffraria.
- 1848. Proclamation of British sovereignty over the territory between the Orange and Vaal rivers.
- 1850. Commencement of eighth Kaffir war.
- 1851. Commencement of first Basuto war.
- 1852. Acknowledgment by Great Britain of the independence of the South African Republic.

CHRONOLOGICAL TABLE OF EVENTS.

A.D.
- 1854. Abandonment by Great Britain of the Orange River Sovereignty.
- —— Establishment of the Orange Free State.
- —— Introduction of a representative legislature in the Cape Colony.
- 1858. Second Basuto war (first with the Orange Free State).
- 1865. Commencement of third Basuto war.
- —— Annexation of British Kaffraria to the Cape Colony.
- 1867. Commencement of fourth Basuto war.
- 1868. Annexation of Basutoland to the British Empire.
- 1869. Discovery of diamonds in South Africa.
- 1871. Creation of the province of Griqualand West.
- 1872. Introduction of responsible government in the Cape Colony.
- 1877. Annexation of the South African Republic to the British Empire.
- —— Commencement of ninth Kaffir war.
- 1879. British conquest of Zululand.
- 1880. Annexation of Griqualand West to the Cape Colony.
- —— Commencement of fifth Basuto war.
- 1881. Recovery of independence by the South African Republic.
- 1884. Commencement of the German Protectorate of the western coast belt north of the Orange river.
- 1885. Creation of the province of British Bechuanaland.
- 1886. Opening of extensive gold-fields in the South African Republic.
- 1887. Annexation of Zululand to the British Empire.
- 1889. Grant of a charter to the British South Africa Company.
- 1893. Introduction of responsible government in Natal.

INDEX.

A

Almeida, Francisco d', is killed in Table Valley, 15
Angra Pequena, discovery of, 8
Anti-convict agitation, account of, 250
Asiatics, introduction into Cape Colony, 35

B

Bantu, description of, 5; suffer severely from small-pox, 81; *see* Bapedi, Baramapulana, Basuto, Cetywayo, Destruction, Dingan, Dinizulu, Fingos, Gaika, Hintsa, Hlubi, Kaffir, Kreli, Langalibalélé, Lobengule, Makana, Mantati, Matabele, Moselekatse, Moshesh, Ndlambe, Panda, Pondo, Sandile, Setyeli, Swaziland, Tembu, Tshaka, and Zulu
Bapedi tribe, war with, 340
Baramapulana tribe, war with, 336
Barberton, foundation of, 349
Basutoland, description of, 263; is annexed to the British empire, 321; is attached to the Cape Colony, 330; is retransferred to the imperial government, 331; present condition of, 331
Basuto treaty state, creation of, 228; destruction of, 247
Basuto tribe, origin of, 171
Basuto wars, account of, 259, 317, 320, 321, 331
Batavian Republic, constitution of the Cape Colony under, 129
Berea, battle of, 265
Bethelsdorp mission station, foundation of, 130
Birkenhead, wreck of the, 254
Black circuit, account of, 146
Bloemfontein, foundation of, 235
Bloemhof arbitration, particulars concerning, 325
Blueberg, battle of, 134
Boomplaats, battle of, 249
Boshof, J. N., presidency of, 315
Brand, J. H., presidency of, 319
British Bechuanaland, history of, 365
British Kaffraria, creation of the province, 246; annexation to the Cape Colony, 289
British Protectorate, reference to, 368
British settlers of 1820, account of, 156
Bronkhorst Spruit, action at, 346
Burgers, T. F., presidency of, 339
Burgher senate, Cape Colony, creation of, 117; abolition of, 176
Bushmen, description of, 1; references to, 44, 63, 73, 88

C

Caledon, Lord, administration of, 139
Cape Colony, foundation of, 23; first surrender to the English, 107; restoration to the Dutch, 128; second surrender to the English, 135; cession to Great Britain, 146; present condition of coloured inhabitants, 380; public schools, 380-3; courts of justice, 383; various institutions, 383; telegraphic and steamship connection with Europe, 385; public debt, 386
Cape of Good Hope, discovery of, 10
Capetown, description of, at various times, 55, 83
Castle of Good Hope, erection of, 40
Cathcart, Sir George, administration of, 255
Cattle farmers, origin of, 49
Census of the Cape Colony, in 1700, 52; in 1791, 97; in 1805, 132; in 1819, 155; in 1890, 380
Census of the Orange Free State in 1890, 328; of Basutoland in 1890, 331; of the South African Republic in 1890, 352; of Kaffraria in 1890, 362; of British Bechuanaland in 1890, 368; of Swaziland in 1890, 376
Cetywayo, Zulu chief, references to, 302, 309
Churches, particulars concerning, 39, 53, 77, 87, 101, 159, 237
Coal, in Natal, 300; in the Orange Free State, 328; in the South African Republic, 350
Cole, Sir Lowry, administration of, 179
Colonists, the first, particulars concerning, 30
Complaints of the burghers against the government of the Dutch East India Company, 92
Constitution of the Cape Colony, description of, 271
Copper, export of, 379
Council of advice, Cape Colony, establishment of, 160
Courts of law, Cape Colony, particulars concerning, 176
Cradock, Sir John, administration of, 142
Craig, General, administration of, 119
Customs union, references to, 328, 369

D

Delagoa Bay, references to, 74, 374
Depopulation of the territory between the Orange and Limpopo rivers, account of, 165
Destruction of all their property by the Kosas, account of, 280 *et seq.*
Diamond mines, annexation to the British empire, 326
Diamonds, discovery of, 322; export of, 379
Dias, Bartholomew, voyage of, 8
Dingan, Zulu chief, references to, 167, 206, 207, 208, 214, 215
Dinizulu, Zulu chief, references to, 310
Drakenstein, settlement of, 51
Durban, description of, 299
D'Urban, Sir Benjamin, administration of, 179
Dutch East India Company, formation of, 18; forms a refreshment station in Table Valley, 23; decline of, 90; insolvency of, 110
Dutch language, is prohibited in public offices, 158; is restored to official equality with English, 275
Dutch reformed church, particulars concerning, 101
Dutch ships, first voyage to India of, 17

INDEX.

E

Eighth Kaffir war, account of, 253
English, the, attempt to seize the Cape Colony in 1781, but fail, 90; conquer it in 1795, 107; restore it to the Dutch in 1803, 128; conquer it again in 1806, 135
English ships, first visit to South Africa of, 17
Etshowe, relief of, 308
Executive council, Cape Colony, creation of, 180
Expansion of the Cape Colony, description of, 61
Exploration of South Africa, particulars concerning, 28; progress of, 83
Exports of South Africa, account of, 378-9

F

Fifth Basuto war, account of, 331
Fifth Kaffir war, account of, 152
Fingos, origin of, 164; references to, 191, 255
First Basuto war, account of, 259
First Hottentot war, account of, 37
First Kaffir war, account of, 88
Form of government of the Cape Colony, before 1795, 53; at present, 271
Fourth Basuto war, account of, 321
Fourth Kaffir war, account of, 143
French, the, take possession of Saldanha Bay, 43; defend the Cape Colony against the English in 1781-3, 90

G

Gaika, Kosa chief, references to, 99, 123, 131, 151, 187
Gama, Vasco da, voyage of, 10
Game, abundance of, in early days, 46

German immigrants, account of, 288
German Protectorate, account of, 372
Ginginhlovu, battle of, 308
Glenelg, Earl, treatment of South Africa by, 192
Gold, discovery of, 349; export of, 349, 379
Government by the Dutch East India Company, particulars concerning, 74
Graaff, van de, C. J., administration of, 96
Graaff-Reinet, foundation of, 87; rebellion of the people, 104, 121
Grahamstown, foundation of, 145; attack by Kosas, 153
Great emigration from the Cape Colony, causes of, 193, 194; account of, 195 et seq.
Grey, Sir George, administration of, 279
Griqualand, West, annexation to the Cape Colony, 326
Griqua treaty state under Adam Kok, creation of, 230; destruction of, 247
Griquas and emigrant farmers: war between, 233
Guano Islands, reference to, 363

H

Haarlem, the, wreck of, in Table Bay, 21
Hintsa, Kosa chief, reference to, 152, 189
Hlobane, disaster at, 307
Hlubi tribe, account of, 292
Hoffman, J., presidency of, 315
Hottentots, description of, 2; first intercourse with Europeans, 11; particulars concerning, 25, 26, 27, 36, 45, 111; purchase of territory from, 42; references to, 44, 72, 81, 87, 103, 121, 123, 130, 140, 141, 177, 178, 179, 254, 364

Hottentot settlement at the Kat river; account of, 179
Hottentot wars, account of, 37, 45
Huguenots, arrival of, 51

I

Immigration from Great Britain, account of, 153, 237
Ingogo, action at, 347
Inyesane, battle of, 307
Isandlwana, destruction of English army at, 305

J

Janssens, J. W., administration of, 129
Johannesburg, foundation of, 349

K

Kaffir wars, account of, 88, 100, 123, 142, 152, 188, 240, 253, 361
Kaffraria, description of, 353; history of, 355; annexation of the greater part to the Cape Colony, 357
Kambula, defence of, 307
Keate award, account of, 326, 338
Kentani, battle of, 361
King-Williamstown, foundation of, 191
Kok, Adam, Griqua captain, references to, 246, 318
Kreli, Kosa chief, references to, 189, 257, 281, 355, 361
Kruger, S. J. Paul, references to, 336, 343, 345

L

Langalibalele, rebellion of, 293
Lang's Nek, action at, 347
Lanyon, Sir Owen, administration of, 343
Lead, export of, 379
Legislative council, Cape Colony, creation of, 180

Livingstone, Rev. Dr., reference to, 335
Loan bank, creation of, 98
Lobengule, Matabele chief, reference to, 370
London missionary society, commences work in South Africa, 126; assumes a hostile attitude towards the colonists, 146; is forsworn by the emigrant farmers, 201
Lovedale missionary institution, foundation of, 279
Lucas, Admiral, surrenders a fleet of nine ships of war to the English, 119
Lutheran church in Capetown, establishment of, 101
Lydenburg, foundation of, 227

M

Macartney, Lord, administration of, 120
Maitland, Sir Peregrine, administration of, 232
Majuba Hill, defeat of British force at, 348
Makana, Kosa seer, account of, 151
Malmesbury, foundation of, 79
Mantati horde, account of, 165
Matabele tribe, origin of, 169; references to, 199, 200, 201, 202, 219, 370
Mauritius, references to, 39, 71
Missionary effort, results of, 4, 186, 291, 380
Mission societies, localities of labour, 173
Mist, J. A. de, references to, 129, 131
Moffat, Rev. Robert, reference to, 170
Mohair, export of, 379
Moravian mission, foundation in South Africa of, 101
Moselekatse, Matabele chief, references to, 167, 370
Moshesh, Basuto chief, references

INDEX. 395

to, 171, 228, 230, 236, 248, 249, 258, 315, 316, 320, 330
Mossamedes, emigration of farmers to, 340

N

Natal, discovery of, 12; depopulation of, 164; description of, 204; occupation by the emigrant farmers, 207; government of the emigrant farmers, 220; possession by British troops, 222; population of, 291; Indian immigrants, 297; constitution of, 301; public debt, 301
Ndlambe, Kosa chief, references to, 99, 123, 130, 143, 150, 151, 152, 187
Nederburgh and Frykenins, reference to, 97, 103, 110
Ninth Kaffir war, account of, 361

O

Ohrigstad, foundation of, 227
Orange Free State, creation of, 269; constitution of, 313; courts of justice, 314; present condition, 327
Orange River Sovereignty, creation of, 248; abandonment of, 269
Ostrich feathers, export of, 379

P

Paarl, description of, 85
Panda, Zulu chief, references to, 215, 217, 218, 225, 302
Paper money, issue of, 92; redemption of, 159
Physical conformation of South Africa, 13
Pietermaritzburg, foundation of, 215
Plettenberg, Joachim van, administration of, 86
Pondoland, reference to, 363
Pondo treaty state, creation of, 230

Port St. John's, reference to, 363
Portuguese discoveries in South Africa, account of, 8 et seq.
Portuguese possessions, account of, 373
Potchefstroom, foundation of, 213
Potgieter, Hendrick, references to, 198-201, 210
Pottinger, Sir Henry, administration of, 242
Pretorius, Andries, references to, 213, 221, 249, 260
Pretorius, M. W., presidency of, 318, 336
Prince Imperial of France, death of, 308
Productions of the Cape Colony, 377
Progress of South African exploration in 1700, account of, 57
Province of Queen Adelaide, creation of, 191; abandonment of, 193
Public debt, of the South African Republic, 351; of Natal, 301; of the Cape Colony, 386

Q

Queenstown, foundation of, 255

R

Railways, in Natal, 300; in the Orange Free State, 328; in the South African Republic, 351; in British Bechuanaland, 368; in the Portuguese possessions, 371, 375; in the Cape Colony, 328
Reitz, F. W., presidency of, 328
Retief, Pieter, references to, 201, 204, 205
Rhodesia, account of, 369
Riebeek, Jan van, references to, 22, 24, 25, 26, 28, 39
Rorke's Drift, gallant defence of, 306

S

Sandile, Kosa chief, references to, 188, 239, 253, 281, 361

Sand River Convention, account of, 261
Schoemansdal, abandonment of, 337
Schools, particulars concerning, 23, 79, 160, 237, 350, 381-3
Scurvy, effects of, 23
Second Basuto war, account of, 317
Second Hottentot war, account of, 45
Second Kaffir was, account of, 100
Setyeli, Bakwena chief, reference to, 335
Seventh Kaffir war, account of, 240
Sheikh Joseph, particulars concerning, 36
Shepstone, Sir T., administration of, 342
Shipwrecks in Table Bay, 76
Silver, export of, 379
Simonstown, foundation of, 77; description of, 85
Sixth Kaffir war, account of, 188
Slachter's Nek rebellion, account of, 149
Slaves, introduction of, 33; emancipation of, 180, 183
Small-pox, ravages of, 71, 80
Smith, Sir Harry, administration of, 244
Somerset, Lord Charles, administration of, 148
South African Republic, independence acknowledged by Great Britain, 262; description of, 332 et seq.; dissensions of people, 333; dealings with Bantu, 334; is annexed to the British empire, 342; recovers its independence, 348; present condition of, 350; constitution of, 351
Stel, van der, Simon, administration of, 50
Stel, van der, W. A., oppressive administraton of, 65, 67; is punished by the directors, 70

Stellaland, reference to, 367
Stellenbosch, foundation of, 50; description of, 85
Stockenstrom, Andries, references to, 192, 193
Swaziland, account of, 10, 376
Swellendam, foundation of, 79; description of, 85; rebellion of the inhabitants of, 104

T

Table Bay, discovery of, 13; improvement of, 77, 385
Taxation of the colonists in the olden times, system of, 55
Tembu tribe, account of, 356
Third Basuto war, account of, 320
Third Kaffir war, account of, 123
Traffic in the seventeenth and eighteenth centuries, account of, 55 et seq.
Treaties, with Andries Waterboer, 187; with Moshesh, 228; with Adam Kok, 230, 235; with Faku, 230
Tshaka, Zulu chief, account of, 162
Tulbagh, foundation of, 79
Tulbagh basin, settlement of, 61
Tulbagh Ryk, administration of, 80

U

Uitenhage, foundation of, 132
Ulundi, battle of, 309

V

Viervoet, battle of, 259
Volksraad, of the Orange Free State, 314; of the South African Republic, 352

W

Walfish Bay, reference to, 364
War between the emigrant farmers and the Zulus, account of, 208, 209
Winburg, foundation of, 201
Wodehouse, Sir Philip, administration of, 320

Wolseley, Sir Garnet, administration of, 308, 344
Wool, export of, 379

Y

Yonge, Sir George, administration of, 126

Z

Zululand, history of, 302 ; is annexed to the British empire, 312
Zulu tribe, origin of, 163 ; references to, 205, 215, 225, 302
Zulu wars, account of, 208, 209, 304

www.ingramcontent.com/pod-product-compliance
Lightning Source LLC
Chambersburg PA
CBHW030556300426
44111CB00009B/1003